ACTA UNIVERSITATIS STOCKHOLMIENSIS

Stockholm Cinema Studies 11

Stockholm University

# Imagining Safe Space

The Politics of Queer, Feminist and Lesbian Pornography

## Ingrid Ryberg

This is a print on demand publication distributed by Stockholm University Library
www.sub.su.se
First issue printed by US-AB 2012

©Ingrid Ryberg and Acta Universitatis Stockholmiensis 2012
ISSN 1653-4859
ISBN 978-91-86071-83-7
Publisher: Acta Universitatis Stockholmiensis, Stockholm
Distributor: Stockholm University Library, Sweden
Printed 2012 by US-AB

Cover image: Still from *Phone Fuck* (Ingrid Ryberg, 2009)

# Contents

1. Introduction ............................................................................................. 13
   Research aims and questions ............................................................... 13
   Queer, feminist and lesbian porn film culture: central debates ............... 19
      Feminism and/vs. pornography ......................................................... 20
      What is queer, feminist and lesbian pornography? ........................... 25
      The sexualized public sphere ............................................................ 27
   Interpretive community as a key concept and theoretical framework ..... 30
      Spectatorial practices and historical context .................................... 33
      Porn studies ..................................................................................... 35
      Embodied spectatorship .................................................................. 37
      Queer, feminist and lesbian cultural production, activism and history ... 40
   Chapter outline ...................................................................................... 42

2. Queer, feminist and lesbian pornography as interpretive community: research methods and material ............................................................... 45
   Research as activism and cultural production ....................................... 47
   Research design and material ............................................................... 51
      Club LASH ....................................................................................... 51
      Pornfilmfestival Berlin ...................................................................... 53
      *Dirty Diaries* .................................................................................. 55
      Films and other material .................................................................. 56
   Research process .................................................................................. 58
      Questionnaires ................................................................................ 58
      Interviews ........................................................................................ 59
      Participant observation .................................................................... 62
   Studying, reading and making porn ....................................................... 66
      Film production as research ............................................................. 68
      Research ethics ............................................................................... 70

3. Constructing a safe space for sexual empowerment: political and aesthetic legacies ..................................................................................... 73
   Film production as politics ..................................................................... 76
      Sexual consciousness-raising on and off stage ................................ 80
   Politicizing pornography ........................................................................ 86
      Legacies of Sex Wars ...................................................................... 89
      Re-vision of porn and sexpert tradition ............................................. 96

>Politics as aesthetics ........................................................................................... 100
>>Avant-garde or documentary? ............................................................... 102
>>Sexual empowerment in private or public? ............................................. 106

4. Affirmation and critique: reception contexts and situations .................... 113
>An affective scene for recognition .................................................................. 115
>>Relying on safe space .............................................................................. 118
>Claiming public space ................................................................................... 121
>>*Dirty Diaries*: public circulation and shifting address ............................. 125
>>Cinemateket, Stockholm, 17 November 2009 ......................................... 130
>>Hamburg International Short Film Festival, 1-7 June 2010 ..................... 131
>>Malmö högskola, 7 September 2009 ....................................................... 132
>Intertwining intimate and counter public trajectories .................................... 133
>>"I wanted to use my body in my queer activism" ..................................... 134

5. Carnal fantasizing: embodied spectatorship ........................................... 141
>Gendered and sexualized body experiences ................................................ 143
>Carnal identification ...................................................................................... 147
>>Habituation to porn consumption ............................................................. 151
>Queer, feminist and lesbian porn as fantasy ................................................ 154
>>Identification vs. desire? .......................................................................... 157
>>Discipline and (politically incorrect) play .................................................. 160
>"Every time we fuck we win" ......................................................................... 164

6. The ethics of shared embodiment ............................................................. 167
>Inviting shared embodiment .......................................................................... 170
>>Shared spaces ......................................................................................... 176
>Embracing trauma, imagining utopia ............................................................ 180

7. The wave and the undertow: summary and conclusions ........................ 189

Appendix ............................................................................................................ 197
>List of *Dirty Diaries* screenings .................................................................... 197
>Questionnaire ................................................................................................ 200

Sources ............................................................................................................. 207

Index .................................................................................................................. 227

# Acknowledgements

This study is based on ethnographic fieldwork made up of interviews, questionnaires and participant observation and would not have been possible without all the generous, personal and insightful contributions from the many research subjects who chose to participate in my project. I am endlessly grateful to everyone that I interviewed – those who chose to participate with their own names and those who participated anonymously – for sharing their thoughts and experiences with me. The efforts of everyone who filled out questionnaires have likewise been invaluable to this research. I am deeply grateful to everyone who participated in meetings during the production of *Dirty Diaries* (Mia Engberg, 2009) and allowed me to record our discussions. My own short for *Dirty Diaries*, *Phone Fuck* (Ingrid Ryberg, 2009), would not have been possible without the fantastic work of the performers Helena Lindblom and Helena Sandström, who are in the photograph on this book's front cover. I dearly appreciate that they made the film happen and thus become a crucial part of my material. It has been a true joy and a great privilege to pursue the research in contexts and with people that I share my queer, feminist and lesbian activist engagement with. I especially want to express my deep gratitude to Marit Östberg for her huge contribution to this project and for her friendship.

I cannot thank my supervisor Anu Koivunen enough for her brilliant guidance and warm support. Without her firm belief in my project I could never have come to this point. She strongly advocated that I conduct fieldwork and participate as a filmmaker in *Dirty Diaries* and gave me the courage to design the project this way. I am so pleased about this. It has been a thrill! Anu's sharp intellect and impressive ability to both map out overarching themes and sort out the complexity of details have been priceless to the structuring and analysis of this project's questions and material. Throughout the writing and editing phase, Anu has provided all the necessary confidence, as well as demands, to get further, rethink and finish up what at times felt as an endless endeavor. She has pushed me to clarify and get to the core arguments that I have struggled to grasp. I am infinitely indebted to Anu for all the time and energy she has put into reading and commenting on countless drafts of the chapters in this dissertation.

I am also deeply grateful to Fanny Ambjörnsson, who became my second supervisor during the writing phase, for all her engagement and encouragement. Fanny's careful readings and crucial comments on various drafts have provided a much-needed perspective on this work. Her deep insights into queer and feminist ethnography have been invaluable to the analysis of the fieldwork material and her sharp editorial eye has been of great help in completing this work. It has been an immense privilege to get feedback from two intellectually luminous supervisors. Our meetings have always left me challenged, but full of inspiration. I will cherish the memory of our intense conversations around the café tables at the genuine bakery Gunnarssons by Skanstull in Stockholm.

Furthermore, I am grateful to Tytti Soila who was my supervisor during my first years as doctoral student. Tytti always encouraged my work and dared me to think further. I also want to thank Tytti for the inspiring trip she organized for doctoral students to go to Hemavan in April 2006.

During this project I have been fortunate to get astute comments from opponents and participants at the research seminar at the Department of Cinema Studies, Stockholm University, where I have presented various versions of chapters and papers. I am grateful to Susanna Paasonen for her crucial comments on the thesis draft that I presented at my final research seminar in May 2011. Ulrika Dahl and Louise Wallenberg have provided invaluable insights to this project through their important readings of texts that I presented on the research seminar in May 2009 and in March 2008. I also want to thank participants at the Queer seminar at Stockholm University where I presented my research in September 2010.

I have had the privilege to follow a number of inspiring courses and participate in many conference panels where I have received essential feedback on my project. In particular I want to express my gratitude to Jane Gaines for the course she taught at the Department of Cinema Studies in spring 2006, where I wrote my first paper on queer, feminist and lesbian pornography, at a time when I strongly doubted I could write my dissertation on this topic. Jane's comments and encouragement helped me to get back on track. I also want to thank Ellen Mortensen and Elizabeth Grosz for their course on feminist theory at the University of Bergen in June 2009 and the Nordic Research School in Interdisciplinary Gender Studies for the generous grant to participate in this course. I am also grateful for the grant I got from the Nordic Research School in Interdisciplinary Gender Studies to participate in the conference The Future of Feminist Theory at Rutgers University in October 2007. Likewise, I am appreciative of the grant from The Danish School of Education that made it possible for me to participate in Beverley Skeggs' inspiring course at the University of Aarhus in June 2008. Richard Dyer's doctoral student seminar at the Department of Cinema Studies, Stockholm University, in December 2010, was also very stimulating.

I am grateful to Eric Schaefer and Patricia White for their vital comments as respondents to panels I participated in at the SCMS conferences in 2010 and 2011. I have participated in many panels and symposiums with Mariah Larsson and our conversations and her work in porn studies in Sweden have always been a source of inspiration. I am grateful to her and to other editors who have given comments on articles that I have written based on this research.

For giving me the opportunity to participate in various conferences and to conduct my fieldwork in Berlin, I want to express my gratitude to the Department of Cinema Studies, Stockholm University, for financing many of my travels and to Lauritzen, KA Wallenberg, J & J Håkansson and Ödlund foundations for different travel grants. I am also grateful to the Department of Cinema Studies for the funding of the language check and printing of the dissertation.

For allowing me to pursue my fieldwork within the three cases that this study is based on, I am grateful to Mia Engberg, who always encouraged that I studied and participated in the production of *Dirty Diaries,* and to Åsa Sandzén for all kinds of assistance; to Jürgen Brüning, Manuela Kay and many others who work with the Pornfilmfestival Berlin; and to Helene Delilah, who invited me to run the questionnaire at Club LASH. I am grateful that they all trusted and saw the value in my project. For generously lending me their impressive collection of films that I would not have been able to see otherwise, I want to thank Helene and Lilaa, who took over the management of Club LASH under the name Club Wish after Helene. I also want to thank Ted McIlvenna and Jerry Zientar at the Institute for the Advanced Study of Human Sexuality in San Francisco, for inviting me to their library in May 2008 and for providing me with a copy of some hard-to-get examples of early lesbian pornography. During my stay in San Francisco I also had the opportunity to visit the Center for Sex and Culture where Carol Queen generously helped me out. Moreover, I am grateful to the staff at The June L. Mazer Lesbian Archives in Los Angeles where I had the opportunity to browse through the first volumes of *On Our Backs* in March 2010.

My colleagues at the Department of Cinema Studies have over the years provided invaluable help and support. I want to express my gratitude in particular to Katariina Kyrölä, Annika Wik, Sofia Bull, Anne Bachmann and Christopher Natzén for encouragement and friendship. I especially want to thank Katariina for her sharp and thoughtful comments on my work at the very last stage of completing the manuscript. I am grateful also to colleagues and friends at other departments and universities whom I have had the pleasure to collaborate with on other projects: Ann Werner, Jenny Sundén, Janne Bromseth and Gunilla Edemo. I want to express my gratitude to Del LaGrace Volcano for inspiration, friendship and collaboration with our porn studies group in the spring 2008. I want to thank Kristoffer Noheden for helping me check references and footnotes and Lawrence Webb for the language check of my manuscript.

In the summer 2011 I was invited to a writing residency at the beautiful countryside house Haga. I am infinitely indebted to Marie Carlsson, Katarina Bonnevier, Joakim Rindå and Stefan Nordberg for all the pampering they provided me with, for their inspiring work with Haga and generous decision to give this opportunity to people engaged in norm critical work.

Aside from the many friends already mentioned above there are many others that I am grateful to for the energy and joy they have brought into my life. For helping me out in all kinds of ways and for keeping me on my feet through the finishing phase of this project, I especially want to thank Åsa Ståhl, Åsa Ekman, Stephen Tapert, C Fox Loft, Andy Candy, Zayera Khan, Inna Bukshtynovich, Anette Ahmed Lebbad, Lotta Nilsson and my dear sister Kristina Ryberg. I want to express my gratitude to my family and in particular to my mother, Eva Ryberg, for support and countless babysitting occasions, without which I could not have completed this thesis. This work is dedicated to my loved children, Isak and Sasha.

Stockholm 9 January 2012

Ingrid Ryberg

# 1. Introduction

## Research aims and questions

> *Dirty Diaries* is a diverse collection of Swedish feminist porn:
> Hardcore action and vanilla sex, queer and straight,
> Flashing and fucking, provocation, penetration and
> poetry.
> Orgasms and art in films for the open adult mind.[1]

In early September 2009, the Swedish feminist porn film collection *Dirty Diaries: Twelve Shorts of Feminist Porn* (Mia Engberg, 2009) premieres at the newly renovated small movie theater Bio Rio in Stockholm. With financial support from the Swedish Film Institute, the filmmaker Mia Engberg has invited a group of artists, filmmakers and activists to make their own shorts interpreting the concept of feminist pornography using mobile phone cameras.[2] The twelve films all differ in length, style and content. Present at this gala premiere are filmmakers and performers, their friends and some press. It is a rainy evening and people squeeze themselves together under the tiny roof outside the cinema when they arrive and when they smoke. Inside it is crowded. People mingle with champagne. There is a tense feeling of anticipation. People are about to see themselves or their friends in sexual situations on the big screen. I myself am both excited and nervous. I have made one of the shorts in the collection, *Phone Fuck* (Ingrid Ryberg, 2009), and arrive together with one of the performers from my film, Helena Lindblom. Once the film starts inside the theater the atmosphere becomes warm, supportive and cheerful. There is applause after each film and a lot of laughter during the 104-minute screening. There is a sense of relief. The film is finally out there.

Actually, in some sense, it has already been out there for a number of weeks now: in articles, columns and blogs, on radio and television. For an-

---

[1] Dirty Diaries: Twelve Shorts of Feminist Porn, "World Wide Success," http://www.dirtydiaries.se/ (accessed 2011-10-13).

[2] *Dirty Diaries* received 500 000 SEK (around 50 000 EUR) in production funding from the Swedish Film Institute.

other few weeks *Dirty Diaries* will continue to be a buzzword in Swedish media. An article about the project on the daily newspaper *Dagens Nyheter*'s website will turn out to be their second most-read article during 2009, outnumbered only by an article about Michael Jackson's death.[3] The reception discusses the possibility of combining the notions of feminism and pornography, the definition of the concept of feminist pornography, and how this state-sanctioned form of pornography differs or relates to the plethora of different sexual images, amateur and professional, already publicly available on the Internet. *Dirty Diaries* also gains attention internationally through the news agency AFP, culminating when Conan O'Brien makes a joking remark and a feature on Swedish state-funded porn on the television program *The Tonight Show*.[4] This prompts the director of the Swedish Film Institute, Cissi Elwin Frenkel, to write a letter to the Swedish minister of culture, Eva Adelsohn Liljeroth, justifying their choice to support the project.[5] After its release, *Dirty Diaries* soon becomes a best-selling DVD at the distribution company Njutafilms. The distribution rights are sold to 12 countries and the film has theatrical releases in Finland and France.[6] The film and the individual shorts circulate broadly at international short film festivals, LGBTQ film festivals, erotic and porn film festivals and at various small alternative festivals, exhibitions and conventions.[7]

*Dirty Diaries* is one example of a current transnational wave of interest in pornography as a potentially vital vehicle for queer, feminist and lesbian activist struggles for sexual, cultural and political empowerment. From the mid-2000s onwards, there has been an extensive and vibrant production of films by directors such as Shine Louise Houston, Madison Young and Courtney Trouble in the US, Emilie Jouvet in France, and Anna Span and Petra Joy in the UK. This activist wave of interest in pornography also consists of performance and production collectives and networks such as Girls Who Like Porno (2003-2007) in Spain and PostPorn (2006-2008) in Sweden and recent launchings of events such as the PostPornPoliticsSymposium held

---

[3] "Mest lästa på DN.se 2009," *DN.se*, 2009-12-31, http://www.dn.se/nyheter/mest-lasta-pa-dnse-2009 (accessed 2011-10-13). Sofia Curman and Maria Ringborg, "Porr för feminister?" *DN.se Kultur&Nöje*, 2009-08-28, http://www.dn.se/kultur-noje/film-tv/porr-for-feminister-1.940378 (accessed 2010-06-17).

[4] The Tonight Show, 10 September 2009, NBC.

[5] Letter written 17 September 2009, received 21 September 2009. The article "Filminstitutet förklarar porrfilmen" by the news agency TT Spektra was published in several papers, for instance in *Dagens Nyheter* 090922, *Göteborgs Posten* 090922, *Svenska Dagbladet* 090922, *Smålandsposten* 090922, *Upsala Nya Tidning* 090922 and *Helsingborgs Dagblad* 090922.

[6] By June 2011 the distribution company Njutafilms had sold over 5,000 DVD copies of *Dirty Diaries*. By October 2011 the distribution rights had been sold to Denmark, France, Belgium, Holland, Luxemburg, Germany, Spain, Hong Kong, USA, Finland and Norway. In June 2010 *Dirty Diaries* opened in 15 cinemas throughout France.

[7] See appendix for a list of screenings of *Dirty Diaries*. LGBTQ refers to lesbian, gay, bisexual, trans and queer.

in Berlin in 2006 and annual events such as Rated X in Amsterdam (2007-), The Feminist Porn Awards in Toronto (2006-), Good Vibrations Independent Erotic Film Festival in San Francisco (2005-) and the Pornfilmfestival Berlin (2006-) with its successors in Athens (2007-) and Paris (2008-). Furthermore, the recent queer, feminist and lesbian activist engagement in pornography is present online at websites such as The Crash Pad Series (2007-) and Queer Porn TV (2010-).[8] This transnational wave of interest includes a wide range of productions, discussions and articulations of notions and categories such as queer porn, feminist porn, female erotica, lesbian erotica, dyke porn, female to male trans porn, BDSM and fetish porn, post porn, meta porn, art porn, sex ed, indie porn and alt porn.[9] It also intersects with discussions about new media technologies and amateur pornography and with discussions about the ongoing proliferation of sexual discourses and representations throughout the public sphere as such, diagnosed as the sexualization of Western culture.[10]

---

[8] The Crash Pad Series, http://www.crashpadseries.com (accessed 2011-11-10). Queer Porn TV, http://queerporn.tv (accessed 2011-11-10). See Jennifer Moorman, "Gay for Pay, Gay For(e)play: The Politics of Taxonomy and Authenticity in LGBTQ Online Porn," in *Porn.com: Making Sense of Online Pornography,* ed. Feona Attwood (New York: Peter Lang Publishing, 2010), 155-170.

[9] See for instance, Tim Stüttgen, ed., *PostPornPolitics* (Berlin: B-Books, 2009); Chris Straayer, *Deviant Eyes, Deviant Bodies: Sexual Re-orientation in Film and Video* (New York: Columbia University Press, 1996), 230-232; Straayer, "The Seduction of Boundaries: Feminist Fluidity in Annie Sprinkle's Art/Life," in *Deviant Eyes, Deviant Bodies*, 1996, 233-252; Gillian Rodgerson, "Lesbian erotic explorations," in *Sex Exposed: Sexuality and the Pornography Debate,* ed. Lynne Segal and Mary McIntosh (New Brunswick, New Jersey: Rutgers University Press, 1993), 275-279; Heather Butler, "What Do You Call A Lesbian With Long Fingers? The Development of Lesbian and Dyke Pornography," in *Porn Studies*, ed. Linda Williams (Durham & London: Duke University Press, 2004a), 167-197; Katrien Jacobs, "'The Lady of the Little Death': Illuminated Encounters and Erotic Duties in the Life and Art of Maria Beatty," *Wide Angle*, 19:3 (1997): 13-40; Mariah Larsson, "Drömmen om den goda pornografin: Om sextio- och sjuttiotalsfilmen och gränsen mellan konst och pornografi," *Tidskrift för genusvetenskap*, 1:2 (2007): 93-107; Michelle Carnes, "Bend Over Boyfriend: Anal Sex Instructional Videos for Women," in *Pornification: Sex and Sexuality in Media Culture,* ed. Susanna Paasonen, Kaarina Nikunen and Laura Saarenmaa (Oxford, New York: Berg, 2007), 151-160. Productions related to these discussions include work by Annie Sprinkle, Maria Beatty, Erika Lust, Buck Angel, Del LaGrace Volcano, Shu Lea Cheang, Todd Verow, Bruce LaBruce and Tristan Taormino, as well as sexually explicit feature films such as *Shortbus* (John Cameron Mitchell, 2006), *Baise-Moi* (Virginie Despentes, 2000), *Romance* (Catherine Breillat, 1999), *A Hole in My Heart* (*Ett hål i mitt hjärta*, Lukas Moodysson, 2004) and the short film collection *Destricted* (Marina Abramovic, Matthew Barney, Marco Brambilla, Larry Clark, Gaspar Noé, Richard Prince, Sam Taylor-Wood, 2006).

[10] Feona Attwood, ed., *Porn.com: Making Sense of Online Pornography* (New York: Peter Lang Publishing, 2010); Feona Attwood, ed., *Mainstreaming Sex: The Sexualization of Western Culture*, (London & New York: I.B. Taurus, 2009); Katrien Jacobs, Marije Janssen, Matteo Pasquinelli, eds., *C'lickme: A Netporn Studies Reader* (Amsterdam: Institute of Network Cultures, 2007); Susanna Paasonen, "Labors of Love: Netporn, Web 2.0 and the Meanings of Amateurism," *New Media and Society,* 12 (2010): 1297-1312; Brian McNair, *Striptease*

The present study examines the current transnational wave of interest in and production of pornography in terms of a queer, feminist and lesbian porn film culture. By invoking such a category of queer, feminist and lesbian pornography, I am not referring to a clear-cut and readily identifiable niche. The dissertation constructs this category in order to investigate the current wave of interest in pornography in different overlapping and at times contradicting contexts where notions of queer, feminist and lesbian activism are central. Through this approach, the dissertation investigates queer, feminist and lesbian pornography as a film culture, rather than as a fixed genre or as specific film texts only. I contend that as a film culture, queer, feminist and lesbian pornography is shaped by several different national as well as cultural contexts of production, distribution and reception and by the circulation of films, people, discourses and practices in between these contexts.[11] The main purpose of the dissertation is to account for this film culture, its historical and cultural legacies, and to understand its politics and ethics.

I discuss queer, feminist and lesbian pornography as a transnational film culture dating back to the emergence of commercially available porn videos from companies such as the women-run Femme Productions and the lesbian-run Fatale Media in the US in the early 1980s, where pornography became part of what was articulated as sex radical activism in the then ongoing heated feminist debates about sexuality usually referred to as the 'Sex Wars.'[12] These debates are also related to the emergence of the category queer as signifying a critique of heteronormative notions of gender and

---

*Culture: Sex, Media and the Democratization of Desire* (London & New York: Routledge, 2002); Anja Hirdman, *Den ensamma fallosen* (Stockholm: Atlas, 2008). Linda Williams proposes the term on/scene for discussing the proliferation of sexual images in public: *Hard Core: Power, Pleasure and the "Frenzy of The Visible"* (Berkeley, Los Angeles & London: University of California Press, 1999[89]), Expanded Paperback Edition, 280-289; Linda Williams, "Porn Studies: Proliferating Pornographies On/Scene: An Introduction," in *Porn Studies,* ed. Williams, 2004a, 2-4; Linda Williams, "Pornographies on/scene, or Diff'rent strokes for diff'rent folks," in *Sex Exposed,* ed. Segal and McIntosh, 1993, 233-265. The notion of pornification has also been coined in order to discuss how pornographic styles, gestures and aesthetics influence Western popular culture. See Paasonen, Nikunen and Saarenmaa, "Pornification and the Education of Desire," in *Pornification: Sex and Sexuality in Media Culture,* ed. Paasonen, Nikunen and Saarenmaa, 2007, 1-20.

[11] For discussions about film as film culture see Janet Harbord, *Film Cultures* (London, Thousand Oaks, California & New Delhi: Sage Publications, 2002); Graeme Turner, "Editor's Introduction," in *The Film Cultures Reader*, ed. Graeme Turner (London & New York: Routledge, 2002), 1-10.

[12] See for instance Drucilla Cornell, ed., *Feminism and Pornography* (Oxford: Oxford University Press, 2000); Carol S. Vance, ed., *Pleasure and Danger: Exploring Female Sexuality* (London: Pandora Press, 1992[84]); Lisa Duggan and Nan D. Hunter, *Sex Wars: Sexual Dissent and Political Culture* (New York & London: Routledge, 2006[96]); Carolyn Bronstein, *Battling Pornography: The American Feminist Anti-Pornography Movement, 1976-1986* (Cambridge: Cambridge University Press, 2011); Williams, 1999, 16-33. In this film culture sex radicalism is accompanied by notions such as sex-positive and pro-sex.

sexuality.[13] In this study I discuss the current transnational queer, feminist and lesbian porn film culture as incorporating these debates, as well as testifying to their wide circulation and legacy also outside of the US.[14] Queer, feminist and lesbian pornography is moreover discussed as building on the legacy of second wave feminism's insistence on sexual pleasure as a key to liberation and empowerment for lesbians as well as heterosexual women.[15] I contend that queer, feminist and lesbian porn film culture builds on the opening up of public and discursive spaces for feminist and lesbian consciousness-raising around and politicizing of sexuality in the 1970s and on explorations of sexuality in literature, art and film by, for instance, Erica Jong, Judy Chicago and Barbara Hammer.[16] Thus, queer, feminist and lesbian pornography is examined as a transnational film culture where diverse activist legacies meet. The conjunction of the three notions of queer, feminist and lesbian reflects the multi-layered character of this film culture as it stretches across several different national and cultural contexts as well as across a complex history of activist engagements with and representations of gender and sexuality.[17] This entails that pornography is discussed not as a fixed notion or genre, but as discursively produced within this film culture and therefore at times intersecting with notions of the erotic.[18] This study takes as a starting point a standard definition of pornography as referring to representations with explicit sexual content aiming at arousing sexual excitement, but it furthermore accounts for how queer, feminist and lesbian pornographic repre-

---

[13] Heather Love, "Rethinking Sex: Introduction," *A Journal of Lesbian and Gay Studies*, 17: 1 (2011): 5.

[14] See for instance, Hanna Hallgren, *När lesbiska blev kvinnor – när kvinnor blev lesbiska: Lesbiskfeministiska kvinnors diskursproduktion rörande kön, sexualitet, kropp och identitet under 1970- och 1980-talen i Sverige* (Göteborg: Kabusa böcker, 2008), 327-338. Hallgren accounts for how questions related to the Sex Wars, such as BDSM and pornography, were brought up among lesbian feminists in Sweden in the 1980s.

[15] Jane Gerhard, *Desiring Revolution: Second-wave Feminism and the Rewriting of American Sexual Thought, 1920 to 1982* (New York: Columbia University Press, 2001).

[16] Erica Jong, *Fear of Flying* (1973), Judy Chicago, *The Dinner Table* (art installation, 1979), Barbara Hammer, *Women I Love* (1979) and *Multiple Orgasm* (1976). For discussions about the legacy of second wave feminist sexual discourse, see Lynn Comella, "Looking Backward: Barnard and its legacies," *The Communication Review*, 11 (2008): 207; Straayer, "Discourse Intercourse," in *Deviant Eyes, Deviant Bodies*, 1996, 184-232.

[17] Love, 2011, 2.

[18] Walter Kendrick, *The Secret Museum: Pornography in Modern Culture* (Berkeley and Los Angeles, California: University of California Press, 1987), ix-xiv; Klara Arnberg, *Motsättningarnas marknad: den pornografiska pressens kommersiella genombrott och regleringen av pornografi i Sverige 1950-1980* (Lund: Sekel bokförlag, 2010), 14-16. For discussions about the notion of the erotic, see Kendrick, 243f; Jane Juffer, "Aesthetics and Access," in *At Home with Pornography: Women, Sex, and Everyday Life* (New York & London: New York University Press, 1998), 104-144. Juffer (107) points out that the notion of women's erotica at times functions more as a "marketing strategy" than as an "indication that the content is less explicit than pornography."

sentations include many different objectives and visual strategies that also challenge and expand the standard definition.[19]

In order to account for the multi-sited, complex and contingent character of this transnational film culture, as well as for its political and ethical implications, I investigate queer, feminist and lesbian pornography as an *interpretive community* where certain shared knowledge and concerns tie its many different participants together.[20] In examining queer, feminist and lesbian pornography as an interpretive community, the dissertation defines its shared knowledge as made up by embodied spectatorial processes and different practices of participation as these take place in specific contexts and situations. This interpretive community has been researched through the methods of ethnographic fieldwork, textual analysis and historicization. My own participation in *Dirty Diaries*, as both researcher and filmmaker, constitutes a vital part of this project. Over the course of 15 months preceding the premiere I followed the production of *Dirty Diaries* through interviews and participation at regular meetings with the other filmmakers in the collection. For another year I continued following the film's reception and distribution at screenings and discussions in Sweden and Germany. My own film, *Phone Fuck*, which features a phone sex meeting between two women, also investigates, creatively and self-reflexively, relationships at play in this film culture. Aside from *Dirty Diaries*, the research project is designed around the annual Pornfilmfestival Berlin, an important platform for this contemporary transnational film culture since the launching in 2006, and Club LASH, a Stockholm-based monthly kinky, fetish and S/M club for women and transsexual people, where lesbian pornography has been screened since the club started in 1995. These three cases – a temporary collective film production and its wide distribution and reception, a festival consisting of screenings, panels, workshops, performances and parties, and a small members-only club where lesbian porn forms part of the setting – are discussed as three different examples of how this film culture materializes in and through different sites, practices and situations.

---

[19] For discussions about the definition of pornography, see Williams, 1999, 9-16, 29f; Linda Williams, "Film Bodies: Gender, Genre and Excess," *Film Quarterly*, 44:4 (1991): 2-13; Annette Kuhn, "The Body in the Machine," in *Women's Pictures: Feminism and Cinema* (London & New York: Verso, 1994[82]), Second Edition, 106-124; Peter Lehman, "Introduction: 'A Dirty Little Secret' – Why Teach and Study Pornography?," in *Pornography, Film and Culture*, ed. Peter Lehman (New Brunswick, New Jersey & London: Rutgers University Press, 2006), 5-10; Magnus Ullén, *Bara för dig: Pornografi, konsumtion, berättande* (Stockholm/Sala: Vertigo förlag, 2009), 38-52; Kendrick, 1-32, 188-239; Paasonen, Nikunen and Saarenmaa, 1f; Arnberg, 35-37.

[20] Stanley Eugene Fish, *Is There a Text in This Class? The Authority of Interpretive Communities* (Cambridge, Massachusetts & London, England: Harvard University Press, 1980); Lynne Pearce, *The Rhetorics of Feminism: Readings in Contemporary Cultural Theory and the Popular Press* (London & New York: Routledge, 2004), 223; Jacqueline Bobo, *Black Women as Cultural Readers*, (New York: Columbia University Press, 1995), 59.

Through these three cases, the study aims at accounting for and historicizing queer, feminist and lesbian pornography and at understanding its politics and ethics. In order to pursue this aim, three research questions have been formulated: 1) What kind of sites, practices, situations, discourses and aesthetics make up the queer, feminist and lesbian porn film culture? 2) What does queer, feminist and lesbian pornography mean to participants in this interpretive community? 3) What are the politics and ethics of queer, feminist and lesbian pornography? In addressing these three questions the study intervenes in wider discussions within gender, queer, cinema, media and cultural studies that the reception and production of *Dirty Diaries* evoke. These include debates about feminism and pornography, the aesthetics and politics of queer, feminist and lesbian pornography, and the sexualization of the public sphere. The study contributes to and reframes these debates by calling attention to how this interpretive community invests in *a figure of safe space*. Through the research process, a notion of queer, feminist and lesbian pornography as a potentially safe space for sexual empowerment has crystallized as central to this interpretive community. Across this film culture's many different sites, practices, situations, discourses and aesthetics this figure reoccurs as a trope which is both imagined and strived for, requested and subsumed, idealized and interrogated. Hence, the dissertation maps out how queer, feminist and lesbian pornography invests in a politics of constructing safe space. However, while this common concern with safe space as a precondition for sexual empowerment defines and ties this interpretive community together, it also results in heterogeneous and at times conflicting strategies for actualizing this space. I contend that queer, feminist and lesbian pornography calls forth an *ethics of shared embodiment* that can accommodate both the movement toward safe space and the conflicts that this entails.

## Queer, feminist and lesbian porn film culture: central debates

In this research project, the production and reception of *Dirty Diaries* are studied as one example of how pornography intertwines with queer, feminist and lesbian activist struggles for sexual empowerment. *Dirty Diaries* activates a series of interrelated debates characteristic of this film culture more generally. These debates revolve around questions about feminism and pornography, politics and aesthetics and sexualization.

## Feminism and/vs. pornography

When *Dirty Diaries* was released several critics commenting on the project took as a starting point the rhetorical question of whether it is possible to combine feminism and pornography.[21] For instance, Camilla Carnmo wrote in a review in the newspaper *Smålandposten*'s cultural section:

> Feminist pornography. Is this not a paradox? At least feminists have fought against pornography, against humiliating images of women and the substandard conditions of production, since the 1960s. But then the 90s came and queer and feminists became sex workers and sex workers became feminists and the discussion became more complicated. And now we have 2009 and the Swedish Film Institute has granted funding for the production of *Dirty Diaries*.[22]

A few feminist voices rejected the possibility of feminist pornography. For instance, Kajsa Ekis Ekman related *Dirty Diaries* to a tendency in left and queer thinking to interpret injustice and status quo as subversive.[23] The Swedish theater director and member of the influential 1970s feminist network Grupp 8, Suzanne Osten, also questioned the possibility of renewing pornography as a genre.[24] These examples apart, *Dirty Diaries* has not resulted in the substantial feminist resistance characteristic of earlier porn debates. Historical research on Swedish feminist porn discourse highlights that these debates have been dominated by anti-porn attitudes.[25] Throughout the 2000s, this critique has been modified through notions of queer feminism, Nordic new feminism and third wave feminism.[26] In the late 1990s questions

---

[21] Linda Fagerström, "Subversivt på sängkanten," *Helsingborgs Dagblad*, 2009-09-03, http://hd.se/kultur/2009/09/03/subversivt-paa-saengkanten/ (accessed 2011-05-17).

[22] Camilla Carnmo, "Dirty Diaries," *Smålandsposten*, 2009-09-04, http://smp.se/noje_o_kultur/film/dirty-diaries(1504761).gm (accessed 2009-09-08). My translation from Swedish.

[23] Kajsa Ekis Ekman, *Varat och varan: Prostitution, surrogatmödraskap och den delade människan* (Stockholm: Leopard, 2010), 85.

[24] Suzanne Osten interviewed by Sofia Curman and Maria Ringborg, "Porr för feminister?" *DN.se Kultur&Nöje*, 2009-08-28, http://www.dn.se/kultur-noje/film-tv/porr-for-feminister-1.940378 (accessed 2010-06-17).

[25] Mariah Larsson, "Contested Pleasures," in *Swedish Film: An Introduction and Reader*, ed. Mariah Larsson and Anders Marklund (Lund: Nordic Academic Press, 2010), 205-214; Tommy Gustafsson and Mariah Larsson, "Porren inför lagen. Två fallstudier angående den officiella attityden till offentligt visad pornografisk film 1921 och 1971," *Historisk tidskrift*, 123:3 (2009): 445-465; Don Kulick "Four Hundred Thousand Swedish Perverts," *GLQ: A Journal of Lesbian and Gay Studies*, 11:2 (2005b): 205-235; Arnberg, 241-261; Ullén, 29-38.

[26] Fanny Ambjörnsson, *Vad är Queer?* (Stockholm: Natur & Kultur, 2006), 171-220; Don Kulick, "Introduction," in *Queersverige*, ed. Don Kulick (Stockholm: Natur & Kultur, 2005a), 11-19; Tiina Rosenberg, *Queerfeministisk agenda* (Stockholm: Bokförlaget Atlas, 2002); Tiina Rosenberg, *L-ordet: Vart tog alla lesbiska vägen?* (Stockholm: Normal förlag, 2006), 116-123; Wencke Mühleisen, "Mainstream Sexualization and the Potential for Nordic *New Feminism*," *NORA – Nordic Journal of Women's Studies*, 15:2-3 (2007): 172-189; Ingrid

about pornography as potentially liberating became part of Swedish public debate through articles by writers such as Petra Östergren, who has since had a central role in discussions about prostitution and pornography in Sweden.[27] The production and reception of Mia Engberg's first feminist porn film, *Selma & Sofie*, in 2002 similarly suggested a reframing of discussions about pornography as a tool for empowerment rather than oppression only.[28] The short *Selma & Sofie*, which, just as *Dirty Diaries*, received production funding from the Swedish Film Institute, features a young woman who fantasizes about and finally has sex with her female swimming teacher.[29] After the film had its theatrical release in February 2002, Mia Engberg was surprised about its positive reception in feminist contexts.[30]

A few years earlier a heated debate had followed the television broadcast of the anti-porn documentary *Shocking Truth* (Alexa Wolf, 2000) in February 2000, a film which was shown in the Swedish Parliament and prompted the then minister of culture, Marita Ulvskog, to consider a strengthening of censorship.[31] The film attacked the porn showed on commercial cable television in Sweden and claimed that women were drugged and abused in these films. In the anthology *Shocking Lies,* a number of writers reacted to the film and to what they perceived as the dominant and biased media discourse about pornography in Sweden at this time.[32] *Shocking Truth* and its impact in

---

Ryberg, "Tant eller queer?" in *Femkamp, Bang om nordisk feminism*, ed. Gunilla Edemo & Ulrika Westerlund (Stockholm: Bang Förlag, 2004), 397-409; Larsson, 2007; Hallgren, 449f.

[27] Petra Östergren, "Kvinnorummets gränser," *Bang*, 2 (1998): 54-55; Per Båvner, "En reproducerad debatt: Svenska ståndpunkter om pornografi," *Res Publica,* 43: 1 (1999): 85-103; Petra Östergren, *Porr, horor och feminister* (Stockholm: Natur och Kultur, 2006); Rasmus Malm, "Slaget om porren," *Ottar*, 2 (2008): 50-55.

[28] Mia Engberg has also commented on how her own approach shifted from anti-porn activism to ideas about feminist pornography in the late 1990s. See Malm, 2008, 54f.

[29] The film was supported with an amount of 320 000 Swedish kronor (about 32 000 EUR). The film was made with an all-female team and the production process was documented in the behind-the-scenes documentary *Bitch & Butch* (2003), which was broadcasted on SVT, 2003-03-30 and 2003-04-05.

[30] Mia Engberg interviewed by Anna Frey, "Intervju med Mia Engberg: 'Feministisk porr vill skaka om,'" *Dagens Nyheter*, 2009-07-25, http://www.dn.se/kultur-noje/film-tv/intervju-med-mia-engberg-feministisk-porr-vill-skaka-om (accessed 2011-11-10).

[31] *Shocking Truth* (Alexa Wolf, 2000), broadcasted on TV4, 2000-02-15. See Förråande pornografiska filmer – en översyn av 4 § lagen (1990:886) om granskning och kontroll av filmer och videogram, PM av hovrättslagmannen Mats Melin, DS 2001:5; Aje Carlbom and Sara Johnsdotter, eds., *Goda sanningar? Debattklimatet och den kritiska forskningens villkor* (Lund: Nordic Academic Press, 2010), 167f; Tomas Kvarnkullen, "Våldsporren i tv ska bort," *Aftonbladet,* 2000-02-14, http://wwwc.aftonbladet.se/nyheter/0002/14/porr.html (accessed 2009-03-16); Mattias Andersson, *Porr: En bästsäljande historia* (Stockholm: Pan, 2006[5]), 90-93; Ullén, 30-36.

[32] Channa Bankier, Daniel Bergqvist, Per Båvner, Xenu Cronström, Pye Jacobsson, Lisa Johansson, Lars Jonsson, Nina Lekander, Stig-Björn Ljunggren, Petra Meyer, Oscar Swartz, Jan Söderqvist, Ylva Maria Thompson, Henrik Tornberg, Petra Österberg, *Shocking Lies: sanningar om lögner och fördomar i porrdebatten* (Stockholm: Periskop, 2000).

the Swedish Parliament can be seen as one example of what Don Kulick discusses as "the hegemonic form of state feminism" in Sweden, referring to the move into power positions by women previously active in 1970s feminist organizations opposing sex liberalism.[33] Kulick comments on how American anti-porn feminists such as Sheila Jeffreys and Janice Raymond have regularly been invited to give talks in the Swedish Parliament.[34] However, in her research on Swedish lesbian feminism, Hanna Hallgren points out that the anti-porn stance was also challenged in discussions about pornography in the 1980s, influenced by the ongoing Sex Wars in North America.[35] Kulick's and Hallgren's respective discussions direct attention to how the Swedish feminist porn debate has been shaped in dialogue with North American feminism.[36] The case of *Dirty Diaries* invokes a specific Swedish feminist context, porn discourse and censorship history, as well as a transnational history of feminist debates about pornography and sexuality.[37] This dissertation examines *Dirty Diaries* as one example of how this interpretive community is shaped by such transnational dialogue between and circulation of people, films, discourses and practices.

The anti-porn struggle in US as well as Swedish feminism has been described as having evolved through a disappointment with and perception that sexual liberation, including legalizations of pornography, benefited only men.[38] This critique was also directed towards sexualized representations of gender in advertisement, television, magazines and not least in film.[39] During

---

[33] Kulick, 2005b, 212.

[34] Kulick, 2005b, 212.

[35] Hallgren, 327-338.

[36] See also Emma Isaksson, *Kvinnokamp: synen på underordning och motstånd i den nya kvinnorörelsen* (Stockholm: Bokförlaget Atlas, 2007), 18f, 122, 349, 374. Isaksson highlights the anthology *Kvinnor i alla länder förena er*, ed. Ursula Armbruster (Stockholm, 1974) as one example of the international orientation of the Swedish women's movement.

[37] The Swedish obscenity clause was abolished in 1971. Film censorship for adults was abolished in 2011 when The National Board of Film Classification merged with The Swedish Media Council. Due to the forthcoming abolition of film censorship *Dirty Diaries*, which had a limited cinematic release of three screenings, including the premiere, in September 2009, was not subject to examination by the board. For an account of the sexuality debates in Sweden in the 1960s, see Lena Lennerhed, *Frihet att njuta: sexualdebatten i Sverige på 1960-talet* (Stockholm: Norstedts, 1994).

[38] Gerhard, 149-153, 173-182; Bronstein, "Seeds of Discontent: The Failed Promise of the Sexual Revolution for Women," 25-37, and "Have You Seen Deep Throat Yet? The Growth of the Commercial Sex Industry in 1970s America," 63-82; Isaksson, 77-79, 86-97; Arnberg, 241-261; Larsson, 2010, 205-214.

[39] Bronstein, "'I'm Black and Blue from the Rolling Stones and I Love It!' Women Against Violence Against Women and the Campaign Against Media Violence," 83-126; Betty Friedan, *The Feminine Mystique* (New York: Norton, 1963); Kate Millet, *Sexual Politics*, (Garden City N.Y., 1970); Molly Haskell, *From Reverence to Rape: The Treatment of Women in the Movies* (New York: Holt, Rinehart and Winston, 1974); Marjorie Rosen, *Popcorn Venus: Women, Movies & the American Dream* (New York: Coward, 1973).

the second half of the 1970s pornography came into focus as epitomizing male violence against women and degrading notions of women as passive objects of male desire.[40] The anti-porn movement problematized pornography's role in reproducing and implicating in its viewers gendered power relations and notions of men as subjects and aggressors and women as submissive objects and receivers of male desire.[41] The anti-porn critique interrelated with what was called cultural feminism, where women's bodies, sexuality and culture were revalued as radically different from male models of genital and penetrative sex.[42] Such conceptualizations of female sexuality as nurturing and non-violent clashed with lesbian sex practices involving dildo penetration, butch/femme roles and BDSM, which were engaged in by the San Francisco-based activist group Samois, for example.[43] Different attitudes in regard to sexuality and pornography within the North American women's movement became more accentuated towards the end of the 1970s and resulted in the heated debates that came to be called the 'Sex Wars.' The Sex Wars are usually exemplified by the conference "Towards a Politics of Sexuality" at Barnard College in 1982 where anti-porn feminists accused conference organizers of promoting anti-feminist sexuality.[44]

Around the same time, the porn actress Candida Royalle and a group of other famous female porn performers started producing their own films through the company Femme Productions and a group of Californian lesbian sex radical activists started the porn magazine *On Our Backs*, soon to be

---

[40] Gerhard, 173-182; Bronstein, "Something Inside Me Just Went 'Click': Women Against Violence in Pornography and Media and the Transition to an Anti-Pornography Movement," 127-172.

[41] Andrea Dworkin, *Pornography: Men Possessing Women* (London: Women's Press, 1981); Diana E. Russell, "Pornography and Rape: A Causal Model [1988]," in *Feminism & Pornography*, ed. Cornell, 2000, 48-93; Katharine A. MacKinnon, "Only Words [1993]," in *Feminism & Pornography*, ed. Cornell, 2000, 94-120; Williams, 1999, 17-23.

[42] Gerhard, 153-173; Hallgren, 275-420; Larsson, 2010, 211f; Isaksson, 181-187. Isaksson and Hallgren both point out that the American notion of "women's culture" and the Swedish "kvinnokultur" diverged from each other. Hallgren (309f, 323-327, 345f, 398-403) discusses how ideas about the specificity of women's culture, sexuality and bodies developed in dialogue with translations into Swedish of American literature such as *Our Bodies, Ourselves: A Book By and For Women by The Boston Women's Health Book Collective* (New York: Simon and Schuster 1973[71]); Shere Hite's *The Hite Rapport: A Nationwide Study of Female Sexuality* (New York: Dell, 1976) and Anne Koed's article "The Myth of the Vaginal Orgasm," in *Notes From the First Years*, ed. Shulamith Firestone (New York, 1968). See also Kathy Davis, "Feminist Body/Politics as World Traveler: Translating Our Bodies, Ourselves," *European Journal of Women's Studies*, 9 (2002): 223-247.

[43] Nan D. Hunter, "Contextualizing the Sexuality Debates: A Chronology 1966-2005," in *Sex Wars*, Duggan and Hunter, 2006, 21f; Bronstein, 282-292.

[44] Carol S. Vance, "More Danger, More Pleasure: A Decade After the Barnard Sexuality Conference," in *Pleasure and Danger*, ed. Carol Vance, 1992, xvi-xxii; Gerhard, 183-195; Bronstein, 397-307; Hunter, 2006, 22.

followed by the launch of the video production company Fatale Media.[45] *On Our Backs* and Fatale Media represented lesbian sex practices considered anti-feminist and patriarchal in the anti-porn discourse, such as BDSM, butch/femme role play and dildo penetration.[46] The sex radical movement and lesbian pornography interrelated with queer activism as it emerged as a reaction to the AIDS crisis, homophobia and assimilationist tendencies in the gay and lesbian movements. In their account of the Sex Wars, based on their own involvement in sex radicalism during this period, Lisa Duggan and Nan D. Hunter contend that "[d]uring the porn wars, many lesbians who were alienated by lesbian-feminists' homogenizing, white, middle-class, anti-gay-male, antisex discourses, refused the category 'lesbian,' and adopted 'queer' as a mark of separation from such politics, a badge of principled dissidence."[47] Research addressing the newly emerged category of lesbian pornography in the 1980s and 1990s emphasized its potential for affirming, recognizing and enhancing visibility of lesbian identity, sexuality and subculture.[48] Lesbian pornography is discussed both in opposition to cultural and anti-porn feminism and in opposition to other pornographic representations of lesbians and women. In this vein, Nan Kinney, the founder of the company Fatale Media states that "I want people to have other images of themselves, a way to bust out of the ingrained images in mainstream porn."[49] Echoing this aim, Mia Engberg asks in the accompanying booklet to the *Dirty Diaries* DVD box: "How do we liberate our own sexual fantasies from the commercial images that we see every day, burying their way into our subconscious?"[50] *Dirty Diaries* as well as the reception of the film activates this complex history of ongoing debates about feminism and pornography and raises questions about the political and aesthetic strategies explored in this film culture.

---

[45] Candida Royalle, "Porn in the USA" in *Feminism and Pornography*, ed. Cornell, 2000, 540-550; "The Evolution of Erotica," TV Series: *Lesbian Sex and Sexuality* 1:3 (2007-); Williams, 1999, 249f; Heather Butler, 2004, 167-197.

[46] Mary T. Conway, "Inhabiting the Phallus: Reading Safe Is Desire," *Camera Obscura*, 13: 2 38 (1996): 133-162; Mary T. Conway, "Spectatorship in Lesbian Porn. The Woman's Woman's Film," *Wide Angel*, 19:3 (July 1997): 94; Ragan Rhyne, "Hard-core Shopping: Educating Consumption in SIR Video Production's Lesbian Porn," *The Velvet Light Trap*, 59 (Spring 2007): 45f; Heather Butler, 181f.

[47] Duggan and Hunter, 2006, 12.

[48] Lisa Henderson, "Lesbian Pornography: Cultural Transgression and Sexual Demystification," in *New Lesbian Criticism: Literary and Cultural Readings*, ed. Sally Munt (New York: Columbia University Press, 1992), 173-191; Becki L. Ross, "It's Merely Designed for Sexual Arousal: Interrogating the Indefensibility of Lesbian Smut [1997]," in *Feminism and Pornography*, ed. Cornell, 2000, 264-317; Cherry Smyth, "The Pleasure Threshold: Looking at Lesbian Pornography on Film," *Feminist Review*, 34 (1990): 154.

[49] Nan Kinney, "About," Fatale Media website, http://www.fatalemedia.com/about.html (accessed 2008-04-04).

[50] Mia Engberg, "What is feminist porn?", *Dirty Diaries* DVD booklet, 2009.

## What is queer, feminist and lesbian pornography?

Besides reactivating the question of feminism and pornography as a matter of intense debate, *Dirty Diaries* and its reception brought up questions about what queer, feminist and lesbian pornography is. Critics had their own different expectations, definitions and ideas. Linda Fagerström wrote in a review in *Helsingborgs dagblad* that the subversive potential in *Dirty Diaries* lies in the films that explicitly challenge and make fun of patriarchy.[51] Elin Sandberg in the online paper *Tidningen Kulturen* contended that the film reinforces a notion of feminism as something "crude and sexually odd."[52] Nasim Aghili in the queer feminist magazine *FUL* is disappointed that there is not more analysis and political strategy.[53] In a column in the tabloid *Aftonbladet*, Annika Marklund critiqued the very lack of a clear definition.[54] Others ask whether the films qualify as pornography in the sense of "jerking-off flick," as Carnmo puts it in *Smålandsposten*. She found the films arousing primarily on an "intellectual level."[55]

These remarks all invoke long-running discussions about feminist film practice, as well as its relation to notions of pornography as aiming at arousing pleasure.[56] Since the 1970s, feminist film scholars have posed questions about what feminist film practice should consist of and many different strategies and notions have been suggested, including notions such as women's cinema, counter-cinema and deconstructive cinema.[57] Parallel to

---

[51] Linda Fagerström, "Subversivt på sängkanten," *Helsingborgs Dagblad*, 2009-09-03, http://hd.se/kultur/2009/09/03/subversivt-paa-saengkanten/ (accessed 2011-05-17). Fagerström refers to the films *Flasher Girl On Tour* (Joanna Rytel), *Body Contact* (Pella Kågerman) and *Dildoman* (Åsa Sandzén).

[52] Elin Sandberg, "Mer provokation än erotik i feministisk porrfilm," *Tidningen Kulturen*, 2009-09-05, http://www.tidningenkulturen.se/artiklar/film/filmkritik/4990-film-dvddirty-diaries-12-short-stories-of-feminist-porn-prod-mia-engberg (accessed 2011-11-11). Lars Böhlin finds that feminist porn in *Dirty Diaries* is ugly, boring, arty, strange and symbolic. Lars Böhlin, "Inte ens feministisk porr känns lovande," *Västerbottens dagblad*, 2009-09-04, http://www.folkbladet.nu/154385/2009/09/04/inte-ens-feministisk-porr-kanns-lovande (accessed 2011-06-16).

[53] Nasim Aghili, "Feministisk? porr," *FUL*, 2-4 (2009), 15.

[54] Annika Marklund, "Dirty Diaries är som hederlig hemmaporr," *Aftonbladet*, 2009-09-11, http://www.aftonbladet.se/nyheter/kolumnister/annikamarklund/article5774851.ab?service=print (accessed 2010-06-21).

[55] Carnmo, 2009. See also Emma Gray Munthe, "Dirty Diaries – bra eller anus?", the blog Weird Science, 2009-09-14, http://www.weirdscience.se/?p=6269 (accessed 2011-11-11).

[56] Jane Gaines, "Women and Representation: Can We Enjoy Alternative Pleasure?" in *Issues in Feminist Film Criticism*, ed. Patricia Erens (Bloomington: Indiana University Press, 1990), 75-92.

[57] Laura Mulvey, "Visual Pleasure and Narrative Cinema," *Screen*, 16:3 (1975): 6-18; Claire Johnston, "Women's Cinema as Counter-Cinema [1973]," in *Feminist Film Theory: A Reader*, ed. Sue Thornham (Edinburgh: Edinburgh University Press, 1999), 31-40; Teresa de Lauretis, "Rethinking Women's Cinema [1985]," in *Figures of Resistance: Essays in Feminist*

and in dialogue with these discussions, female filmmakers have developed a vast repertoire of aesthetic strategies. As Alison Butler contends in her summary of debates around the concept of women's cinema, it is not possible to talk about *a* feminist film practice, but rather "women produce feminist work in a wide variety of forms and styles."[58] The aesthetic diversity of *Dirty Diaries* and the film's reception reactivates these discussions about feminist film practice. This dissertation discusses *Dirty Diaries*, one example of the current queer, feminist and lesbian porn film culture, as building on the legacy of these discussions. The different shorts in the collection invoke, in Butler's words, "a wide variety" of documentary, narrative, educational and experimental "forms and styles." In her introduction to the project in the *Dirty Diaries* DVD booklet Mia Engberg also rhetorically asks what feminist pornography is and replies that: "All the filmmakers in the project have their own interpretation of the concept of feminist porn, and as such have chosen different ways of expressing it. It makes me very proud to see the range of inventiveness and the diversity among the films."[59] This study discusses *Dirty Diaries* as reflecting the heterogeneity of the queer, feminist and lesbian porn film culture. Visual strategies in this film culture involve, for instance, both emphasizing and rejecting genital display and orgasms. Hence, as pornography it relates to porn conventions in many different ways. The dissertation contends that the political and aesthetic heterogeneity of queer, feminist and lesbian pornography builds on legacies of feminist film critique and practice as these intertwine with multilayered discussions and debates about sexuality and pornography since the second wave feminist movement. Drawing from Teresa de Lauretis, queer, feminist and lesbian pornography is discussed as characterized by a tension between affirmation and critique, constitutive of the women's movement and cinema as such.[60] It builds on the legacies of both feminist cultural critique, not least of pornography, and sex radical challenges to anti-porn and cultural feminism. The heterogeneity that arises from this tension between affirmation and critique is also articulated in the call for participants on *Dirty Diaries*' first website:

> *Dirty Diaries* is a project where women make their own short erotic films. The purpose is to make feminist and queer erotica as an alternative to the mainstream porn. We believe it is possible to make sexy films with a female perspective and high artistic quality. The need for a change unites us, but every short film in *Dirty Diaries* is unique.
>
> There will be vanilla-sex and hard core, lesbian love, trans porn and straight fucking. Poetry and filth and animations even. We make films that

---

*Theory*, ed. Patricia White (Urbana & Chicago: University of Illinois Press, 2007a), 25-47; Kuhn, 1992, 151-171.
[58] Alison Butler, *Women's Cinema: The Contested Screen* (London & New York: Wallflower, 2002), 19.
[59] Engberg, *Dirty Diaries* DVD booklet, 2009.
[60] De Lauretis, 2007a, 25f.

emerge from our own sexuality and creativity. The rules are simple; no one should be harmed and everyone must be older than 18. Otherwise, you're free to do exactly what you want. The creators are artists, film-makers, amateurs, queer-activists, straight, gay, trans, bi, and one or two queens who identify as women. Sexuality is diverse.[61]

The heterogeneity in discussions about queer, feminist and lesbian pornography, both in the subcultural contexts where I myself first learned about this film culture and in research addressing this film culture, was one starting point for this research project. The project grew out of an aim of grappling with parallel and intertwining understandings of queer, feminist and lesbian pornography as affirming lesbian sexuality through "authentic" representations, interrogating and troubling gender and sexual categories and aiming at sexual arousal.[62] The recurrence of these complex and partly contradictory discussions across this film culture, reflected also in the *Dirty Diaries* call for participants, prompted the conceptualization of this film culture as an interpretive community. I discuss this interpretive community as made up by the transnational circulation of discourses, aesthetics, practices and people engaging in pornography as queer, feminist and lesbian activism. As such, I also discuss this film culture as interrelated with questions about the sexualization of the public sphere.

## The sexualized public sphere

When *Dirty Diaries* was released in September 2009, the reception revolved largely around the fact that the Swedish Film Institute had supported the project. While many critics were positive, others, such as Beatrice Fredriksson, a member of the Moderate Party's youth organization, claimed that *Dirty Diaries* is "definitely not something that the state should be paying for."[63] According to her, "feminism has earned a special status and has somehow been deemed deserving of people's tax money in order to fund everything from seminars to pornography."[64] In an article on the political debate website *Newsmill*, Ester Martin Bergsmark, one of the directors in the collection, argued that *Dirty Diaries* to a much higher degree than other Swedish film projects fulfils the Swedish Film Institute's commission to support "quality" films "renewing the cinematic expression," providing "so-

---

[61] Dirty Diaries website, www.dirtydiaries.se (accessed 2008-06-09).
[62] Teralee Bensinger, "Lesbian Pornography: The Re/Making of (a) Community," *Discourse*, 15:1 (Fall 1992), 69-93; Tiina Rosenberg, "Varför så rädda för sex?" *Arena*, 3 (2003): 15-17; Heather Butler, 2004; Henderson, 192.
[63] Beatrice Fredriksson, "Taxpayers should not have to fund feminist porn," *The Local*, 2009-09-03, http://www.thelocal.se/21870/20090903/ (accessed 2011-09-14).
[64] Fredriksson, 2009.

cial critique," "playfulness" and "visionary strength."[65] Some critics interrogated the very need for a specifically labeled "feminist" pornography and the difference between *Dirty Diaries* and other contemporary pornographies, not least amateur porn on the Internet.[66] In her column in *Aftonbladet* Annika Marklund ironically remarked that "contrarily to what most people masturbate to this pornography is feminist."[67] She continued:

> Over the last years there has been an extensive amateur revolution on the Internet. Pornography has also become a kind of grassroots movement. Ordinary horny people film themselves and share the films on the net. Ordinary horny people watch.[68]

In a blog post, the film critic Emma Gray Munthe warned that the Swedish Film Institute's support of *Dirty Diaries* risks reinforcing gendered notions of good and bad sexuality unless the same amount of money is earmarked for men making alternative pornography.[69]

These examples again invoke both a specific Swedish context of film production and feminist debate and current discussions in gender, queer, cinema, media and cultural studies about the sexualization of the public sphere. The comments invoke Kulick's critical discussion about Swedish state feminism and the construction of a notion of a national, healthy, natural and good sexuality, through denouncing and rejecting bad, decadent and perverse sexualities (such as prostitution).[70] Lena Lennerhed demonstrates how sexual life in Sweden since the 1950s came to be defined as sound, rational and enlightened and as a social concern for the state to intervene into.[71] The notion of "good sex" in Sweden interrelates with the notion of the 'Swedish Sin' as it emerged in the 1950s and came to signify the perceived sexual liberty in Sweden, related to the mandatory sex education in Swedish schools, as well as to sexually charged films by art film directors such as Ingmar Bergman, Mai Zetterling and Vilgot Sjöman, but also by soft porn

---

[65] Ester Martin Bergsmark, "Rätt att skattebetalarna finansierar våra porrfilmer," *Newsmill*, 2009-08-27, http://www.newsmill.se/artikel/2009/08/27/r-tt-att-skattebetalarna-finansierar-v-ra-porrfilmer (accessed 2011-11-12).
[66] Munthe, 2009. In the commentary field to Munthe's blog post on Weird Science the signature "Palmodovar" finds that "home porn" where "[t]he unshaved and natural looks and the fact that the persons largely are real couples is a reaction to the silicone porn," already provides a challenge to the porn industry. My translation from Swedish.
[67] Marklund, 2009. My translation from Swedish.
[68] Ibid.
[69] Munthe, 2009. See also Rasmus Malm, "Ett annat sätt att berätta om lusta," *Göteborgs-Posten*, 2009-09-03, http://www.gp.se/kulturnoje/1.16170-rasmus-malm-ett-annat-satt-att-beratta-om-lusta (accessed 2009-09-11).
[70] Kulick, 2005b.
[71] Lennerhed, 1994.

and sex education directors such as Torgny Wickman and Mac Ahlberg.[72] These films pushed the boundaries for what could be represented on the screen and influenced the debates that led to the legalization of pornography in 1971. Mariah Larsson shows how a concept of good and quality pornography formed part of the legislation debates and how this notion was tied to notions of female sexuality.[73] She relates the recent interest in "fairtrade," "post" and "feminist" porn to this history, pointing out how these discussions also mobilize gendered notions of women's sexuality as morally and aesthetically superior.[74]

These discussions all raise questions about the implications of queer, feminist and lesbian pornography's circulation in and relation to the sexualized public sphere. Brian McNair's understands sexualization as forming part of an ongoing "democratization of desire" where the visibility of female, gay and lesbian sexuality in the mainstream contributes to a shift in the norms regulating sexuality and where the blurring of boundaries between what has traditionally been seen as private and the public helps breaking down sexual hierarchies."[75] However, sexualization has also been discussed as a backlash where conservative norms are re-established in the face of presumed free choices and individualization and where feminist politics is reduced to the right to belong to a commodity culture.[76] Feona Attwood points out how sex in this present condition is understood more as lifestyle, recreation and self-expression than as reproduction or relationships.[77] As such, sexualization is also "associated with the rise of neo-liberalism in which the individual becomes a self-regulatory unit within society" and with "a refusal of genuine social politics."[78] *Dirty Diaries*, especially through its

---

[72] Erik Hedling, "Breaking the Swedish Sex Barrier: Painful Lustfulness in Ingmar Bergman's The Silence," *Film International*, 6:6 (2008): 17-27; Lennerhed, 1994; Kulick, 2005, 210f; Larsson, 2007. In 1955, Sweden became the first country in the world to make sex education in schools obligatory. Ingmar Bergman, *Summer With Monica* (*Sommaren med Monika*, 1953), *The Virgin Spring* (*Jungfrukällan*, 1960), *The Silence* (*Tystnaden*, 1963); Vilgot Sjöman, *491* (1964), *I Am Curious Yellow* (*Jag är nyfiken gul*, 1967); Mai Zetterling, *Night Games* (*Nattlek*, 1966); Torgny Wickman, *Swedish Marriage Manual* (*Ur kärlekens språk*, 1969); Mac Ahlberg, *Flossie* (1975).

[73] Larsson, 2007, 103-107.

[74] Larsson, 2007, 107. "Fairtrade-labeled" ("kravmärkt") porn was called for by ethics researcher Ann Heberlein in the article "Ge oss bra porr – för båda könen," *Aftonbladet*, 2004-05-13, http://www.aftonbladet.se/debatt/article210841.ab (accessed 2009-03-16).

[75] McNair, 2002. See also Lauren Berlant and Michael Warner, "Sex in Public," *Critical Inquiry*, 24:2, Intimacy (Winter 1998), 547-566.

[76] Angela McRobbie, *The Aftermath of Feminism: Gender, Culture and Social Change* (London: SAGE, 2009); Angela McRobbie, "Pornographic Permutations," *The Communication Review*, 11 (2008), 225-236; Rebecca Munford, "BUST-ing the Third Wave: Barbies, Blowjobs and Girlie Feminism," in *Mainstreaming Sex,* ed. Attwood, 2009, 183-198; Hirdman, 2008.

[77] Attwood, 2009, xiii-xxiv.

[78] Attwood, 2009, xxiii.

wide circulation across different public contexts in Sweden and internationally, invokes this debate and raises questions about how this wide accessibility mobilizes different notions of gender and sexuality. These questions also relate to a tension in queer and feminist theory and activism between gay male and lesbian sex cultures. Whereas gay male practices of public sex, risky sex and promiscuity have been framed as expressions of the fundamental anti-sociality, aggressiveness and self-shattering of sexuality, queer and lesbian feminists have insisted on discussing issues of ethics and safety.[79] Critiques have been raised against idealizations of a privileged white, middle class, gay male sexuality publicly mobile and unrestricted by gender, race, sexuality or class.[80] This dissertation discusses how the public expansion and mobility of queer, feminist and lesbian pornography rearticulates these debates.

## Interpretive community as a key concept and theoretical framework

*Dirty Diaries* evokes debates that are central in queer, feminist and lesbian porn film culture and that this dissertation engages in its aim at accounting for, historicizing and understanding this film culture and its political and ethical implications. The questions articulated in the production and reception of *Dirty Diaries* evoke a specific Swedish context and history but also echo larger contemporary debates regarding feminism and pornography, activist and aesthetic strategies and sexualization of the public sphere. This study intervenes into these debates through its three research questions regarding: 1) what this film culture is made up of; 2) what it means to its participants; and 3) what its politics and ethics are. The case of *Dirty Diaries* testifies to the transnational character of this film culture as shaped by the circulation of films, people, practices and discourses. In order to account for the multi-sited character of this film culture as it stretches across different national, cultural and historical contexts, but nevertheless engages with a number of common and overarching discussions, the dissertation investigates queer, feminist and lesbian pornography in terms of an *interpretive community*.

---

[79] Leo Bersani, "Is the Rectum a Grave?" *October*, 43 (Winter 1987), 197-222; Lee Edelman, "Unbecoming: Pornography and the Queer Event," in *PostPornPolitics,* ed. Stüttgen, 2009, 194-211; Ann Cvetkovich, *An Archive of Feelings: Trauma, Sexuality and Lesbian Public Cultures* (Durham & London: Duke University Press, 2003), 49-82; Judith Halberstam, "The Anti-Social Turn in Queer Studies," *Graduate Journal of Social Science*, 5:2 (2008): 140-156; Elizabeth Freeman, *Time Binds: Queer Temporalities, Queer Histories* (Durham & London: Duke University Press, 2010), 140-143.
[80] Sara Ahmed, *The Cultural Politics of Emotion* (New York: Routledge, 2004), 151-153, 163f.

Coined by Stanley Fish in the field of literary studies, the concept of interpretive community implies that meaning and interpretation originate not formally from the text or from the individual reader as an independent agent, but are shaped by the interpretive community within which the text is written and read.[81] According to Fish, different "ways of reading" are "extensions of community perspectives."[82] Scholars such as Janice Radway, Lynne Pearce, Jacqueline Bobo and Janet Staiger have further discussed the concept in the fields of feminist literary, cultural and cinema studies.[83] Pearce defines interpretive communities as sharing "specialist knowledge" that enables certain interpretations, but also stresses that rather than representing a fixed set of values, these communities in themselves become sites of struggles and disagreements.[84] For instance, she discusses film critics and feminist academics in terms of interpretive communities. Bobo discusses black women as an interpretive community characterized by an "instant intimacy" and a "bond of collective concerns" that contribute to a "transformation of black women's consciousness" and therefore also "unification as social force."[85]

In this study, interpretive community is a key concept for accounting for the shared knowledge, perspectives and concerns that circulate and unfold in various contexts where queer, feminist and lesbian porn film culture materializes. Following Pearce and Bobo, the interpretive community of queer, feminist and lesbian pornography is discussed as a site of struggle where a number of debates are mobilized, but where a collective concern with the figure of safe space for sexual empowerment is also articulated. As suggested above, I maintain throughout the dissertation that this interpretive community is characterized by a politics of constructing safe space for sexual empowerment, resulting, however, in heterogeneous and sometimes conflicting strategies.

Drawing further from Pearce, the interpretive community of queer, feminist and lesbian pornography is discussed in this study as a "[site] where a number of [...] discourses meet" and as a "[site] of social interaction."[86]

---

[81] Fish, 14f.

[82] Fish, 16.

[83] Janice Radway, "Interpretive Communities and Variable Literacies: The Functions of Romance Reading," *Daedalus*, 113:3 (Summer 1984): 49-73; Lynne Pearce, *Feminism and the Politics of Reading* (London, New York, Sydney, Aukland: Arnold, 1997), 211-213, 220f, 230-234; Janet Staiger, *Interpreting Films: Studies in the Historical Reception of American Cinema* (Princeton, New Jersey: Princeton University Press, 1992), 38, 154; and Janet Staiger, "Fans and Fan Behavior," in *Media Reception Studies* (New York & London: New York University Press, 2005), 95-114; Bobo, 33-60.

[84] Pearce, 2004, 223; 1997, 212f.

[85] Bobo, 59-60.

[86] Pearce, 1997, 231. Pearce distinguishes between interpretive community, audience and text-reader interaction as different instances of the reading process. In my definition interpretive community encompasses spectatorial processes, practices of participating and interacting in this film culture, as well as the contexts within which these take place.

Hence, shared knowledge is discussed as formed by discourses, as well as by specific practices, sites, situations and aesthetics that constitute this film culture. Interpretive community is defined in a broad sense as encompassing embodied spectatorial processes, practices of participation in the film culture and the specific sites and situations where these take place. In this definition, the concept of interpretive community reactivates a number of discussions in cinema, literary, media and cultural studies directing attention to how readers of cultural texts in different historical and social contexts produce different interpretations.[87] Central to this study is Jane Juffer's research on the home as a place for women's porn consumption and her highlighting of how "particular sites at which pornography is produced, obtained, and consumed shape its meanings and uses."[88] Grounded in ethnographic fieldwork, this study follows Juffer's insistence on locating the analysis of pornography in specific contexts of production, distribution and consumption and on considering specific conditions of "access" and "agency" that shape women's consumption of porn.[89] Juffer argues that these conditions need to be analyzed in relation to the forces that enable and constrict women's consumption of porn. Drawing from Sara Ahmed's discussion about queer phenomenology, this study understands these forces as also involving how norms and power hierarchies related to gender, sexuality, class and race shape and direct bodies.[90]

The concept of interpretive community and increased attention to specific contexts and practices of consumption in cultural research interrelate, not least, with a development in cinema studies towards notions of spectatorship as historically and socially situated and as embodied.[91] This development is related to the vast film theoretical work dedicated to modifying, rejecting and reconsidering psychoanalytic and semiotic spectatorship models estab-

---

[87] Ien Ang, *Watching Dallas: Soap Opera and the Melodramatic Imagination* (London: Methuen, 1985); Janice Radway, *Reading the Romance: Women, Patriarchy and Popular Literature* (Chapel Hill, NC, & London: University of North Carolina Press, 1984); Angela McRobbie, *Feminism and Youth Culture* (London: Macmillan Press Ltd, 1991).
[88] Jane Juffer, *At Home With Pornography, Women, Sex, and Everyday Life* (New York and London: New York University Press 1998), 2.
[89] Juffer, 8.
[90] Sara Ahmed, *Queer Phenomenology: Orientations, Objects, Others* (Durham & London: Duke University Press, 2006).
[91] Tom Gunning, "The Cinema of Attractions: Early Film, Its Spectator and the Avant-Garde," *Wide Angle*, 8:3-4 (1986), 1-14; Judith Mayne, *Cinema and Spectatorship* (London & New York: Routledge, 1993); Vivian Sobchack, *The Address of the Eye: A Phenomenology of Film Experience* (Princeton, New Jersey: Princeton University Press, 1992); Miriam Hansen, *Babel and Babylon: Spectatorship in American Silent Film* (Cambridge, Massachusetts & London, England: Harvard University Press, 1991); Jackie Stacey, *Star Gazing: Hollywood Cinema and Female Spectatorship*, (London and New York: Routledge, 1994); Staiger, 1992.

lished by film theorists such as Christian Metz and Laura Mulvey.[92] Notions of the apparatus and the gaze and discussions about film's ideological mastery over the audience have been problematized for reducing the spectator to a disembodied, fixed and passive position depriving especially the female spectator of agency and erasing lesbians and black women from the spectatorial process.[93] Throughout the 1980s and 1990s a considerable amount of research engaged in expanding the understanding of film spectatorship. This dissertation's theoretical framework draws from some of this work towards understanding spectatorship as, in Linda Williams' words in the mid-1990s: "historically specific, grounded in the specific spectatorial practices, the specific narratives, *and* the specific attractions of the mobilized and embodied gaze of viewers."[94]

## Spectatorial practices and historical context

In discussing queer, feminist and lesbian pornography as an interpretive community involving spectatorial processes and different practices of participation taking place in specific contexts and situations, this dissertation relates to Miriam Hansen's historical study of spectatorship and early cinema.[95] Hansen argues for an understanding of film reception as an interactive and ambivalent experience and for "formations of spectatorship" as "public horizons" and "structural conditions for the articulation and reflection of experience."[96] Hansen conceptualizes cinema as an alternative public sphere where in particular women potentially could come into contact with an alternative experiential horizon.[97] Early cinema opens up an arena for a new discourse on femininity and a redefinition of norms and codes of sexual conduct.[98] As Hansen points out, this arena involves both the physical space of

---

[92] Christian Metz, *The Imaginary Signifier: Psychoanalysis and the Cinema*, trans. Celia Britton et al. (Bloomington: Indiana University Press, 1986[77]); Mulvey, 1975, 6-18. See also Mary Ann Doane, "Film and the Masquerade: Theorising the Female Spectator," *Screen*, 23:4-4 (1982): 74-88.

[93] bell hooks, "The Oppositional Gaze: Black Female Spectators," in *Reel to Real: Race, Sex and Class at the Movies* (New York & London: Routledge, 1996), 197-213; Patricia White, "Lesbian Cinephilia," in *UnInvited: Classical Hollywood Cinema and Lesbian Representability* (Bloomington & Indianapolis: Indiana University Press, 1999), 29-60; Teresa de Lauretis, "Recasting the Primal Scene: Film and Lesbian Representation," in *The Practice of Love: Lesbian Sexuality and Perverse Desire* (Bloomington & Indianapolis: Indiana University Press, 1994), 81-148; Bobo, 101-2.

[94] Linda Williams, "Introduction," in *Viewing Positions: Ways of Seeing Film*, ed. Williams (New Brunswick, New Jersey: Rutgers University Press, 1997), 18.

[95] Hansen, 1991.

[96] Hansen, 1991, 24f.

[97] Hansen, 1991, 114-125

[98] Hansen, 1991, 118.

the theater and "the phantasmagoric space on the screen, and the multiple and dynamic transactions between these spaces."[99]

In this dissertation I similarly define queer, feminist and lesbian porn film culture as a public arena where new sexual discourses and conduct can be articulated and expressed and where a new experiential horizon is provided. As an alternative public sphere, the interpretive community of queer, feminist and lesbian pornography is characterized by activist struggles aiming at constructing a safe space for sexual empowerment.[100] I discuss how this interpretive community functions both as an *intimate public* and as a *counter public*.[101] The notion of a counter public has been theorized as an alternative space where marginalized groups formulate and circulate "counter discourses" and where new understandings and ideas of their experiences, identities and interests are encouraged and mobilized in order to challenge the wider public.[102] I account for how queer, feminist and lesbian pornography functions as a counter public sphere where dominant notions of sexuality and gender are contested and challenged, but also how this film culture simultaneously functions as an intimate space for recognition and belonging. In her work on intimate public spheres, Lauren Berlant defines alternative publics centered around national, sexual, racial, gendered or class identity as "affective scene[s] of identification" where a particular group's claimed core interests and desires are circulated.[103] According to her, intimate publics are organized by a promise of affective recognition and social belonging rather than by political aspirations.[104] I discuss how these functions intertwine in queer, feminist and lesbian pornography and how they mobilize and sometimes put the figure of safe space at stake.

Drawing from film theoretical discussions about spectatorship as historically and socially located, this study also builds on related developments of ethnographic approaches to specific film cultures, audiences and spectators. In this context, Jacqueline Bobo's study of black women as an interpretive

---

[99] Hansen, 1991, 118.

[100] See also Rhyne, 2007.

[101] Lauren Berlant, Preface to *The Female Complaint: The Unfinished Business of Sentimentality in American Culture* (Durham & London: Duke University Press, 2008), vii-xiv; and Berlant, "Introduction: The Intimate Public Sphere," in *The Queen of America Goes to Washington City: Essays on Sex and Citizenship* (Durham & London: Duke University Press, 1997), 1-24; Michael Warner, "Publics and Counterpublics," *Public Culture*, 14: 1 (Winter 2002a), 49-90; Warner and Berlant, 1998, 558-564.

[101] Berlant, 2008, viii.

[102] Nancy Fraser, "Rethinking the Public Sphere: A Contribution to the Critique of Actually Existing Democracy," *Social Text*, 25-26 (1990): 67-68; Iris Marion Young, "Unruly Categories: A Critique of Nancy Fraser's Dual Systems Theory," *New Left Review,* 1/222 (March-April 1997), http://www.newleftreview.org/?page=artivle&view=1899 (accessed 2010-08-25); Warner, 2002a, 86.

[103] Berlant, 2008, viii.

[104] Berlant, 2008, viii.

community, based on interviews, is again important.[105] Jackie Stacey's study *Star Gazing: Hollywood Cinema and Female Spectatorship* bridges film studies and audience research in its combination of film theory and ethnographic material consisting of questionnaires and letters from female cinema-goers accounting for their relations to Hollywood stars in the 1940s and 1950s.[106] In their respective work they have challenged the methodological separation between cinema studies' "textual spectator" and cultural studies' ethnographic research on empirical audiences in crucial ways.[107]

## Porn studies

As a research field, porn studies also emerged from aims at contextualizing and historicizing pornography as a multidimensional cultural phenomenon in need of theoretical analysis.[108] The emergence of porn studies in the 1980s and 1990s has been described as a development, or a paradigm shift, from Sex Wars and porn debates towards investigations of different contextualized pornographies.[109] When Linda Williams, as one of the founders of the field published *Hard Core* in 1989, her purpose was not to take sides in the debate about porn's negative or positive effects, but "to get beyond the question of whether pornography should exist to a consideration of what pornography is and what it has offered those viewers – primarily men but, now,

---

[105] Bobo, 1995.

[106] Stacey, 1994.

[107] Jackie Stacey, 1994, 11ff, 47. See also Annette Kuhn, *An Everyday Magic: Cinema and Cultural Memory*, (London, New York: I.B. Tauris, 2002) and Annette Kuhn, *Family Secrets: Acts of Memory and Imagination* (London & New York: Verso, 1995). In her research, based on methods such as interviews and memory work, on private photographs as well as film, Annette Kuhn has investigated personal, collective and cultural memory and the role in people's lives of cinemagoing and film culture. For an account of cinemagoing in Sweden in the 1940s and 1950s, see Carina Sjöholm, *Gå på bio: Rum för drömmar i folkhemmets Sverige* (Stockholm/Stehag: Brutus Östlings Bokförlag Symposion, 2003). See also Janet McCabe, *Feminist Film Studies, Writing the Woman into Cinema* (London & New York: Wallflower, 2004). McCabe (39) emphasizes the contributions of cultural studies to feminist film theory and contends that: "Alternative subjectivities were proposed from these findings based on class, gender identity, sexual orientation, regional identity, race and ethnicity, and personal experience. It further identified never before discussed generic material as well as complex viewing positions related to identities beyond the white, middle class heterosexual norm."

[108] See anthologies such as Peter Lehman, ed., *Pornography, Film and Culture,* (New Brunswick, New Jersey and London: Rutgers University Press, 2006); Pamela Church Gibson, ed., *More Dirty Looks, Gender, Pornography and Power*, (London: BFI Publishing, 2004); Linda Williams, ed., *Porn Studies*, (Durham and London: Duke University Press, 2004a).

[109] Feona Attwood, "Reading Porn: The Paradigm Shift in Pornography Research," *Sexualities,* 5 (2002): 91-105; Pat Kirkham and Beverley Skeggs, "Pornographies, Pleasures and Pedagogies in UK and US," *Jump Cut*, 40 (1996): 106-113; Laura Kipnis, *Bound and Gagged: Pornography and the Politics of Fantasy in America* (Durham: Duke University Press, 1999), viii; Paasonen, Nikunen and Saarenmaa, 2007, 17f; Williams, 1999, xvii.

women in increasing numbers – who have been 'caught looking' at it."[110] *Hard Core* accounts for pornography as a discourse of sexuality, a discourse which from *Deep Throat* (Gerhard Damiano, 1972) and onwards, deals with sexuality as a diverse field where different people are turned on and satisfied by different things.[111] Drawing on Michel Foucault, Williams discusses pornography in terms of "scientia sexualis," of a scientific will to know, understand and explain sex. She demonstrates how the genre is obsessed with finding the truth about sex, understood as being able to capture and represent through visible evidence of sexual pleasure. Williams argues that pornography builds on a principle of maximum visibility, where lighting, framing, camera angles, close-ups, body positions, and not least editing form part of the machinery that works to unveil the secrets about what sex is, resulting in a number of formal conventions such as the the meat shot and the money shot.[112]

Queer, feminist and lesbian pornography has been addressed by scholars analyzing work by filmmakers such as Candida Royalle and Annie Sprinkle, and films produced by American companies such as Tigress Productions, Fatale Media and SIR Video.[113] The majority of this literature was published in the 1990s and often reads films in relation to the Sex Wars, defending the emerging queer, feminist and lesbian porn film culture by emphasizing its empowering, affirming and liberating potential.[114] However, questions about queer, feminist and lesbian pornography, as they have resurfaced during the last decade through a wave of productions, as well as public events and festivals both in the US and in Europe, have not been addressed in depth. In accounting for and historicizing the contemporary queer, feminist and lesbian porn film culture as it materializes in this project's three case studies, *Dirty Diaries*, Pornfilmfestival Berlin and Club LASH in Stockholm, this dissertation sheds light on an under-investigated area of the present sexualization of the public sphere.

Furthermore, this study answers calls for more empirically grounded research of pornography in relation to specific contexts and practices of both production and consumption. For instance, as Feona Attwood notes, in porn studies "[a] 'turn to the audience,' apparent in many other forms of cultural analysis, remains underdeveloped."[115] Similarly, Susanna Paasonen, Kaarina

---

[110] Williams, 1999, xvii. Williams here refers to the anthology *Caught Looking: Feminism, Pornography, and Censorship,* ed. Kate Ellis, Nan D. Hunter, Beth Jaker, Barbara O'Dair and Abby Tallmer (New York, 1986).

[111] Williams stresses this point through the famous *Deep Throat* quote: "diff'rent strokes for diff'rent folks."

[112] Williams, 1999, 72-74.

[113] See Straayer, 1996, 199-217, 233-252; Williams, 1993, 233-265; Williams, 1999, 246-264.

[114] Smyth, 1990; Becki L. Ross, 2000; Bensinger, 1992; Henderson, 1992.

[115] Attwood, 2002, 103.

Nikunen and Laura Saarenmaa comment on the lack of empirical studies of the reception and production of pornography, remarking that pornography concerns practices and "physical sensations and acts (be these auto-erotic or other)."[116] In her research on online pornography, Paasonen also points out that porn produces all kinds of "gut reactions," not just arousal, but also disgust, amusement and puzzlement, evident in accounts of hurt, violence and grief as well as pleasure and empowerment throughout the porn debates.[117] Highlighting the need for analyzing the affective "stickiness" and dynamics of pornographic images beyond interpretive attempts at determining their meanings, she argues that "we need to dig deeper into the complex ways in which pornographic images resonate with the bodies of their viewers and the affective complexities that this engenders."[118] This dissertation accounts for embodied sensations articulated within the interpretive community of queer, feminist and lesbian pornography. Building on the work of Linda Williams, Vivian Sobchack and Teresa de Lauretis it investigates the corporeal dimension of the relation between porn and viewers in terms of *embodied spectatorship*.[119]

## Embodied spectatorship

In her work, Linda Williams has directed attention to pornography as a "body genre." Williams argues that pornography, alongside body genres such as horror and melodrama, aims at arousing the same sensations represented in the film in the viewer: sorrow in relation to melodrama, fear in relation to horror and sexual excitement in relation to porn.[120] However, ar-

---

[116] Paasonen, Nikunen and Saarenmaa, 2007, 18.

[117] Susanna Paasonen, "Strange Bedfellows, Pornography, Affect and Feminist Reading," *Feminist Theory*, 8 (2007): 43-57.

[118] Susanna Paasonen, "Disturbing, fleshy texts: Close looking at Pornography," in *Working with Affect in Feminist Readings: Disturbing Differences*, ed. Marianne Liljeström and Susanna Paasonen (New York & London: Routledge, 2010), 69. See also Paasonen, *Carnal Resonance: Affect and Online Pornography* (Massachusetts Institute of Technology, 2011).

[119] Sobchack, 1992, and Sobchack, *Carnal Thoughts, Embodiment and Moving Image Culture* (Berkeley & Los Angeles: University of California Press, 2004); Williams, 1999, and Williams *Screening Sex* (Duke University Press, 2008); De Lauretis, 1994, 81-148; De Lauretis, *Technologies of Gender: Essays on Theory, Film, and Fiction* (Bloomington & Indianapolis: Indiana University Press, 1987); De Lauretis, "On the Subject of Fantasy," in *Feminisms in the Cinema*, ed. Laura Pietropaolo and Ada Testeferri (Bloomington: Indiana University Press, 1995), 63-85; De Lauretis, "Popular Culture, Public and Private Fantasies: Femininity and Fetishism in David Cronenberg's M. Butterfly," *Signs: Journal of Women in Culture and Society*, 24: 2 (1999a): 303-324; De Lauretis, "Film and the Visible," in *How Do I Look? Queer Film and Video*, ed. Bad Object-Choices (Seattle: Bay Press, 1991), 223-264.

[120] Williams, "Film Bodies: Gender, Genre, and Excess," *Film Quarterly*, 44:4 (1991): 2-13. Williams (4) famously describes the body genres as manipulating the audience in such a way that "[the] body of the spectator is caught up in an almost involuntary mimicry of the emotion or sensation of the body on the screen."

guing against rigid categorizations of pornographic films and spectators, Williams claims that porn does not have to address the viewer in accordance with established sexual identities. She finds that what she herself learned from writing *Hard Core* was actually how easy it was to identify with and desire different subject positions.[121] She argues in favor of an interactive spectatorship model that "includes the visceral," where the viewer is "vulnerable to and implicated in the images he or she sees."[122] Furthering this discussion in her book *Screening Sex*, Williams contends that the sexual revolution and the "on/scenity" and current accessibility of sexual explicit materials to all classes and genders has brought with it a crucial transformation in people's relation to sexual images.[123] With reference to Foucault she sees pornography as forming part of a proliferation of sexual discourses intertwined with both sexual liberation and new forms of discipline. She argues that through screening sex, bodies become "habituated to diverse qualities and kinds of sexual experiences" and that "sexual sensations previously viewed as private" become socially integrated.[124]

Williams' discussions about embodied spectatorship draws from the film phenomenological work of Vivian Sobchack, which is also central to the present study. Sobchack theorizes spectatorial processes as simultaneously engaging the viewer's body and consciousness. In her discussion, film is not just seen and understood with the eyes, but experienced and felt with the entire body through an embodied vision. Cinematic intelligibility, hence, is carnally founded. Sobchack argues that "*to understand movies figurally, we first must make literal sense of them* [emphasis in original]."[125] She coins the term "cinesthetic subject" in order to describe "the film viewer (and, for that matter, the filmmaker) who, through an embodied vision in-formed by the knowledge of the other senses, 'makes sense' of what it is to 'see' a movie – both 'in the flesh' and as it 'matters'."[126] In Sobchack's analysis sense then is

---

[121] Williams, 1999, 315. See also Peter Lehman, "Revelations About Pornography," in Peter Lehman, ed., *Pornography, Film and Culture* (New Brunswick, New Jersey & London: Rutgers University Press, 2006), 95; and Paasonen, 2007, 46. Paasonen (46) argues that "[v]iewer sensations do not necessarily result from engagement with characters and their assumed emotions but can be generated by far more random and fleeting encounters with scenes, genres and characters, or even music and dialogue." Similarly, Lehman (95) argues that the erotic pleasures of porn lie outside narration, thematization and characterization. Porn spectators do not identify with fictional characters or bodies on screen but direct their attention to their own bodies, masturbating. Arousal and pleasure are derived from fleeting moments, "brief, fragmentary visual or aural moments such as a passing facial expression or a particular moan."

[122] Williams, 1999, 291f.

[123] Williams, 2008.

[124] Williams, 2008, 18.

[125] Vivian Sobchack, "What My Fingers Knew: The Cinesthetic Subject, or Vision in the Flesh," in *Carnal Thoughts, Embodiment and Moving Image Culture* (Berkeley & Los Angeles: University of California Press, 2004), 59.

[126] Sobchack, 2004, 67, 70f.

both a carnal matter and a conscious meaning. Sense, and to make sense, emerges simultaneously in "that *single system of flesh and consciousness* synthesized as the *lived body* [emphasis in original]."[127]

Furthermore, in this study the discussion about embodied spectatorship draws from the work of Teresa de Lauretis and her emphasis on the social and corporeal aspects of the psychic processes at play in the film experience. De Lauretis importantly addresses the specificity of the individual film experience as a process "formed, but also shattered, disrupted, or reshaped, by the discourses, practices, and representations that surround and traverse each spectator as the subject of social, racial, and cultural, as well as personal, history."[128] In her work, film, along with other discursive and visual representations (emanating from institutions such as the family, educational system, media, medicine, law, language, art, literature and theory), is famously theorized as a technology of gender.[129] Through a rearticulation of the psychoanalytic notion of fantasy, de Lauretis discusses film as forming part of the ongoing reworkings of external and internal through which embodied subjectivity is constituted.[130] As she argues, fantasy is "the dynamic grid through which external reality is adapted/reworked in psychic reality."[131] In regard to film spectatorship, fantasy, understood as the setting rather than the object of desire, implies that the spectator does not simply identify with the protagonist or with any specific role or character in the film. However, de Lauretis also stresses that the idea that the spectator can choose and move in and out of any of the subject positions inscribed in the film regardless of gender or sexual difference is an oversimplification. A public representation is not the same thing as a private fantasy.[132]

Following Williams, Sobchack and de Lauretis, I discuss spectatorship as embodied and as historically and culturally situated within the specific interpretive community of queer, feminist and lesbian pornography. As such, I maintain that embodied experiences of queer, feminist and lesbian pornography are shaped by the specific sites, practices, situations, discourses and aesthetics that constitute this film culture. In this definition, embodied spectatorship is then not a matter of a realm beyond culture or politics. This study's focus on embodiment therefore differs from recent discussions about new materialism across the field of cultural research engaged in challenging

---

[127] Sobchack, 2004, 73.
[128] De Lauretis, 1995, 75.
[129] De Lauretis, 1987.
[130] De Lauretis, 1995, 63-68; 1999a, 306f.
[131] Teresa de Lauretis, *Freud's Drive: Psychoanalysis, Literature and Film* (New York: Palgrave MacMillan, 2008), 17.
[132] De Lauretis, 1994, 139-142.

poststructuralist concerns with representation and signification.[133] Building on Deleuzian notions of virtuality and becoming, theorists such as Elizabeth Grosz and Brian Massumi cast affect in opposition to questions of meaning and subjectivity as a way of addressing intensities, forces and potential for change beyond discourse and culture.[134] In a similar vein, Patricia MacCormack discusses the relation between films and viewers as unbound by specific representations, identifications and viewers and instead as a matter of "cinesexuality" and as inherently queer.[135] Contrarily, this study discusses how embodied experiences of queer, feminist and lesbian pornography are articulated within this interpretive community and hence shaped by specific film texts, as well as by specific contexts and situations. As such this study belongs to what Anu Koivunen calls "an affective turn [...] *within* the poststructuralist, social constructionist theories of subject and power."[136]

## Queer, feminist and lesbian cultural production, activism and history

Finally, in order to historicize queer, feminist and lesbian pornography as intertwining with activist struggles for sexual empowerment and in order to discuss this film culture's political and ethical implications, I draw from the work of Clare Hemmings, Elizabeth Freeman, José Esteban Muñoz, Ann Cvetkovich and Sara Ahmed.[137] Ahmed's phenomenological work on queer feelings, orientations and pleasures are tied to Williams', Sobchack's and de Lauretis' theories on embodied spectatorship. Her discussion about how bodies can be reshaped "through the enjoyment of what or who has been barred" and how this reshaping of bodies "can 'impress' differently upon the surface of social space" is a central backdrop throughout this study.[138] In accounting for how queer, feminist and lesbian pornography activates a number of discussions involved in politicizing sexuality since the emergence of second wave feminism, the study builds on Hemmings' call for a non-

---

[133] Anu Koivunen, "An affective turn? Reimagining the subject of feminist theory," in *Working with Affect in Feminist Readings*, ed. Marianne Liljeström and Susanna Paasonen (Routledge, 2010), 8-28.

[134] Brian Massumi, *Parables for the Virtual: Movement, Affect, Sensation* (Durham & London: Duke University Press, 2002); Elizabeth Grosz, *Chaos, Territory, Art: Deleuze and the Framing of the Earth* (New York: Columbia University Press, 2008).

[135] Patricia MacCormack, *Cinesexuality* (Aldershot, Hampshire: Ashgate, 2008).

[136] Koivunen, 2010, 9. See also Ahmed, 2004, 40.

[137] Clare Hemmings, "Telling Feminist Stories," *Feminist Theory*, 6 (2005), 114-139; José Esteban Muñoz, *Cruising Utopia: The Then and There of Queer Futurity* (New York: New York University Press, 2009); Ann Cvetkovich, *An Archive of Feelings: Trauma, Sexuality and Lesbian Public Cultures* (Durham: Duke University Press, 2003); Ahmed, 2004, 2006; Freeman, 2010.

[138] Ahmed, 2004, 165.

linear conceptualization of the feminist past.[139] Hemmings critiques common and pervasive narratives of Western feminist theory as a progressive and decade-specific development from 1970s concerns with unity, through 1980s discussions about diversity and 1990s focus on difference in general. She highlights how this trajectory is constructed as a story about the 1980s as signifying a growing awareness of racial and sexual differences where black feminist critique and the Sex Wars are contrasted to 1970s essentialism. Hemmings instead suggests approaches that stress links rather than discontinuities and that read different perspectives on common problems in more productive ways.[140] Freeman critiques a similar progressive narrative in regard to lesbianism, feminism and queer activism, where, in particular, the notion of lesbian feminism is associated with "essentialized bodies, normative visions of women's sexuality, and single-issue identity politics that exclude people of color, the working class, and the transgendered."[141] Instead of disavowing feminism and its histories in queer politics and theory, Freeman proposes a notion of "temporal drag" in order to complicate notions of progressive time and political generations or waves. She highlights how the forward movement of the wave is always also a drag back through the undertow. Freeman's discussion about temporal drag as signifying "the movement time of collective political fantasy" is central to how this study accounts for queer, feminist and lesbian pornography's investment in the figure of a safe space for sexual empowerment.[142]

In linking this film culture's "collective political fantasy" of safe space to a history of queer, feminist and lesbian activism and cultural production, the dissertation furthermore relates to Muñoz's work on cultural production around the time of the Stonewall rebellion in 1969. Muñoz defines queer cultural production as a world-making and utopian practice, as "a 'doing' in response to that status of nothing assigned to us by the heteronormative world."[143] In a similar vein, Cvetkovich discusses lesbian cultural production as making up for "the failures of the public sphere" by "providing space for emotional expression that is not available elsewhere."[144] She discusses the building of lesbian public cultures around the sharing of sexual experience in terms of "archives of feeling."[145] These conceptualizations of queer, feminists and lesbian cultural production in terms of building worlds and publics and of collective fantasies and feelings inform how the dissertation will

---

[139] Hemmings, 2005, 131.
[140] Hemmings, 2005, 130f.
[141] Freeman, 62. See also Judith Halberstam, *In A Queer Time and Place: Trangendered Bodies, Subcultural Lives* (New York: New York University Press, 2005), 179-187.
[142] Freeman, 65. See also de Lauretis' (1995, 68) suggestion that gay and lesbian subcultural practices work as public forms of fantasy.
[143] Muñoz, 2009, 118.
[144] Cvetkovich, 82.
[145] Cvetkovich, 80.

come to understand the politics and ethics of queer, feminist and lesbian pornography.

## Chapter outline

Chapter 2 accounts for this study's research process, methods and material. It accounts for how the three cases of *Dirty Diaries*, Pornfilmfestival Berlin and Club LASH have been studied through questionnaires, interviews and participant observation, amounting to a large body of ethnographic material. I point out the value of an ethnographic approach to questions about the implications of pornography and describe how the fieldwork and these three case studies contribute to the knowledge production about this film culture. The chapter highlights the importance of investigating spectatorial processes, practices of participation and specific contexts and situations as interrelated and informing each other. It also accounts for how the fieldwork has contributed to the conceptualization of queer, feminist and lesbian pornography as an interpretive community. I furthermore discuss research ethics and my own participation in the film culture, including participating as one of the filmmakers in *Dirty Diaries,* as a basis for the research project. As such the chapter responds primarily to the first research question regarding the sites, practices, situations, discourses and aesthetics that make up this film culture, but also discusses methodological concerns in regard to the second research question about what queer, feminist and lesbian pornography means to participants in this interpretive community.

The first research question is further explored in chapter 3. Based on fieldwork and textual analysis the chapter historicizes queer, feminist and lesbian pornography. The film culture is discussed as building on political and aesthetic legacies of sexuality debates since second wave feminism. I read the production of *Dirty Diaries* in relation to a history of queer, feminist and lesbian discussion, politicizing and cultural production concerning sexuality. The chapter proposes a non-linear understanding of the queer, feminist and lesbian past and highlights how a recurrent figure of safe space supports this conceptualization. It demonstrates how a concern with constructing safe space for sexual empowerment runs throughout this history, but that this concern also results in heterogeneous strategies. Queer, feminist and lesbian pornography is analyzed as made up by an overarching tension between affirmation and critique played out politically as well as aesthetically. The chapter hence examines how the production of queer, feminist and lesbian pornography also produces this interpretive community. In accounting for this interpretive community as engaging a collective political fantasy of safe space for sexual empowerment, the chapter also addresses the second and third research questions.

In chapter 4, the production of this interpretive community is discussed from the point of view of reception. It examines different distribution and reception sites, practices and situations within the three case studies of *Dirty Diaries*, Pornfilmfestival Berlin and Club LASH and discusses different meanings and experiences articulated in these contexts. I point out how participation in this film culture often implies a blurring of boundaries between audience, producers and performers. The chapter addresses the second research question as inseparable from the first and interrogates how meanings and experiences of queer, feminist and lesbian pornography are shaped by the contexts within which they take place. I point out how a tension between affirmation and critique in this film culture is played out also as a tension between the notions of intimate and counter publics. Drawing on questionnaires, interviews and participant observation, the chapter accounts for how participation in this film culture produces experiences both of empowerment, belonging and affirmation and of exposure, shame and unsafety.

Chapter 5 digs deeper into the question about what queer, feminist and lesbian pornography means to participants in this interpretive community. I analyze interview accounts through the notion of embodied spectatorship and discuss in what sense queer, feminist and lesbian pornography can form part of processes of sexual empowerment. Accounting for participation in this film culture through Williams', Sobchack's, de Lauretis' and Ahmed's respective discussions about habituation, carnal identification, fantasy and orientation, the chapter examines how queer, feminist and lesbian pornography shape embodied subjectivities. The chapter considers how queer, feminist and lesbian pornography as a public and collective political fantasy has the potential to shape and extend bodies in new directions. Hence, the chapter opens up for an understanding of the politics and ethics of queer, feminist and lesbian pornography as located in this process of shaping embodied subjectivities.

Chapter 6 specifically addresses the question about the politics and ethics of queer, feminist and lesbian pornography and looks into how recording and screening technology shapes embodiment in this film culture. I read *Dirty Diaries* and other films in relation to Laura U. Marks' discussions about the notions of the haptic and the indexical and point out how queer, feminist and lesbian pornography invests in a shared embodiment. Such shared embodiment is also produced through this interpretive community's shared social contexts. The chapter relates the question about shared embodiment to the work of Cvetkovich and Muñoz and concludes that queer, feminist and lesbian pornography calls forth an ethics capable of harboring both the collective political fantasy of safe space for sexual empowerment and the conflicts and difficulties that this politics entails.

Chapter 7, finally, offers a concluding discussion where the threads from the previous chapters are collected.

# 2. Queer, feminist and lesbian pornography as interpretive community: research methods and material

It is early June 2008. We have gathered at the queer feminist café Copacabana near the water by Hornstull in the Södermalm area of Stockholm. We drink champagne. There is excitement in the air. We have been invited to an "inspirational evening with Dirty Diaries."[1] The filmmaker Mia Engberg has just received 350 000 SEK (around 35 000 EUR) from the Swedish Film Institute to produce an erotic short film collection aimed at "redefining pornography and making it queer, feminist and innovative," as the motivation for the funding reads:[2]

> *Dirty Diaries* is a collection of erotic short films made by women with mobile phone cameras. The project aims at redefining pornography and making it queer, feminist and innovative. The directors are known and unknown and have made their films with only two rules in common: Nobody should get hurt during the shooting and the entire cast is over 18 years of age.[3]

At Copacabana we are about twenty-five people who have been invited to participate as filmmakers in the project. People find their seats at the retro-style tables, forming a kind of circle in the small space. While not everyone knows exactly what *Dirty Diaries* is or will be, many in the crowd know each other – and Mia Engberg from before, if not personally then as a director. In 2002 she produced the first Swedish feminist porn film *Selma & Sofie*, a short feature about the erotic meeting between a young woman and her swimming teacher. Mia Engberg and her assistant at the time also started the company Sexy Film in order to distribute alternative porn. As such, Mia

---

[1] Email received from Mia Engberg and assistant Åsa Sandzén, 2008-05-27.
[2] Svensk Filmdatabas, "Dirty Diaries," http://www.sfi.se/sv/svensk-film/Filmdatabasen/?type=MOVIE&itemid=66210&ref=%2ftemplates%2fSwedishFilmSearchResult.aspx%3fid%3d1225%26epslanguage%3dsv%26searchword%3ddirty+diaries%26type%3dMovieTitle%26match%3dBegin%26page%3d1 (accessed 2009-05-09). My translation from Swedish. At a later stage in the production process, the project received another 150 000 SEK (around 15 000 EUR) from the Swedish Film Institute.
[3] Ibid.

Engberg has been a central figure in the public discussion about queer, feminist and lesbian pornography in Sweden since the early 2000s. *Selma & Sofie* was discussed at conferences and festivals where questions about intersexuality, sex work and the notion of queer were also brought up.[4] As such, the film is related to what has been described as a shift into queer feminism in Sweden.[5] This shift in Swedish activism during the 2000s is also a process I have experienced and participated in, and a history I share with many others at this meeting at Copacabana in June 2008. In fact, this café is also part of this history.[6] In her talk, Mia Engberg also reflects over how she sees the development in Swedish feminist porn discussions since she and Kajsa Åman started Sexy Film:

> At that time when we started it was like 'why porn?'... but now it feels as if there are parallel things happening in the world. Things are written about alternative porn, research is done about alternative porn, there are more and more women and artists who experiment around the topic of sexuality and identity... I also think that the feminist movement has developed a lot during these last ten years. You're not just against porn but you can also affirm your own sexuality in a good way.[7]

At the meeting, Mia Engberg describes the background to and purpose of *Dirty Diaries* and stresses that it is an experimental project and that the aim is to produce a diverse collection. Filmmakers will have the option to contribute anonymously and do not have to have any previous film skills. Some more people drop in while Mia Engberg talks. One is the distributor Nicolas Debot from the company Njutafilms, a company specialized in underground and cult movies. We do a round where we all introduce ourselves and say something about our ideas. I start off by introducing this research project and making sure I can record the discussion. The film ideas presented at this meeting include topics such as jealousy, the objectification of men, gay male butch-femme dynamics and anal sex. After the round, questions are asked about the distribution and about the gender of participants, among other things. Mia Engberg says that the purpose is to get a wide circulation of the project through the company Njutafilms and that the project also invites biological men who identify as women. We drink more champagne and mingle. We are encouraged to book the camera for filming during the summer. I personally also feel a certain excitement at this meeting. I have recently made two crucial methodological decisions. I am going to base my

---

[4] "HBTH" conference in Stockholm March 2-3, 2002 and the festival "Shame" in Stockholm September 14, 2002.

[5] Ambjörnsson, 2006, 171-220; Kulick, 2005a, 11-19; Rosenberg, 2002; Rosenberg, 2006), 116-123; Ryberg, 2004, 397-409.

[6] The Café Copacabana is discussed in Katarina Bonnevier's *Behind Straight Curtains: Towards a Queer Feminist Theory of Architecture* (Stockholm: Axl Books, 2007), 117-127.

[7] Mia Engberg, *Dirty Diaries* meeting, 2008-06-12. My translation from Swedish.

research project on ethnographic fieldwork, and, as part of this fieldwork, I am going to take part in *Dirty Diaries* as one of the filmmakers. This chapter accounts for the background to these decisions and for this project's research methods, design and material. I also discuss how the research process has contributed to an understanding of this film culture as an interpretive community.

*Invitation to the first Dirty Diaries meeting. Image by Åsa Sandzén.*

## Research as activism and cultural production

On a personal level the decision to ground the research in fieldwork and participate in *Dirty Diaries* was exciting and crucial because it allowed me to bring into academic research my background as documentary filmmaker and television journalist dedicated to portraying queer, feminist and lesbian cultural production. In 2002, I had made the documentary *Dragkingdom of Sweden* together with Åsa Ekman.[8] The film portrays the then emerging Swedish dragking scene and follows six women and their dragking characters, on and off stage. Working at different cultural and arts programs for Swedish television I had often made features with queer, feminist and lesbian artists. Participating in *Dirty Diaries* now became an opportunity for me to explore queer, feminist and lesbian activism and cultural production by bringing together my practical and academic skills. As such this project aligns itself with a legacy in queer and gender studies, as well as in feminist

---

[8] The one-hour film was made as part of the Swedish National Television cultural documentary series *K-Special* and was broadcast on 2002-08-02 and 2002-08-04. Louise Wallenberg discusses *Dragkingdom of Sweden* along with Mia Engberg's *Manhood* (1999) and *Selma & Sofie* (2002) in "Transgressive Drag Kings Defying Dildoed Dykes: A Look at Contemporary Swedish Queer Film," in *Queer Cinema in Europe*, ed. Robin Griffiths (Bristol: Intellect, 2008), 207-227.

film studies, where research is anchored in subcultural activism and cultural production. Judith Halberstam finds that in doing research on queer subcultures one needs to rethink distinctions between theorist, activist and cultural producer.[9] She points out that these roles are often fluid in the sense that the activist or cultural producer may also be an academic. Just as the subculture often feeds into research, research also feeds back into the subculture, for instance in the form of documentation and in constructing queer archives and memory.[10]

In cinema studies, the work of B. Ruby Rich and Alexandra Juhasz on the feminist film movement serve as examples of such construction of activist memory.[11] As they and other feminist film scholars have often pointed out, feminist film theory and practice sprung from the second wave women's movement and feminist activism.[12] Recently, Juhasz has argued that feminist media scholarship needs to return "to the feminist media community and movement from whence it was born."[13] Similarly, Patricia White, drawing on her own engagement in independent feminist and LGBTQ media distribution and exhibition, highlights how "women, people of color, international scholars, and queers in the profession remain connected to community-based media organizations as sustaining contexts for their work."[14] In this vein, Jacqueline Bobo also contends that "[i]t is as a participant, not a detached observer, that the work of the critic becomes vitally important within the inter-

---

[9] Judith Halberstam, *In a Queer Time and Place: Transgender Bodies, Subcultural Lives* (New York and London: New York University Press, 2005), 161-63.

[10] Halberstam, 2005, 159. See also Ulrika Dahl, "Femme on Femme: Reflections on Collaborative Methods and Queer Femme-inist Ethnography," *SQS* 1 (2011): 1-22; Kelly Hankin, "And Introducing…The Female Director: Documentaries about Women Filmmakers as Feminist Activism," *NWSA Journal*, 19:1 (Spring 2007): 59-88; Mariam Fraser and Nirmal Puwar, "Introduction: Intimacy in Research," *History of the Human Sciences*, 21:4 (2008): 3f; Cvetkovich, 2003.

[11] B. Ruby Rich, *Chick Flicks: Theories and Memories of the Feminist Film Movement* (Durham, North Carolina: Duke University Press, 1998); Alexandra Juhasz, ed., *Women of Vision: Histories in Feminist Film and Video* (Minneapolis: University of Minnesota Press, 2001). The book consists of transcriptions from her documentary *Women of Vision* (1998).

[12] Rich, 1; Mary Ann Doane, Patricia Mellencamp and Linda Williams, "Feminist Film Criticism: An Introduction," in *Re-vision: Essays in Feminist Film Criticism*, ed. Doane, Mellencamp and Williams (The American Film Institute Monograph Series 3, 1984), 1, 4f; Claire Johnston, "The Subject of Feminist Film Theory/Practice," *Screen*, 21: 2 (Summer 1980): 27-34.

[13] Alexandra Juhasz, "The Future Was Then: Reinvesting in Feminist Media Practice and Politics," *Camera Obscura* 61, 21: 1 (2006): 53. See also Alexandra Juhasz, "No Woman Is an Object: Realizing the Feminist Collaborative Video," *Camera Obscura* 54, 18: 3 (2003): 71-98. Juhasz herself has produced several documentaries as well as the features *The Owls* (Cheryl Dunye, 2010) and *The Watermelon Woman* (Cheryl Dunye, 1996).

[14] Patricia White, "Feminist Commitment and Feminized Service: Nonprofits and Journals," *Cinema Journal*, 49: 3 (Spring 2010): 100.

pretive community."[15] Research on queer, feminist and lesbian film cultures often also entails research methods such as fieldwork and interviews.[16]

The rethinking of boundaries between activist, cultural producer and theorist implies in my case that the method of participant observation is understood in its most literal sense.[17] Rather than accompanying and observing, as the method is often applied in ethnographic fieldwork today, I have *participated* in the field, and built on my own experience as well as the experience of others. Through this approach, the project draws on discussions about queer and feminist ethnography and epistemology where notions of objectivity are interrogated and situated knowledge emphasized.[18] The fieldwork and my participation as a filmmaker in *Dirty Diaries* have served as methods for productively acknowledging, reflecting on and accounting for my own embodied and situated knowledge. As such, this research project grew out of my own participation in contexts where pornography was screened and discussed in the early 2000s. In these contexts, I became aware of how multiple and at times contradictory conceptualizations were intertwined in this film culture. On the one hand, queer, feminist and lesbian porn was discussed as offering authentic representations that would reflect and affirm viewers' sexual identities.[19] On the other hand, pornography in all forms was framed as potentially liberating. In this perspective it was emphasized that viewers should not be seen as passive victims but as active subjects taking queer pleasure in pornographic material through subversive reading strategies. Thus, while these discussions focused on pornography as empowering and

---

[15] Bobo, 51. See also Corinn Columpar and Sophie Mayer, "Introduction," in *There She Goes: Feminist Film Making and Beyond,* ed. Corinn Columpar and Sophie Mayer (Detroit: Wayne State University Press, 2009), 7.

[16] Lisa Henderson, "Queer Relay," *GLQ*, 14:4 (2008): 569-597; Patricia White, B. Ruby Rich, Eric O. Clarke and Richard Fung, "Queer Publicity, A Dossier on Lesbian and Gay Film Festivals," *GLQ*, 5:1 (1999): 73-93; Skadi Loist, "Precarious Cultural Work: About the Organization of (Queer) Film Festivals," *Screen*, 52:2 (2011): 268-273. In cinema studies in general such methods have also been discussed recently, for instance in production studies. For example, see Christine Cornea, "Introduction: Interviews in Film and Television Studies," *Cinema Journal* 47: 2 (Winter 2008): 117; Vicki Mayer, Miranda J. Banks and John Thornton Caldwell, eds., *Production Studies, Cultural Studies of Media Industries* (New York: Routledge 2009); Vicki Mayer, "Guys Gone Wild," Cinema *Journal*, 47: 2 (2008): 97-116; Marc Jancovich, Lucy Faire, Sarah Stubbings, "From Spectatorship to Film Consumption," in *The Place of the Audience: Cultural Geographies of Film Consumption* (London: BFI Publishing, 2003), 3-15.

[17] Fanny Ambjörnsson, *I en klass för sig, Genus, klass och sexualitet bland gymnasietjejer* (Stockholm: Ordfront 2004), 38f. Anna Sofia Lundgren, *Tre år i G. Perspektiv på kropp och kön i skolan* (Eslöv: Symposion, 2000), 11f.

[18] Donna Haraway, "Situated Knowledges: The Science Question in Feminism and the Privilege of Partial Perspective," *Feminist Studies*, 14: 3 (Autumn, 1988): 575-599; Alison Rooke, "Queer in the Field: On Emotions, Temporality, and Performativity in Ethnography," *Journal of Lesbian Studies*, 13 (2009): 149-160; Dahl, 2010.

[19] Rosenberg, 2003.

liberating, the processes this involved were imagined in radically different terms.

This project was formulated out of an aim to interrogate these recurring and conflicting conceptualizations as they also echo discussions in cinema, media and cultural studies where attention has been directed to audiences within different social and cultural contexts.[20] These discussions also inform the field of porn studies as it has grappled with conceptualizations of the spectator: on the one hand, the porn spectator as passively absorbing patriarchal ideology, teaching men to be aggressors and women to be submissive; on the other hand, the celebration of viewer agency, pleasure and mobility unrestricted by gender or sexual identity.[21] As Jane Juffer points out, pornography's oppressive or liberating qualities have often been conceptualized in terms of either "universal power" or "individual appropriation."[22] Discussions about queer, feminist and lesbian pornography activate both conceptualizations. In research addressing lesbian pornography, the relation between film and viewer is often understood more in terms of identification, reflection and affirmation, than as fluid, mobile or unbound by gender or sexual identity.[23]

Hence, this project's research focus and questions grew out of a perceived conceptual gap in the discussions about pornography and its potentially empowering and liberating meanings in both academic writing and in the subcultural context where I first came into contact with this film culture. Attention to the recurring tension between notions of porn spectatorship as either fluid and unbound or determined by identity paved the way for an understanding of this film culture as an interpretive community sharing certain knowledge and engaging in a number of common debates.[24] This conceptualization, as well as the decision to ground the research on ethnographic

---

[20] John Fiske, *Television Culture* (London: Methuen & Co. Ltd, 1987); Ien Ang, *Watching Dallas: Soap Opera and the Melodramatic Imagination* (London: Methuen, 1985); Angela McRobbie, *Feminism and Youth Culture* (London: Macmillan Press Ltd, 1991); Janice Radway, *Reading the Romance: Women, Patriarchy and Popular Literature* (Chapel Hill, NC, and London: University of North Carolina Press, 1984); Stuart Hall, "Encoding/Decoding," in *Culture, Media, Language: Working Papers in Cultural Studies, 1972-79*, ed. Stuart Hall, Dorothy Hobson, Andrew Lowe and Paul Willis (London & New York: Routledge, 2005 [1980]), 117- 127; Pertti Alasuutari, "Introduction: Three Phases of Reception Studies," in *Rethinking the Media Audience: The New Agenda*, ed. Pertti Alasuutari (London: SAGE Publications, 1999), 1-21; Will Brooker and Deborah Jermyn, "Reading as Resistance: The Active Audience, Introduction," in *The Audience Studies Reader*, ed. Brooker and Jermyn (London & New York: Routledge, 2003), 91-93.

[21] Catharine A. MacKinnon, "Only Words,", in *Feminism & Pornography,* ed. Cornell, 2000, 94-120; Loretta Loach, "Bad Girls: Women who use pornography," in *Sex Exposed*, ed. Segal and McIntosh, 1993, 266-274; Juffer, 9-21.

[22] Juffer, 8.

[23] Smyth, 1990; Henderson, 1992; Bensinger, 1992; Heather Butler, 2004.

[24] Pearce, 2004, 223.

fieldwork, formed a crucial part in specifying the research aim to historicize and understand this interpretive community and its central and intertwining debates. Drawing on Clare Hemmings' conceptualization of the feminist past "as a series of ongoing contests and relationships rather than a process of imagined linear displacement," this aim involves accounting for the heterogeneity of this film culture beyond dichotomies of repression or liberation, reflection or appropriation.[25] In order to do so, I direct attention to the discourses and aesthetics, as well as to the practices, sites and situations that make up this film culture.

## Research design and material

The research project revolves around three cases: Club LASH, Pornfilmfestival Berlin and *Dirty Diaries*. These three cases are understood as examples of how this film culture materializes in different locations: the basement space of a members-only kinky, fetish and S/M club; the cinemas, bars, cafés and clubs hosting a film festival; and the many spaces of production and consumption of a short film collection. The cases also involve different practices, including watching, socializing, having sex, networking, discussing, performing, directing and many more. The dissertation understands these cases as tied together through and at the same time shaping this interpretive community.

## Club LASH

The fieldwork was initiated in late May 2008 when, with the assistance of a friend and colleague, I ran a questionnaire at the monthly members-only Club LASH in Stockholm. Club LASH, "the kinky/fetish/SM-club for chicks and TS," is the one permanent site in Stockholm where queer, feminist and lesbian porn is regularly screened.[26] I had been a member of Club LASH since the early 2000s and this was one of the first contexts where I first took part in screenings of lesbian pornography. When the club started in 1995 in a basement space belonging to Scandinavian Leather Men (SLM), they followed their concept of screening porn and made use of the small monitor located in the bar area. For the sex educator and activist Helene Delilah, who started up the club, this entailed embarking on a long search for "flatporr," roughly translatable to "dyke porn," as she preferred to call it when I interviewed her in November 2008.[27] The films screened at Club LASH were

---

[25] Hemmings, 2005, 131.
[26] LASH newsletter, "LASH-info maj 2008," received through email, 2008-05-26. Since 2009 the club is managed under the name Club Wish.
[27] Interview with Helene Delilah, Stockholm, 2008-11-25.

selected by Helene Delilah according to criteria that shifted over the years. For instance, Delilah mentioned concerns about diversity and communication in BDSM scenarios.

The evening when I ran the questionnaire the theme for the night was Bad Birds Ball, where the "most depraved and daring" outfit would be nominated the Bad Bird of the year.[28] The evening also featured a burlesque striptease show and the display, sales and ordering of leather skirts and corsets. Such activities, as well as lectures and workshops regularly form part of the program at Club LASH. Besides a bar area and a small dance-floor, the space is also made up by a darkroom space with smaller booths. Practices engaged in by visitors at Club LASH include bar mingling, dancing, sex and BDSM scenes. There is also a separate space for getting dressed according to the dress code.[29] Hence, at Club LASH the screening of pornography on a small monitor attached to the ceiling near the DJ-booth in the bar area is one of many parallel activities going on at the club. The questionnaire I ran in May 2008 asked questions about viewing practices and consumer habits and aimed at engaging research subjects for further participation in the research project.[30] 28 out of approximately 60 guests were willing to take their time to fill out the four-sheet document. Out of these, I did interviews with four research subjects who I saw in pairs and individually in a seminar room at the Department of Cinema studies on four occasions in November 2008. Their respective participation in the film culture included organizing (2), performing (1) and being regular visitors to Club LASH (1).

*Club LASH flyer.*

---

[28] LASH newsletter, 2008-05-26.
[29] According to newsletter 2008-05-26: "LEATHER – Rubber – Uniform – PVC – Corset – or otherwise Kinky… Minimum = Basic Black. No sneakers, track suit etc."
[30] See appendix for a copy of the questionnaire.

## Pornfilmfestival Berlin

In October 2008, I attended the third Pornfilmfestival Berlin, where I conducted participant observation, carried out interviews and ran the same questionnaire again. Pornfilmfestival Berlin is an annual four-day festival, mainly located at Moviemento cinema, "Germany's oldest cinema" in the Kreuzberg district of Berlin.[31] In 2006 I had participated in the first Pornfilmfestival Berlin with a lecture about the notion of authenticity in lesbian pornography. On the website, the organizers of the first Pornfilmfestival Berlin declared that "there is growing demand for explicit sex that empowers individuals to make their own decisions and choices free of social stigma" and "an appetite for accessible erotica and sexual explicit images that is no longer limited to the top shelf."[32] Their background motivation to the festival also reads:

> The filmmakers, photographers and artists involved in **PORN**filmfestival**BERLIN** have been exploring sex through their work for years and the fact that they have been invited to be with **PORN**filmfestival**BERLIN** gives you the experience to participate in a universe that seems so fabulously, tantalizingly exciting.
>
> **PORN**filmfestival**BERLIN** will showcase the most innovative, risk-taking visionaries from film, photography, performance, music, the art scene, pornoland and even porn karaoke to challenge the genre of erotic film. All works shown form a collection of uncensored responses to the social and aesthetic questions of how we represent ourselves as sexual beings. The curation of diverse talent ensures a wide spectrum of interests and points of view.
>
> **PORN**filmfestival**BERLIN** seeks to harness these developing attitudes and trends by inviting artists, photographers and filmmakers whose work invokes sex, curiosity, desire, fantasy and satisfaction in it's own right. So be part of this adventure and submit your films and other works to create Entertainment for the reasonable Adult.[33]

The focus here is on diversity and inclusion. The gay porn producer and festival organizer Jürgen Brüning emphasized that the festival was called porn film festival without any prefixes such as "alternative" or "queer."[34] In an interview with another of the organizers, Manuela Kay, in October 2008, she also stressed that one purpose of the festival was to bring together different communities interested in pornography and to encourage gay men to see lesbian films and lesbians to see gay male porn.[35] The program shows films

---

[31] According to the website: http://www.moviemento.de/ (accessed 2011-10-10).

[32] Jürgen Brüning et al., "What is the difference between pornography and art? ART IS MORE EXPANSIVE!", Pornfilmfestival Berlin 2006 website, http://www.pornfilmfestivalberlin.de/archiv/background.html (accessed 2011-02-12).

[33] Brüning et al., 2006. Emphasis in original.

[34] Jürgen Brüning, opening talk Pornfilmfestival Berlin 2006-10-18 and notes from conversation with Brüning.

[35] Interview with Manuela Kay, Berlin, 2008-10-26.

in categories such as hetero, gay, lesbian, female director, non-explicit and documentary and consists of film competitions, panels and workshops, often covering aspects of feminism, pornography and sexuality. Even if not exclusively dedicated to queer, feminist and lesbian porn or addressed only to women, the festival is a central arena for this film culture. Over the years the festival has invited directors such as Emilie Jouvet, Maria Beatty, Petra Joy, Anna Span, Candida Royalle, Shine Louise Houston, Courtney Trouble, Madison Young, Cheryl Dunye and Tristan Taormino. The screenings take place in the theaters at Moviemento and in other cinemas. The program also consists of performances, workshops, art exhibitions, parties and industry networking, taking place in locations such as cafés, bars, clubs and galleries. As such, the festival involves many different spaces and practices, although, significantly, the screenings take place in theaters.

With the assistance of a friend, I ran the same questionnaire from Club LASH at Pornfilmfestival Berlin 2008, at the screening of the main feature in the category lesbian film, *In Search of the Wild Kingdom* (Shine Louise Houston, 2007).[36] The film was screened in Moviemento 1, a theater with 103 seats that were sold out for this screening. We approached people waiting in the foyer and standing in line to enter the theater and collected the filled-out questionnaires both before and after the screening. Again I got 28 completed questionnaires back and managed to meet with four research subjects during the festival and interviewed one person over Skype during the following month. These research subjects were participating in the festival as filmmakers (2), an activist working in a queer feminist sex shop (1), a researcher (1), and an organizer and researcher (1). The interviews were conducted wherever it was possible to fit them in during the four intense festival days: at the festival cinema, in cafés and in private apartments. I also did participant observation throughout the festival, particularly at screenings and Q&As in the program "lesbian shorts" and in the category lesbian, and at the workshop "What does feminist porn look like?" held by the producer, director and model Audacia Ray.[37] I also interviewed the French director Emilie Jouvet, the festival organizer, magazine editor and director of the lesbian porn film *Airport* (1994), Manuela Kay, as well as the sexpert, porn distributor and lecturer, Laura Méritt. In October 2009 I returned to the Pornfilmfestival Berlin where my short *Phone Fuck* together with three other *Dirty Diaries*-films were screened as part of a "Swedish Sex" program. This year I also did participant observation, particularly at Candida Royalle's presentation of her own work and at a panel discussion called "Chicks With Guts."[38] I also interviewed the San Francisco-based director Shine Louise Houston. I returned to the festival in 2010 and did participant observation, in particular

---

[36] Screened in Moviemento 1, 2008-10-23.
[37] Workshop held at the queer feminist café WirrWarr, 2008-10-25.
[38] Candida Royalle presentation, 2009-10-22; panel "Chicks with Guts," 2009-10-24.

at the premiere of Emilie Jouvet's *Much More Pussy* (2010) and at a panel discussion about Cheryl Dunye's then under-production feature *Mommy Is Coming* (2012).[39]

*Pornfilmfestival Berlin website.*

## Dirty Diaries

In between June 2008 and June 2010, I followed the process of the production, distribution and reception of *Dirty Diaries* and directed my own film *Phone Fuck*. This case includes many different locations and practices and makes up a large amount of material consisting of: six meetings with other participants in the *Dirty Diaries* project between June 2008 and January 2010; directing and editing *Phone Fuck* and conversations and meetings with

---

[39] *Much More Pussy*, screening, 2010-10-29; panel "Mother Fucker," 2010-10-31.

the performers prior to and after the shooting and editing; and participation at the premiere and eight other screenings of *Phone Fuck* and other or all of the *Dirty Diaries* shorts during the fall 2009 and spring 2010 (Malmö University in September 2009, Malmö Queer Art & Film Festival in September 2009, HBTH conference in Stockholm in October 2009, Uppsala International Short Film Festival in October 2009, the Pornfilmfestival Berlin in October 2009, the Cinematheque in Stockholm in November 2009, the festival FilmIdyll in Stockholm in November 2009, Hamburg International Short Film Festival in June 2010). Furthermore, this material includes emails from Mia Engberg to the filmmakers in *Dirty Diaries*; reception material such as news articles, reviews and blogs; articles written by *Dirty Diaries* filmmakers; interviews that I myself did for newspapers and magazines at the time of the release; emails from viewers to Mia Engberg.

I furthermore interviewed Mia Engberg in September 2008 and January 2010. I did eight interviews with Marit Östberg, the director of the *Dirty Diaries* film *Authority*, between August 2008 and June 2011. Marit Östberg became involved in queer, feminist and lesbian porn film culture at the same time that I started up the fieldwork and her process of directing three films, performing in two and starting up a consciousness-raising group for porn activists in Berlin, has run parallel with my fieldwork. The opportunity to follow this process over the course of almost three years has provided a rich insight into some of the personal and political implications of this film culture. In this sense, Marit Östberg has become a key research subject in this study.

## Films and other material

The research material also consists of films, many of which I have seen, obtained and learned about through the three case studies. The project focuses in particular on the shorts in *Dirty Diaries*.[40] These are: *Skin* (Elin Magnusson, 2009), *Fruitcake* (Sara Kaaman & Ester Martin Bergsmark, 2009), *Night Time* (Nelli Roselli, 2009), *Dildoman* (Åsa Sandzén, 2009), *Body Contact* (Pella Kågerman, 2009), *Red Like Cherry* (Tora Mårtens, 2009), *On Your Back Woman!* (Wolf Madame, 2009), *Phone Fuck* (Ingrid Ryberg, 2009), *Flasher Girl On Tour* (Joanna Rytel, 2009), *Authority* (Marit Östberg, 2009) and *For the Liberation of Men* (Jennifer Rainsford, 2009). The dissertation also discusses Mia Engberg's *Selma & Sofie* (2002), *Bitch & Butch* (2003) and *Come Together* (2006), which is included as a bonus track on the *Dirty Diaries* DVD. Marit Östberg's short *Uniform* (2008), which was made for *Dirty Diaries* but did not form part of the final collection, and her film *Share* (2010) are also addressed.

---

[40] On request from the anonymous filmmakers, one short in the collection has been left out of the research material.

Other films forming part of the research material are Emilie Jouvet's films *One Night Stand* (2006), *Too Much Pussy: Feminist Sluts in the Queer X Show* (2010) and *Much More Pussy* (2010); Shine Louise Houston's *The Crash Pad* (2006) and *In Search of the Wild Kingdom* (2007); Morty Diamond's *Trans Entities: The Nasty Love of Papi and Wil* (2007); SIR Video's *Hard Love and How to Fuck in High Heels* (2000); Fatale Media's *Clips* (1988), *Suburban Dykes* (1990), *Safe Is Desire* (1993), *Bathroom Sluts* (1991); Blush Entertainment's *Shadows* (1985); Tigress Productions' *Erotic In Nature* (1985). Furthermore, works by Carolee Schneemann, Valie Export, Barbara Hammer, Annie Sprinkle and Candida Royalle function as points of reference in discussions throughout this study. Films by Courtney Trouble, Madison Young, Anna Span, Petra Joy, Maria Beatty, Bruce LaBruce and Todd Verow, many of which have been screened at the Pornfilmfestival Berlin, also inform the discussion, although they are not addressed directly.

The research process has additionally included archival work. In April 2008 I visited the Institute for the Advanced Study of Human Sexuality in San Francisco where I was generously provided with a DVD copy from an old VCR cassette with early lesbian porn videos such as *Erotic in Nature* and *Shadows*, films that I thus far had only read about. During this trip I also visited the Center for Sex & Culture in San Francisco where I interviewed the sex educator Carol Queen. In 2010 I visited the June L. Mazer Lesbian Archives in Los Angeles where I studied articles and advertisement related to early lesbian porn productions in the first volumes of the magazine *On Our Backs* (1984-1988). Furthermore, the material includes websites, blogs, facebook pages and newsletters from, in particular, Fatale Media, *The Queer X Show*, Pornfilmfestival Berlin and The Good for Her Feminist Porn Awards.[41] Finally, the material also includes events related to queer, feminist and lesbian pornography that has taken place in Stockholm over the course of the research process, such as a presentation by Barbara Hammer at Iaspis (The Swedish Arts Grants Committee's International Program for Visual Artists) in early June 2010 and an interview that I did with her during her stay. It also includes a program called "Community Action Center and Be-

---

[41] The Queer X Show blog, http://queerxshow.wordpress.com/ (accessed 2011-11-15) and facebook page,
https://www.facebook.com/note.php?note_id=334096238387&id=119867167658&ref=mf (accessed 2011-11-15);
The Feminist Porn Awards, http://goodforher.com/feminist_porn_awards (accessed 2011-11-15); Pornfilmfestival Berlin, http://www.pornfilmfestivalberlin.de/pffb_2011/en/ (accessed 2011-11-15) and facebook page, https://www.facebook.com/#!/pages/Pornfilmfestival-Berlin/259816320725799 (accessed 2011-11-15);
Fatale Media website, http://www.fatalemedia.com/ (accessed 2011-11-15), facebook page, https://www.facebook.com/#!/FataleMedia (accessed 2011-11-15) and email newsletter.

yond – Two Days of Sociosexual Affinity," held at the art space Konsthall C in Stockholm, in early June 2011.

# Research process

## Questionnaires

The questionnaire was designed in order to provide qualitative background information about the participants in the contexts of Club LASH and Pornfilmfestival Berlin and about their consumer habits and views on lesbian pornography. It asked questions about age, gender, sexuality, profession, education and about consumer habits regarding where, how, in what form and with whom pornography is obtained and consumed. Some of the total of 56 filled-out questionnaires are incomplete, certain questions and pages have been skipped, some comments are difficult to make out and some checked options ambivalent. In Berlin the questionnaire language was in English and thus presumed a certain level of language skills, although this leaves open a possibility of misunderstanding. However, rather than making up statistical or quantitative data, the information from the questionnaires is understood as providing qualitative background information and as indicative rather than representative facts.[42]

At this stage in the research process I used the categorization lesbian porn in the questionnaire, but also asked about how research subjects themselves described the lesbian porn that they were watching and if they watched other kinds of pornography. The wide and multi-layered definition of lesbian pornography that the questionnaires indicate contributed to the conceptualization of this film culture as queer, feminist and lesbian pornography. Other frequently mentioned notions in the questionnaires, both in Stockholm and Berlin, are BDSM, bisexual and transgender porn. The 28 participants filling out questionnaires at Club LASH stated that they were born between 1957 and 1985, with the majority born in the 1970s, thus at this time (2008) they were between 23 and 51 years old. The majority defined themselves as women and as lesbian and bisexual. Aside from one they all lived in Stockholm. The majority had more than three years of college education and were working full time or studying. The questionnaires indicated that lesbian pornography is consumed predominantly at home but almost as often at a club, which reflects the fact that the participants were all members of Club LASH. They indicated that research subjects watch pornography with a frequency in between watching every month and watching three to six times a year, in order to get sexually aroused but equally often for other reasons, such as

---

[42] Ambjörnsson, 2004, 42.

entertainment, research, inspiration, education and curiosity. Masturbation and sex with partner/s were indicated to happen less than half of the times that they are watching.

The participants in the questionnaires completed at the Pornfilmfestival Berlin were born between 1960 and 1986, with the majority born between 1977 and 1983. Whereas Club LASH is a members-only space for women and transgendered persons, Pornfilmfestival Berlin is a publicly open and gender-mixed space. Nevertheless, the majority who filled out the questionnaires defined themselves as women and as lesbian, bisexual and queer. The majority lived in Berlin but also in other German cities and in Utrecht, Vienna and Madrid. The majority had college education and were presently working or studying. Many stated that they were self-employed and freelancers. Participants stated most often that they watch lesbian pornography three to six times per year, followed by the option every week. They stated that they watch both in order to get aroused and for other reasons such as empowerment, in order to learn about sexual practices and behavior and related to academic and research interest. About half stated that they masturbate more than half of the times or always, while the other half stated they do it less than half of the times or never. The majority stated that they have sex with partner/s while or after watching less than half of the times or never. Lesbian pornography here is indicated to be consumed predominantly at home, but almost as often at a festival, thus similarly to Club LASH, reflecting the context and particular audience where the questionnaire was run.

The results from the questionnaires ran at Club LASH and at Pornfilmfestival Berlin resemble each other largely in how participants describe their identities, background and habits. Furthermore, many of the same titles, filmmakers and websites are mentioned repeatedly in both cases, most notably Maria Beatty, Annie Sprinkle and Mia Engberg. As such, the questionnaires indicate a shared knowledge within and in between these different contexts, which supports the conceptualization of this film culture as an interpretive community. The total of 56 filled-out questionnaires also indicate that porn consumption in this interpretive community is a social practice and that access to material depends on specific spaces for learning about and obtaining pornographic material, such as festivals, sex shops, magazines, Internet sites and friendship networks. Thus the questionnaires indicate that this interpretive community is also engaged in online practices and activities, such as obtaining information, buying, watching and downloading. However, as will be addressed below, an in-depth discussion about these activities falls outside the scope of this dissertation.

## Interviews

The interviews conducted for this research project were semi-structured and had different characters and focus. Interviews with filmmakers (Mia Engberg, Emilie Jouvet, Shine Louise Houston and Barbara Hammer) and organizers (Manuela Kay, Laura Méritt) have focused on their objectives and reflections around their work, in terms of both production and reception. The eight interviews I made with Marit Östberg focused on her experiences and reflections of participating in this film culture as activist, filmmaker and performer. The interviews I conducted with nine research subjects who signed up for further participation through the questionnaires that I ran at Club LASH (4) and at Pornfilmfestival Berlin (5), focused on the different meanings that queer, feminist and lesbian porn had for them. In what ways did or did not queer, feminist and lesbian porn matter to them personally? What kind of representations did they like and dislike? How were films experienced in relation to their own sexual practices? How would they describe the embodied experience of watching queer, feminist and lesbian porn? The interviews did not specifically ask about how they engaged in films in terms of identity related to gender, sexuality, class, race or age, but asked more open questions about how they did or did not recognize themselves, their desires and practices in films. I tried avoiding the term "identification," unless it was brought up by research subjects themselves, which it often was, but in a broad and everyday sense. Also, in their accounts, research subjects often did reflect over how they saw their gender and sexual identities in relation to pornographic representations.

Interviews with Swedish research subjects were done in Swedish and the rest of the interviews in English, both with research subjects with English as their first language and with research subjects with other first languages. Significantly then, both the questionnaires and the interviews conducted in Berlin presumed certain English skills. The questionnaires indicate that to a large extent participants in this interpretive community have college education. Many research subjects signing up for interviews through the questionnaires participate in this film culture as directors, performers, organizers, distributors and activists. In accounting for their relation to pornography, research subjects have possessed significant abilities to reflect over and verbalize both their ideas about and their embodied experiences of pornography.[43] This self-reflexive ability can also be understood as a form of cultural capital that participation in this interpretive community entails, as well as a reflection of the present condition of sexualization of the public sphere as such.

Importantly, these interview accounts are understood as discourse and as articulations to be analyzed in relation to their specific contexts, rather than

---

[43] For discussions about audiences' accounts of their relation to media, see Helen Wood, *Talking With Television: Women, Talk Shows and Modern Self-Reflexivity* (Urbana & Chicago: University of Illinois Press, 2009) 58; Bev Skeggs, Nancy Thumim and Helen Wood, "'Oh Goodness, I Am Watching Reality TV': How Methods Make Class in Audience Research," *European Journal of Cultural Studies*, 11:1 (2008): 17f.

as providing access to authentic or isolated viewing experiences.[44] The project draws on Jackie Stacey's methodological discussion about shifting from "the textual spectator" to "the spectator as text," and her emphasis on dealing with audiences' stories as narrative accounts. Audiences' accounts, she argues, need to be understood and contextualized as "specific kinds of texts produced within a specific set of conditions."[45] Importantly, however, this does not imply that they are seen as fictional. When analyzing the transcribed interviews, I used different colored highlighter pens in order to identify to what degree the accounts shared common themes, concerns and conceptualizations. Significantly, notions such as empowerment, recognition and affirmation are often present in these accounts as they also echo the wider debates about feminism and pornography, aesthetics and politics in queer, feminist and lesbian cultural production and the question of public sexualization. Most crucially the interviews also invoke the figure of queer, feminist and lesbian pornography as a potentially safe space for sexual empowerment. The shared conceptual framework in the interview accounts has further supported the conceptualization of this film culture as an interpretive community.[46]

Investigating the meanings produced within this interpretive community as involving practices of participation and specific sites and situations, but also embodied spectatorship, the interviews have asked questions about the physical experience of watching porn and about how films are felt in the body. In analyzing this material I have paid attention to how the embodied experience of queer, feminist and lesbian pornography is described and how it relates to research subjects' accounts of their own identities and practices. These accounts, as well as the questionnaires, indicate that many different modes of reading are activated in the reading process. Films are watched both for the purposes of sexual arousal and for research purposes or out of curiosity. Hence, these accounts invoke Linda Williams' remark about the different sensations arising from her own different approaches to pornography, as a feminist, as a porn consumer seeking "to stimulate [her] sensorium" and as a woman.[47] They also direct attention to Lynne Pearce's discussion about how interpretive communities can encourage or restrict reading modes that are more "implicated" or more "hermeneutic."[48] The interview accounts in this project focus on the aesthetic and political meanings of the films as well as on the personal and physical sensations they evoke and

---

[44] See Elspeth Probyn, *Sexing the Self, Gendered Positions in Cultural Studies* (London & New York: Routledge, 1993), 28; Juffer, 14.
[45] Stacey, 1994, 76. See also Wood, 2009, 112.
[46] Bobo, 22, 60; Fish, 16; Pearce, 1997, 211f.
[47] Williams, 1999, 314.
[48] Pearce, 1997, 228, 244, 247.

indicate that different modes of reading intertwine and are not separable in the reading process.[49]

In studying embodied spectatorship this project has primarily considered articulations of experiences through verbal accounts. As Feona Attwood notes, in the small amount of qualitative work in this area, "*talking* has emerged as a vitally important way of way of examining how pornography is used and experienced, or of exploring the range of attitudes, feelings, beliefs, and political positions taken up in relation to a range of explicit media [emphasis in original]."[50] These verbal accounts of the embodied film experience are not regarded as transparent records of or as direct and unmediated expressions of the research subjects' sensations, but are, in the same way as the interview material in large, understood as enabled by and articulated within this interpretive community and as such shaped by the discourses, aesthetics, practices, sites and situations that it is made up by. These have also been studied through participant observation.

## Participant observation

Participant observation has been conducted throughout the fieldwork as a means of investigating this interpretive community within the three case studies. In her work on the home as a site for women's porn consumption, Juffer critiques the sex radical conceptualization of female porn reader agency as individual and isolated acts of resistance and liberation in an undifferentiated public sphere. Against such a "placeless" understanding of agency, Juffer argues for a consideration of how "representations shape individual consciousness only insofar as they exist within sets of social relations that shape the material transformation of the sites at which women purchase and consume pornography."[51] She further claims that "[a] cultural studies critic engaged in pursuit of the mundane implications of consumption, then, acknowledges that the text's meaning is determined as much by factors outside the text as by factors within it."[52] In a similar move, but regarding the case of gay male porn, John Champagne rejects the methods of close analysis and reception studies concerned with audiences' interpretations and instead highlights the importance of theorizing "the porno film viewing experience as part of a larger set of cultural and social rituals and practices."[53] He finds that "the exhibition of gay pornography makes possible a social space

---

[49] Paasonen, 2010, 59.

[50] Attwood, "What Do People Do with Porn? Qualitative Research into the Consumption, Use, and Experience of Pornography and Other Sexually Explicit Media," *Sexuality & Culture*, 9:2 (Spring 2005): 69.

[51] Juffer, 16f.

[52] Juffer, 23.

[53] John Champagne, "'Stop Reading Films!': Film Studies, Close Analysis and Gay Pornography," *Cinema Journal*, 36: 4, (Summer 1997), 81.

in which dominant forms of (sexual) subjectivity might be (re)produced, challenged, countered, and violated."[54] Therefore, gay porn films "signify culturally and socially *regardless* of whether they are 'actually' watched or not [emphasis in original]."[55]

In this study, participant observation in a range of different contexts of both production and exhibition, in screening situations in theaters, as well as in situations engaged in other practices, such as discussions, has demonstrated that the implications of this interpretive community stretch beyond close readings of film texts. It has become evident that the meanings of films are shaped both by the "film experience" and by the "theater experience," in Miriam Hansen's words.[56] Participant observation in different screening contexts has provided crucial insights into how different audiences react, conduct and express themselves in relation to different films and moments in films. Screenings of *Dirty Diaries* have demonstrated that laughter, but also moving about nervously or covering one's eyes are all more acceptable than expressions indicating arousal or pleasure. This has implied that non-verbal expressions in different screening contexts have not been regarded as more authentic or less mediated than verbal accounts, but as shaped by these very contexts and situations and by what conduct is imagined appropriate in these.[57] The embodied dimension of the relation between films and viewers in this film culture has then been investigated primarily through research subjects' accounts, including also accounts of my own embodied experiences of certain films. Hence, this project draws on recent attention to how affective responses to media constitute a crucial dimension of the text-reader relation, while also being cautious about the methodological challenges that this presents.[58]

This approach also implies that the embodied experience of queer, feminist and lesbian pornography has not been studied in research subjects' private homes. The presence of a researcher in the situation of porn consump-

---

[54] Champagne, 77.

[55] Champagne, 77.

[56] Miriam Hansen, 1991, 93f.

[57] See Hansen, 1991, 95f, for a discussion about audience behavior. For a famous account of visiting porn theaters, see Scott MacDonald, "Confessions of a Feminist Porn Watcher," *Film Quarterly*, 36: 3 (Spring 1983), 10-17.

[58] See Skeggs, Thumim and Wood, 2008; 11, 5, 17f. In their attempt to grasp viewers' affective encounters with television Wood, Thumim and Skeggs apply a method of "text-in-action" paying close attention to non-verbal expressions of affect in relation to specific moments of the media text. They find that attention to affect provides insight into dimensions of the relation between television and viewers that research subjects, depending on class and ethnicity, may not be able to articulate in words. See also Attwood, 2005, 67. Attwood discusses how quantitative methods such as surveys but also physical experiments have been applied in research on the "effects" of pornography and how these "[m]ethods tend to be inadequate, generally involving the performance of experiments that bear little relation to the actual conditions in which pornography is consumed."

tion would provide radically different conditions for this experience than private consumption. However, I have watched excerpts of porn together with research subjects during interviews, but the purpose of showing these clips has mainly been to stir and stimulate the discussion rather than to analyze their embodied experiences of this particular excerpt. In these situations research subjects have sometimes told me that they find the excerpts arousing and sometimes that they think they could find them arousing under other premises, highlighting some of the complexities involved in researching porn consumption and embodied meanings. Similar methodological challenges also formed part of the decision to delimit the fieldwork from online practices related to queer, feminist and lesbian porn film culture. As Sonia Livingstone remarks, internet use is often a private practice "located in the bedroom or study" and "at times highly personal, even transgressive – including intimate conversations, pornography, personal concerns, etc., making observation or interviews difficult."[59] Moreover, this delimitation has been supported by research subjects' accounts, where online forms of participation in this film culture have been marginal, which of course may depend on the questions asked. While sites such as The Crash Pad Series and Queer Porn TV provide online platforms for this film culture, the research project's focus has been shaped primarily by how the recent wave of interest in queer, feminist and lesbian pornography has materialized in events with physical locations, not least the Pornfilmfestival Berlin, where the producers of these online sites importantly also participate.[60]

In doing participant observation the emphasis, as pointed out above, has been on participation, not least in the case of *Dirty Diaries*. This implies that I use my own experiences of different practices of participation as research material. As such, my experience of directing the *Dirty Diaries* short *Phone Fuck* forms part of the research material and process. My work with the film consisted of writing a manuscript, casting, directing, shooting and editing. Since the film would be a short feature and based on dialogue I searched for people with previous experience of acting. I also wanted performers who were familiar with Mia Engberg and this project and with the queer, feminist and lesbian activism that this film culture forms part of. Just as many of the other filmmakers, I therefore engaged performers from my own subcultural contexts and networks in Stockholm: Helena Lindblom from the queer thea-

---

[59] Sonia Livingstone, "The Challenge of Changing Audiences: Or, What Is the Audience Researcher to Do in the Age of the Internet," *European Journal of Communication,* 19: 1 (2004): 82. See also Attwood, "Toward the Study of Online Porn Cultures and Practices," in *Porn.com*, ed. Attwood, 2010, 236-244.

[60] The Crash Pad Series, http://www.crashpadseries.com (accessed 2011-11-10); Queer Porn TV, http://queerporn.tv (accessed 2011-11-10). Shine Louise Houston, the creator of The Crash Pad Series and Courtney Trouble, the creator of Queer Porn TV have both participated in the Pornfilmfestival Berlin. For a recent account of this film culture's online existence, see Moorman, 2010, 155-170. See also Jacobs, Janssen, Pasquinelli, 2007.

ter group Kunq and Helena Sandström, the performer and director of performance productions such as *You Give Gay People A Bad Name* and *Dragana*. In November 2008 the three of us rehearsed and shot the film during three days, in my apartment at the time and in the apartment of one of the other filmmakers in *Dirty Diaries*. Over the next few months we had a couple of meetings where we evaluated the process and looked at first a rough cut that I edited and then a final version of the film, edited by Hanna Lejonqvist. This process and the dialogue with Helena Lindblom and Helena Sandström has formed a vital part of the research project as such and has provided rich material for considering production strategies and their practical implications within this film culture.

Throughout this research project my own experiences of participation have provided a crucial basis for analysis. Following Donna Haraway's influential work on feminist epistemology, this approach has also served as a means of acknowledging how knowledge production in this study is produced from a specific embodied location.[61] Importantly, however, while my own experiences are more directly available to me, I discuss them too as shaped by this interpretive community, or in Stanley Fish's words as "extensions of community perspectives."[62] My own accounts of film experiences or of participating in this film culture are as culturally and historically located and constructed as the interview accounts. As Alison Rooke states in her work on queer ethnography, "[t]he ethnographic self is as contingent, plural, and shifting as that of many of the informants we are concerned with."[63] Similarly, Elspeth Probyn emphasizes that "critics, like anyone else, are a part of the social and [...] their experience of it should be put to work theoretically."[64] In this vein, rather than "[guaranteeing] a true referent" I use my experiences as "an articulated position which allows [me] to speak as an embodied individual within the process of cultural interpretation."[65] Building on and "[putting] to work" my own experiences has shaped the research process in crucial ways.[66] In particular my experiences from the release and reception phase of *Dirty Diaries* have informed the discussion of this film culture in terms of both intimate and counter public. Participating in the wide

---

[61] Haraway, 1988.
[62] Fish, 16. See also Bobo, 51.
[63] Rooke, 2009, 157.
[64] Probyn, 21.
[65] Probyn, 29, 31. See also Pearce, "First person strategic," in *The Rhetorics of Feminism*, 2004, 85-107; and Sobchack, 2004, 6. Sobchack argues that "grounding broader social claims in autobiographical and anecdotal experience [...] provides the phenomenological – and embodied – premises for a more processual, expansive, and resonant materialist logic through which we, as subjects, can understand (and perhaps guide) what passes as our objective history and cultural existence."
[66] See also Fraser and Puwar, 2008, 2. They contend that "sensory, emotional and affective relations are central to the ways in which researchers engage with, produce, understand and translate what becomes 'research'."

public circulation of the film and in different reception situations directed my attention to questions about how the figure of safe space is mobilized differently across this film culture. The dissertation aims at making this integral part of research visible in a productive way, not in the form of confession or autobiographical notes for the sake of it, nor for transparency only, but in order to demonstrate how research questions and findings are interrelated with and affected by my own embodied position and experience within the film culture.[67]

## Studying, reading and making porn

The research process has also involved methodological reflections concerning studying queer, feminist and lesbian porn film material. Contrarily to Champagne's argument about the exhibition of gay porn films, I do not find it possible to reject the film texts and their meanings in these contexts.[68] Following Miriam Hansen's understanding of film as an alternative public sphere, the alternative experiential horizon offered in this film culture is understood in terms of "multiple and dynamic transactions" between the space of the theater and the space on the screen.[69] In his study on activities in gay male theaters and in response to Champagne, José Capino finds that the social space, rather than being separated from the film content, may lead viewers to the film.[70] In her discussion about women's porn consumption, Juffer regards the pornographic texts, their content and aesthetics, as "participants in determining conditions of access."[71] Similarly, I discuss films circulating in this film culture as a central part of this interpretive community and its shared knowledge, concerns and perspectives. Pornographic film texts are central not only from the point of view of reception, but also in terms of production and distribution. Hence, in this study films form part of the research material both in the sense of being experienced, produced and accounted for by research subjects, and in the sense of texts articulating the interpretive community's shared knowledge.

In Susanna Paasonen's work the question of affective engagements with pornographic texts relates to methodological questions of how to read and engage with the material. Exploring the affective dynamics of pornography rather than focusing on meaning she highlights "modes of interpretation that

---

[67] Fraser and Puwar, 6.
[68] See also Alasuutari, 7.
[69] Hansen, 1991, 118.
[70] José B. Capino, "Homologies of Space: Text and Spectatorship in All-Male Adult Theaters," *Cinema Journal,* 45: 1 (Fall 2005): 50-65. See also Amy Herzog, "In the Flesh: Space and Embodiment in the Pornographic Peep Show Arcade," *The Velvet Light Trap*, 62 (Fall 2009): 29-43.
[71] Juffer, 23.

remain open to surprises and uncertainties while accounting for the affective power, or force, of the texts studied," such as Pearce's notions of implicated reading and Eve Kosofsky Sedgwick's notion of reparative reading.[72] However, rather than a question of maintaining a separation between affect and signification or sensation and interpretation, she finds that awareness of different modes of readings is a question of self-reflexivity and accountability.[73] In line with Paasonen, this dissertation understands different modes of reading as intertwining in research subjects' as well as in my own accounts of film experiences. I engage with the pornographic material both through implicated and hermeneutic readings. The meaning I make out of some films, especially my account of *Much More Pussy* (Jouvet, 2010) in the context of the Pornfilmfestival Berlin in chapter 5, is evidently shaped both by the film and the theater experience, as Hansen puts it. Film texts are also engaged through more hermeneutic reading modes in order to historicize this film culture's aesthetic and political features. Through textual analysis, chapter 3 reads films in relation to a history of queer, feminist and lesbian sexual representations since second wave feminism. Nevertheless, this does not mean these films have not touched me corporeally or that my affective engagement in them has not shaped the analysis.

Rather, I find that affectively charged experiences have often prompted theoretical analysis, similarly to how Don Kulick argues that "erotic subjectivity in the field is a potentially useful source of insight," as it may provoke questions and "draw attention to the conditions of its own production."[74] Importantly, however, erotic subjectivity does not only imply desire as a positive eye-opener, but also include more ambiguous and sometimes uncomfortable experiences. Such experiences also form the basis of the discussions in this study, for instance in chapter 5. Kulick contends that:

> It is because erotic experience can be 'messy', 'unsettling', and a 'between-thing', capable of provoking a whole gamut of both pleasurable and painful feelings, that it has great capacity to prod us into moving, gingerly and with a lot at stake, onto the terrain of others, with the goal of extending positions, both our own and theirs.[75]

In an afterthought to *Hard Core*, Linda Williams also reflects on how her personal reactions were embedded in the attention she gave to different films

---

[72] Paasonen, 2010, 59; Pearce, 1997, 1-33; Eve Kosofsky Sedgwick, "Paranoid Reading and Reparative Reading, Or, You're so Paranoid, You Probably Think This Essay Is About You," in *Touching Feeling: Affect, Pedagogy, Performativity* (Durham: Duke University Press, 2003), 123-151.
[73] Paasonen, 2010, 59.
[74] Don Kulick, "Introduction: The Sexual Life of Anthropologists: Erotic Subjectivity and Ethnographic Work," in *Taboo: Sex, Identity and Erotic Subjectivity in Anthropological Fieldwork*, ed. Don Kulick and Margaret Wilson (London & New York: Routledge, 1995), 5.
[75] Kulick, 1995, 22.

in her study, despite her aim at being neutral in relation to the material.[76] Paasonen argues that in order to make the critiques of pornography more situated it is important to make oneself "vulnerable" to texts and to "reflect on one's own affective investments in the texts."[77]

*Phone Fuck (Ingrid Ryberg, 2009).*

## Film production as research

By the time I developed my idea for *Phone Fuck*, in the spring and summer of 2008, one pornographic scene in particular heightened my awareness of my own affective investment in my research material. It was a scene that intrigued me theoretically and excited me sexually and made me reflect on what kinds of knowledge and questions were produced in my own encounters with pornographic texts. The scene is from the film *Hard Love* (SIR Video, 2000) and features a butch-femme couple and a sexual encounter played out in dirty talk while both are masturbating. They are not naked and there is hardly any physical contact between them. The femme sits on a table, masturbating with one hand in her panties. The butch stands in front of

---

[76] Linda Williams, "Second Thoughts on Hard-Core," in *More Dirty Looks, Gender, Pornography and Power*, ed. Pamela Church Gibson 2004b[93], 171-172.
[77] Susanna Paasonen, "Strange Bedfellows, Pornography, Affect and Feminist Reading," *Feminist Theory*, 8 (2007): 55.

her jerking off a dildo with the other hand down her pants masturbating. From the first time I saw the clip it stuck to my mind and this affective investment triggered analysis. I interpreted the film as thematizing the same tension between touching and still not reaching that also characterizes an erotic encounter with a pornographic film. It represents a sexual encounter without physical contact as an interactive meeting played out in imagination. It also plays on the tension between the fantasy scenario in the dirty talk and the masturbation as well as on a tension and fusion between body and technology through the jerking off and having the dildo "come."[78] Thus, my embodied experience of *Hard Love* became the basis for theorizing and affected the research, not so much in terms of attention that I give to this particular film text, but attention that I give to questions of fantasy and touch in the embodied film experience. Here *Dirty Diaries* became a platform where I could explore these ideas further. Inspired by *Hard Love*, my film *Phone Fuck* features a sexual encounter between two women, taking place over telephone and in a mutual fantasy while both are masturbating in their separate apartments. My summary and presentation of the film in the *Dirty Diaries* DVD booklet reads:

> *Phone Fuck* explores the idea of longing and absence – and the tension between touching and not touching – as a trigger for desire. The film is a post break up phone sex scene between two women. It is an erotic encounter played out in fantasy while the women masturbate in their separate apartments. The phone call is cross-edited with fragments of intimate contact between them – images that can be seen as memories or fantasies alike.
>
> I wanted to work with the theme of a sexual experience played out on different levels – not necessarily physically between the two women in my film, but as a meeting created verbally between them, in a shared fantasy. A meeting produced in imagination, but also an autoerotic meeting, as well as a meeting between the film and the viewer. Where the viewer is invited to interact with the fantasy scenario and perhaps inspired to reach for and feel herself.
>
> Even though the women cannot physically reach each other over the phone they still manage to touch eachother. Likewise, I think an erotic encounter with a pornographic – or any other kind of film – is characterized precisely by the tension between touching and not touching, between touching and still not reaching. Watching film is a sensual experience. It is about how the film touches the viewer. *Phone Fuck* wants to enhance this encounter.[79]

The production of *Phone Fuck* served as one way of creatively investigating questions both of production strategies within this film culture and of the embodied experience of porn spectatorship. *Phone Fuck* also became a method for reflecting on my own affective investments in the research material and in particular in the film *Hard Love*. It has been one productive way

---

[78] See also Rhyne, 2007, 46-48.
[79] Ingrid Ryberg, "Phone Fuck," *Dirty Diaries* DVD booklet, 2009.

of including and accounting for my personal reactions in the research process.

## Research ethics

As Halberstam points out, in queer subcultures distinctions between research, activism and cultural production are often blurred. In queer, feminist and lesbian pornography there is no sharp distinction between detached audience and active participants. Many research subjects actively engage in the film culture as filmmakers, programmers, sex educators, performers or researchers themselves. While my own involvement in this film culture implied that "getting access" was not a big concern and that research subjects may have chosen to participate in the project because they knew me or assumed I was engaged in queer, feminist and lesbian activism, the production of knowledge also forms an integral part of this interpretive community.[80] For instance, at Club LASH in Stockholm some guests did express intimidation when I and my assistant for the evening approached them, but filling out questionnaires dominated the activities at an early stage of the evening, and while this was odd and awkward in some sense, it was also not a too surprising or out-of-context activity in this space. As one arriving visitor jokingly commented: "You're going to a lesbian BDSM club in a basement – and you're met by two feminist researchers…" Consequently, I do not consider research subjects only as informants, but rather as research collaborators and co-producers of knowledge.[81] Several research subjects signing up for interviews through the questionnaires participate in this film culture publicly as organizers, researchers or filmmakers. Therefore research subjects who I interviewed were given the choice to participate with their own names, to get credit for their activist work and knowledge production within this film culture.[82] Importantly, the choice to participate anonymously was also made clear and some research subjects have chosen to do so. In order to clarify this

---

[80] For discussions about "getting access" and insidership in queer, feminist and lesbian communities, see Rooke, 2009; and Alison L. Bain and Catherine J. Nash, "Undressing the researcher: feminism, embodiment and sexuality at a queer bathhouse event," *Area*, 38: 1 (2006): 99-106.

[81] Dahl, 2010, 7.

[82] The ethical guidelines from the Swedish Research Council, that this project is designed in line with, emphasize confidentiality, but also state that this is not a general rule. See Forskningsetiska principer inom humanistisk-samhällsvetenskaplig forskning (Vetenskapsrådet, 1990), 12. In her research on young queer activists, Fanny Ambjörnsson points out that anonymity can be problematic in the sense that it risks reproducing both the historical and the present invisibility and discrimination of non-heterosexual subjects. See Fanny Ambjörnsson, "En rosa revolution i vardagen: Om femininitet, queera strategier och motstånd," in *Motstånd*, ed. Mona Lilja & Stellan Vinthagen (Malmö: Liber, 2009), 177. See also Ingeborg Svensson, *Liket i garderoben: En studie av sexualitet, livsstil och begravning* (Stockholm: Normal, 2003), 109-114.

in the dissertation, research subjects who participate anonymously are mentioned with a first name pseudonym, while research subjects participating with their own names are mentioned with first and last names.

Besides following the ethical guidelines from the Swedish Research Council about informed consent, I have also had to consider how to handle the fact that people I know form part of the research. As Julia O'Connell Davidson points out: "[I]ntimate, collaborative relationships between ethnographers and their research subjects represent ethical terrain that is no less difficult than research relationships that are more bounded and hierarchical."[83] Whereas issues of building close relations with research subjects lie at the heart of all ethnographic research, in this project I still found it necessary to structure the research relations in some kind of bounded way. As I did not want my previous knowledge about people and their personal experiences impact who would take part of the project, I decided to engage research subjects only through and after I had decided on the three case studies, primarily through the questionnaires. In other words, research subjects are people who were present in the specific contexts and situations that the fieldwork was made up by. This also implies that research subjects do not form part of the project as representatives of specific subject positions or identities related to age, class, race, ethnicity, nationality, sexuality or gender. However, and not without relevance, research subjects participating in the study are predominantly white, just as the contexts of the three case studies also are. Still, research subjects are not seen as directly reflecting the film culture as such. They also reflect who, at these specific occasions and sometimes under rather intense circumstances, could make the fast decision to sign up for interviews where they would reflect over their own relation to pornography, sometimes in a language that was not their first language. This also includes who in these situations felt comfortable, compelled and invited to sign up for a research project conducted by a 30-something white femme Swedish academic.

Thus, research relations and situations have been bounded by and limited to specific occasions, to interviews and participant observation at certain meetings, clubs, festivals and screenings. I have not considered all contact, meetings or conversation with research subjects as research data that I could build on without consent, although it is not unlikely that social contact with research subjects has influenced how I perceive the interviews I have done with them. With interviewed research subjects, informed consent has been made in written form, as a method of increasing the validity of the consent by separating friendly agreements from a formal one and as a means of also providing information about the project and my contact information in written form. At meetings with *Dirty Diaries* filmmakers I have been cautious

---

[83] Julia O'Connell Davidson, "If No Means No, Does Yes Mean Yes? Consenting to Research Intimacies," *History of the Human Sciences*, 21: 4 (2008): 56.

about informing each new participant about the purpose of recording the conversations. Here the dictaphone has also functioned as a reminder of my role as researcher.

Nevertheless, as O'Connell Davidson asks: "Is it possible for anyone to genuinely consent to being objectified through the research process?"[84] In the end, she contends, it is impossible not to appropriate the voices and experiences of research subjects, especially since over time they will continue to be objectified not as their full selves, but as the role they represent or are assigned to at the time of the research.[85] In this project I have the power to interpret research subjects' accounts and select which ones to represent more fully and put in dialogue with the theoretical framework I choose.[86] Importantly, however, research subjects have been given the opportunity to read and comment on the text and have through their readings contributed further to the process. There has also been a case where research subjects withdrew their participation. On request from the filmmakers, one of the *Dirty Diaries* films does not form part of the research material. Hence, consent has remained an ethical principle throughout this project. As will be discussed more in the next chapter, this is also a principal characteristic of queer, feminist and lesbian porn film culture.

---

[84] O'Connell Davidson, 51
[85] O'Connell Davidson, 57. See also Rooke, 2009.
[86] See Stacey, 1994, 77f.

# 3. Constructing a safe space for sexual empowerment: political and aesthetic legacies

In September 2008, the day after we have had our second *Dirty Diaries* meeting with the participating filmmakers, I do an interview with Mia Engberg, at her working space by Mariatorget, in the Södermalm area of Stockholm. I ask if she thinks differently about this project than she did about *Selma & Sofie*, her first feminist porn film from 2002. *Selma & Sofie*, along with the behind-the-scenes documentary *Bitch & Butch*, was one starting point when I embarked on this project. As the first lesbian porn film made in Sweden, *Selma & Sofie* reactivated the feminist discussion about pornography and raised questions about production and distribution strategies in feminist pornography. It was highlighted that the film was produced by an all-female team and that it featured a real life lesbian couple and "authentic sex scenes."[1] When I see her now, I ask Mia Engberg about the notion of authenticity and what she thinks about this notion in relation to *Dirty Diaries*. Her rich answer brings up several questions that this chapter grapples with as it historicizes contemporary transnational queer, feminist and lesbian porn film culture.

> What I thought about yesterday when we had our rally – I like the word rally because you get the feeling that *we are a movement* and that we have rallies – was that so much has happened *during the last years*. Just in how our conversations were last night and how we want to make our films and how one thinks about sexual fantasies and about *expressing sexual fantasies*. Those conversations would not have been possible among feminists *just a few years ago*...
>
> We have stopped defining ourselves only *in opposition to something* that we are against. It is about *what we are for* and how we can express that. This thing with *authenticity* – yes it feels as if we have come *a step further*. Since *Selma & Sofie* felt as if it was the first film we made it was important to *get away from the artificiality*. What characterizes *sexist mainstream porn* is that it is so artificial. There are no real breasts and no real nails, there are no real eyelashes, there are *no real orgasms*. So then it was natural to start with authenticity – that they would be in love for real, they would have sex for real. And *Selma & Sofie*, when you watch it today, it feels almost like *a documentary*, in a way like – yes we shoot when they have sex, they do not act and

---

[1] *Selma & Sofie* VHS case and DVD case; "Selma & Sofie," Sexyfilm website, www.sexyfilm.se (accessed 2006-06-09). See also *Bitch & Butch* (Mia Engberg, 2003).

they are not performers who enact. But it is just real, just real body, real feelings. But now it feels more important to make... *an artistic expression* of, not sexuality, but of *horniness* or of the *sexual fantasy* – which is what I think porn is...

Most of the films in *Dirty Diaries* move beyond the idea of authenticity.[2]
[My emphasis.]

Just like Mia Engberg's presentation of the project at our first *Dirty Diaries* meeting a few months earlier, this answer echoes how feminism in Sweden has been described as shifting into queer feminism in the 2000s and how this parallels articulations of concepts such as Nordic new feminism and third wave feminism, as contemporary formations of feminism where pornography and sexuality are articulated as tools for empowerment rather than for oppression.[3] Her description of *Dirty Diaries* as belonging to a movement organized through rallies invokes an understanding of this film culture as an interpretive community engaged in activist struggles and a shared concern about sexual empowerment. Furthermore, Mia Engberg's reflections about whether *Dirty Diaries* will define itself in opposition to the "artificiality" of "sexist mainstream porn," or focus on "what we are for" and make "artistic expressions" of "horniness" and "sexual fantasy," raise questions about the objectives of these activist struggles. Her answer evokes a tension between critique (of artificiality in mainstream porn) and affirmation (of horniness and fantasy), and raises questions about the relationship between these. Her invocation of movement rallies, as well as our regular *Dirty Diaries* meetings as such, also direct attention to questions about the production practices and strategies that make up queer, feminist and lesbian pornography. The contrast between authenticity and fantasy, as well as documentary and artistic expression similarly brings up questions about the many different aesthetic strategies of queer, feminist and lesbian pornography. Finally, Mia Engberg's consideration of these issues in relation to a development within the feminist movement "during the last years" raises questions about the history of queer, feminist and lesbian pornography, about its political and aesthetic legacies, and about how to account for them.

This chapter scrutinizes production and aesthetic strategies within this interpretive community in relation to a history of queer, feminist and lesbian discussions and productions of sexual representations. Through textual analysis, primarily of the shorts in *Dirty Diaries*, as well as of ethnographic material from meetings and statements made by the filmmakers in articles and in the DVD booklet, it accounts for the political and aesthetic legacies of

---

[2] Interview with Mia Engberg, 2008-09-19. My translation from Swedish.
[3] Ambjörnsson, 2006, 171-220; Kulick, 2005a, 11-19; Rosenberg, 2002; Rosenberg, 2006, 116-123; Mühleisen, 2007: 172-189; Ryberg, 2004, 397-409.

queer, feminist and lesbian pornography.⁴ I examine how the many different production and aesthetic strategies explored within this interpretive community all revolve around a politics of constructing safe space for sexual empowerment. This politics is characterized by a tension between affirmation and critique, as also manifested in Mia Engberg's formulation. I argue that the current transnational queer, feminist and lesbian porn film culture embodies what Teresa de Lauretis describes as a constitutive contradiction specific to the women's movement: "a twofold pressure, a simultaneous pull in opposite directions, a tension toward the positivity of politics, or affirmative action in behalf of women as social subjects, on one front, and the negativity inherent in the radical critique of patriarchal, bourgeois culture, on the other."⁵ This contradiction between affirmation and critique in the women's movement, de Lauretis points out, "was also central to the debate on women's cinema, its politics and its language, as it was articulated within Anglo-American film theory in the early 1970s."⁶ I account for how this twofold pressure is played out politically and aesthetically in queer, feminist and lesbian pornography.

In highlighting this internal pull and the ongoing struggles around the safe space trope across queer, feminist and lesbian pornography's political and aesthetic legacies, I also argue for a non-linear conceptualization of the queer, feminist and lesbian past. As such, I draw on Chris Straayer's chronicling of lesbian sexual representations in film and video as an overlapping of feminist discourses that are not mutually exclusive.⁷ Straayer argues that the ideologies of both cultural feminism and "pro-sex" lesbians "frequently intersect in independent video," where women's struggle for control over their bodies and sexuality prevail as a central concern.⁸ For instance, she highlights how female sexual agency, self-definition and empowerment are equally central to the 1970s work of Barbara Hammer and to the 1990s "bad-girl" videos by Sadie Benning.⁹ Jane Gerhard and Lynn Comella also disrupt understandings of second wave feminism as standing in opposition to later feminist discussions about sex.¹⁰ They both highlight that the issues of sexual

---

[4] One of the shorts in the collection is excluded from this discussion on request from its filmmakers.
[5] De Lauretis, 2007a, 25.
[6] De Lauretis, 2007a, 26.
[7] Straayer, 1996, 201.
[8] Straayer, 1996, 204. The notions "pro-sex" and "sex-positive" emerged along with "sex radical" during the North American Sex Wars. See Gayle Rubin, "Thinking Sex: Notes for a Radical Theory of the Politics of Sexuality," in *Pleasure and Danger: Exploring Female Sexuality*, ed. Carol S. Vance (London: Pandora Press, 1992[84]), 267-319; Carol Queen, "Sex Radical Politics, Sex-Positive Feminist Thought, and Whore Stigma," in *Whores and Other Feminists*, ed. Jill Nagle (New York & London: Routledge, 1997), 125-137.
[9] Straayer, 204. See also Halberstam, 2005, 179-187.
[10] Gerhard, 2001, 9; Comella, "Looking Backward: Barnard and its Legacies," *The Communication Review*, 11 (2000): 205. See also Vance, 1996, xvii.

pleasure and self-determination that the Barnard Conference put on the agenda in 1982 were already emphasized in the 1960s and 1970s, for instance at the NOW (National Organization for Women) conference in New York in 1973.

In queer and feminist studies, Elizabeth Freeman, Judith Halberstam and Clare Hemmings have all complicated frameworks of displacement, "conflict or mandatory continuity" when accounting for the feminist past and its relation to the present.[11] Hemmings calls for a conceptualization of the feminist past "as a series of ongoing contests and relationships rather than a process of imagined linear displacement."[12] In cinema studies, Annette Kuhn similarly contends that rather than a progressive evolution, feminist film theory could better be described as "a series of circles or spirals" where some issues are "repeatedly returned to."[13] Lynn Spigel and Vicki Callahan both also problematize conceptualizations of feminist media studies, as well as film history in terms of waves and historical timeline.[14] Freeman points out that "the undertow is a constitutive part of the wave; its forward movement is also a drag back."[15] She proposes a notion of "temporal drag" in order to "complicate the idea of horizontal political generations or waves succeeding each other in progressive time," and highlights "the movement time of collective political fantasy."[16] Drawing on Freeman this chapter discusses how this interpretive community, in *Dirty Diaries* and other examples, "[registers] on [its] very surface the co-presence of several historically contingent events, social movements, and/or collective pleasures."[17]

## Film production as politics

The *Dirty Diaries* meeting the day before I interview Mia Engberg in September 2008 also takes place at her workspace, where we squeeze ourselves together around a table with wine and cheese.[18] There are some new faces. We discuss our different projects and processes. Some have already started filming and we get to see some rough cuts. For inspiration we watch a porn

---

[11] Halberstam, 2005, 185.
[12] Hemmings, 2005, 131.
[13] Kuhn, "Bent on Deconstruction," in *Women's Pictures: Feminism and Cinema*, 1994, 193.
[14] Lynn Spigel, "Theorizing the Bachelorette: 'Waves' of Feminist Media Studies," *Signs: Journal of Women in Culture and Society*, 30: 1 (2004), 1209-1221; Vicki Callahan, "Introduction: Reclaiming the Archive: Archeological Explorations toward a Feminism 3.0," in *Reclaiming the Archive: Feminism and Film History*, ed. Vicki Callahan (Detroit, Michigan: Wayne State University Press, 2010), 1-7.
[15] Freeman, 65.
[16] Freeman, 65.
[17] Freeman, 63.
[18] *Dirty Diaries* meeting, 2008-09-18.

short by Ester Martin Bergsmark, one of the attending filmmakers. *My Cock Is A Dildo* (2007), made together with Emanuel Nyberg, was inspired by the queer researcher Beatriz Preciado's *Contra-sexual Manifesto*.[19] The project is starting to take shape and already feels much more concrete, not least since the purpose of the meeting is also to go through legal details regarding profit and rights.

Mia Engberg hands out two different contracts. One is for the filmmakers to sign. It states that the filmmakers own the rights to their own films while Mia Engberg as producer owns the general rights to the project. It states that any profit will be shared between all the filmmakers. It also states that the filmmakers guarantee that the performers in their respective shorts participate out of free will and approve that the film will be exhibited as a part of *Dirty Diaries* "in all media in all territories infinitely."[20] The other contract is to be signed by the filmmakers and the performers in the individual shorts. It states that performers are over 18 years of age, participate out of free will and consent to the film being screened as part of *Dirty Diaries* in "all media in all territories infinitely."[21] It also states that the performers consent to any kind of distribution and exhibition of the film "in all territories and media." Mia Engberg talks about her own previous experiences of performers regretting their participation and about not wanting to risk this again. However, if we as filmmakers want to make any special agreements with performers giving them the right to approve of the result, we may add this to our individual contracts. Just as at the first meeting, Mia Engberg stresses that it is possible for both performers and filmmakers to participate anonymously in the project.

With its collective and collaborative structure, regular meetings, shared profit and concern about not "[harming] anyone during the shooting," as it was also put in the first descriptions of the project, *Dirty Diaries* invokes principles and strategies central to and evolved from the second wave feminist movement.[22] Starting each meeting with a round where everyone is given the opportunity to talk, the project echoes models for non-hierarchical and democratic meetings associated with second wave feminist organization

---

[19] Beatriz Preciado, *Manifiesto Contra-sexual* (Opera Prima, 2002); Ingrid Ryberg, interview with Ester Martin Bergsmark and Emmanuel Nyberg, "Röra upp," *Kom Ut*, 7 (2007): 20-21.
[20] My translation from Swedish.
[21] In Swedish it states that performers need to be "myndiga."
[22] Dirty Diaries website, www.dirtydiaries.se (accessed 2008-06-09); Svensk Filmdatabas, "Dirty Diaries,"
http://www.sfi.se/sv/svensk-film/Filmdatabasen/?type=MOVIE&itemid=66210&ref=%2ftemplates%2fSwedishFilmSearchRe-sult.aspx%3fid%3d1225%26epslanguage%3dsv%26searchword%3ddirty+diaries%26type%3dMovieTitle%26match%3dBegin%26page%3d1 (accessed 2009-05-09); and email from Mia Engberg, 2008-04-11.

structures and consciousness-raising groups.²³ At this and other meetings Mia Engberg also underscores that people do not have to talk if they do not want to, just as they have the possibility to participate anonymously in the project:

> One does not have to feel an obligation to be able to formulate oneself in front of everybody else. And one has the right to participate anonymously… One does not have to be afraid of what grandmother will think [giggles] or whatever reason one might have for not wanting one's name… on the film. That is an important detail, because I think one of the reasons why there is not more women-produced pornography is… self-censorship and not daring to reveal one's dirty fantasies.²⁴

Inviting participants without previous film skills also enables activists outside of the established Swedish film production culture to contribute with their "diaries." Here the group process and support is central. During the production phase there are many collaborations between the different filmmakers in the project. Mia Engberg also stresses, especially at our fifth *Dirty Diaries* meeting in August 2009, a few weeks before the release of the film, that "we are together" in this project:

> Within the next few weeks there will also be bad comments about this, especially on the net… People will blog and write mean things… People are angry and think it is disgusting or unnecessary… But then it is important to remember that we are many together in this and not to get sad or broken down.²⁵

As such, *Dirty Diaries* also evokes the feminist film movement of the 1970s as organized through networks and collectives where women would help, support and teach each other.²⁶ In 1975, E. Ann Kaplan underscored that collective film work makes "[w]omen's movies […] as valuable in terms of the process of making them as for the products that result."²⁷ Reflecting on women's film in 1973, Claire Johnston similarly proposed that collective work "constitutes a formidable challenge to male privilege in the film industry; as an expression of sisterhood, it suggests a viable alternative to the rigid

---

²³ Isaksson, 2007, 122-132. Isaksson points out that ideas about democratic and egalitarian organization structures also characterized the left movement at this time. See also Gerhard, 6, 101; and Stacey K. Sowards and Valerie R. Renegar, "The Rhetorical Functions of Consciousness-raising in Third Wave Feminism," *Communication Studies*, 55: 4 (Winter 2004), 535-552.
²⁴ *Dirty Diaries* meeting, 2008-09-18. My translation from Swedish.
²⁵ *Dirty Diaries* meeting at the lesbian-run restaurant Roxy in Stockholm, 2009-08-25. My translation from Swedish.
²⁶ Rich, 1; Doane, Mellencamp and Williams, 1984, 1-8; Johnston, 1980, 27-34.
²⁷ E. Ann Kaplan, "Women's Happytime Commune: New Departures in Women's Films," *Jump Cut: A Review of Contemporary Media*, 9 (1975), http://www.ejumpcut.org/archive/onlinessays/JC09folder/WomensHappytmCom.html (accessed 2011-11-16).

hierarchical structures of male-dominated cinema and offers real opportunities for a dialogue about the nature of women's cinema within it."[28] In this vein, *Dirty Diaries* has also constituted a challenge to male privilege in the Swedish film industry today.

*Dirty Diaries* and the contracts we sign at the meeting in August 2008 moreover raise questions about the collaboration between filmmakers and performers, about how this relation is handled and about principles of safety and consent. During the production phase of *Dirty Diaries* these principles result in one case in the exclusion of one short from the final collection after one of the performers withdraws her participation.[29] These principles also involve discussions about the shooting of the sex scenes. When Mia Engberg's film *Selma & Sofie* was released in 2002 it was forwarded that the performers were not told what to do in the sex scene but were allowed to do what they felt comfortable with.[30] In my interview with the French director Emilie Jouvet in Berlin in October 2008 she described how she and her performers discuss and decide together about the content of the sex scene and how she gives minimal direction during the shooting.[31] When I myself shot *Phone Fuck* I learned that the performers preferred being directed rather than having to improvise or bring out too much of their own experiences in the performance. They saw their participation in the project as acting rather than as documentary portraying. Thus, the shooting of and performance in queer, feminist and lesbian pornography raise questions about its heterogeneous generic nature where documentary, narrative, educational and experimental features interweave, as Mia Engberg's formulation in the opening of this chapter also echoes. These questions will be returned to later on in this chapter.

For the shooting of *Phone Fuck* I found it important that only I and the performers would be present in order to make possible a close collaboration and ongoing dialogue about the process without stress. In queer, feminist and lesbian pornography, concerns about safety and consent in regard to shooting sex scenes also include discussions about safer sex. For instance, at a panel at the Pornfilmfestival Berlin in 2010 the artist, sex worker and activist Sadie Lune stressed the importance of providing lube, gloves, condoms and other safer sex products during the shooting.[32] In several interviews, Marit Östberg underscores that she has learned that it is important to be aware of and reduce stress factors, for instance by taking many breaks and providing plenty

---

[28] Johnston, 1999, 39. See also Michelle Citron, "Women's Film Production: Going Mainstream," in *Female Spectators, Looking At Film and Television*, ed. Deidre Pribram (London, New York: Verso, 1988), 54.
[29] Other examples of cancelled productions in this film culture include a film shot by Emilie Jouvet in Berlin 2008 and a Danish project called *Female Fist*.
[30] See *Bitch & Butch* (Mia Engberg, 2003).
[31] Interview with Emilie Jouvet, Berlin, 2008-10-25.
[32] Panel "Mother Fucker," Pornfilmfestival Berlin, 2010-10-31.

of food.[33] In her case she has also chosen to cross boundaries between director and performer by performing in her own *Dirty Diaries* film *Authority* as well as in productions by Emilie Jouvet and Cheryl Dunye. In the case of *Selma & Sofie* it was also suggested that the all-female team would provide safe conditions for the performers.[34] Questions about whom the sexual performance is addressed to are, in some cases, also raised in relation to the distribution of the film.[35] In our interview in Berlin 2008 Emilie Jouvet told me that she and the performers in *One Night Stand* made an agreement that the film would only be shown in queer, feminist and lesbian spaces.[36] The *Dirty Diaries* contract approving of the film's exhibition in all media and territories resulted in my case that one performer who was interested in participating in the project chose not to.

As these examples demonstrate, a number of different production and distribution practices and strategies are proposed, discussed and circulated in queer, feminist and lesbian porn film culture. Similarly to how the foundational principles in *Dirty Diaries* were safety and consent, at a workshop on feminist pornography held by the sex worker and activist Audacia Ray in Berlin 2008, it was suggested that feminist porn could be defined by the same principles that guide practices of BDSM: safe, sane and consensual.[37] Thus, while the production of queer, feminist and lesbian pornography includes a variety of practices and strategies, the figure of safe space is central throughout all of these. As will be discussed below, films often stylistically emphasize these principles of safety and consent by including interviews or behind-the-scenes material where performers reflect over their participation in the film.

## Sexual consciousness-raising on and off stage

> *Dirty Diaries* is a project where women make their own short erotic films. The purpose is to make feminist and queer erotica as an alternative to the mainstream porn. We believe it is possible to make sexy films with a female perspective and high artistic quality. The need for a change unites us, but every short film in *Dirty Diaries* is unique.

---

[33] Interviews with Marit Östberg, for instance, 2008-10-22 and 2009-10-24.
[34] See *Bitch & Butch* (Mia Engberg, 2003).
[35] A Danish project called *Female Fist* that ended up being cancelled considered separatism throughout the distribution. See *Female Fist* (Kajsa Dahlberg, 2006) where one of the organizers of the project is interviewed. The London-based queer Klub Fukk produced films for exhibition only within the space of the club. See Ingo & The Fukk Crew X, "Klub Fukk – The End," http://woteverworld.com/2010/11/klub-fukk-the-end/ (accessed 2011-11-17).
[36] Interview with Emilie Jouvet, Berlin 2008-10-25. See Ingrid Ryberg, "Tips från pornografen," *FLM: En kulturtidskrift om film*, 5 (2009), 16-17.
[37] Workshop "What does feminist porn look like," Pornfilmfestival Berlin, 2008-10-25.

> There will be vanilla-sex and hard core, lesbian love, trans porn and straight fucking. Poetry and filth and animations even. We make films that emerge from our own sexuality and creativity. The rules are simple; no one should be harmed and everyone must be older than 18. Otherwise, you're free to do exactly what you want. The creators are artists, film-makers, amateurs, queer-activists, straight, gay, trans, bi, and one or two queens who identify as women. Sexuality is diverse.
> Do you want to make a film yourself? Contact us!
> No technical skills are required. The films are made with a mobile telephone camera provided by us.
> Let's come together and make creative porn on our own terms. Let's empower ourselves and change the view of sexuality and gender. It's a revolution and it starts NOW![38]

In this call for participants from the first *Dirty Diaries* website the project is described in terms of activist struggles for change and for alternatives to mainstream porn. Empowerment here is paralleled with "[coming] together" and with "[changing] the view on sexuality and gender." As such it echoes de Lauretis' notion of the twofold pull between affirmation – in the sense of collective and supportive coming together in a group – and critique – in the sense of aiming at "revolution" and change in dominant notions of gender and sexuality. The call, furthermore, evokes second wave feminism's focus on sexual pleasure and on collective consciousness-raising around this topic. As an activist strategy aiming both at critical awareness and analysis and at encouraging new forms of knowing and being based on women's own experiences, consciousness-raising also embodies the pull between affirmation and critique.[39] In her account of the many different conceptualizations of sexuality in American second wave feminism, Jane Gerhard points out that before what came to be defined as radical feminism had fractured into different interests, groups and sexual agendas towards the end of the 1970s, sexual pleasure was framed as the key to liberation and became synonymous with empowerment and self-determination.[40] Gerhard argues that the impulses to both anti-porn critique and sex radicalism coexisted in radical feminism in the late 1960s and early 1970s and "resulted in a productive moment of activism" where sexual pleasure was claimed as every woman's right.[41] Similarly, and also resonating with the *Dirty Diaries* call for participants,

---

[38] Dirty Diaries website, www.dirtydiaries.se (accessed 2008-06-09).

[39] Gerhard, 101; Sowards and Renegar, 2004, 535f.

[40] Gerhard, 2, 4, 6. Radical feminism refers to the analysis of women's oppression in terms of patriarchy that emerged in the US in the early 1970s, associated with widely circulated texts such as Kate Millet's *Sexual Politics* and Shulamith Firestone's *The Dialectic of Sex: The Case for Feminist Revolution* (New York: Morrow, 1970). Isaksson (151-154) and Hallgren (138-141) both discuss how radical feminism was central to the Swedish women's movement and lesbian feminism in the 1970s, but also how Swedish feminism, unlike these texts, insisted on socialism.

[41] Gerhard, 153.

pants, Lynn Comella discusses the NOW Conference on Female Sexuality in New York City in 1973 as a pivotal moment in creating "a public space for women to *come together* and talk openly about their sexuality at a time when women had few opportunities to do so [my emphasis]."[42] She quotes one of the conference organizers who at the time described it as a "marathon consciousness-raising experience."[43] Gerhard, as well as Jane Juffer, also discuss the importance of the discursive space opened up by second wave feminist literature explicitly engaging with and politicizing sexuality and women's pleasure, such as Betty Friedan's *The Feminine Mystique* (1963), Germaine Greer's *The Female Eunuch* (1970), Nancy Friday's *My Secret Garden* (1973), Erica Jong's *Fear of Flying* (1973) and Rita Mae Brown's *Rubyfruit Jungle* (1973).[44] One of the most influential examples of this activism based on consciousness-raising in small groups as well as on the public sharing and circulation of new knowledge, is the Boston Women's Health Collective classic *Our Bodies, Ourselves*.[45] Describing their sense of empowerment through their coming together, sharing of experiences and learning about their bodies and sexualities on their own terms, the collective write:

> [W]e have felt exhilarated and energized by our new knowledge. Finding out about our bodies and our bodies' needs, starting to take control over that area of our life, has released for us an energy that has overflowed into our work, our friendships, our relationships with men and women, for some of us our marriages and our parenthood.[46] [---]
>
> For us, body education is core education. Our bodies are the physical bases from which we move out into the world; ignorance, uncertainty – even, at worst, shame – about our physical selves create in us an alienation from ourselves that keeps us from being the whole people that we could be.[47] [---]
>
> As we managed to be more trusting with each other we found that talking about ourselves and our sexuality can be very liberating. [...]
>
> [W]ith each other's support, we have become more accepting of our sexuality, and we have begun to explore aspects of ourselves that we hadn't thought much about before. [---]
>
> We are learning to define our sexuality in our own terms. [---]
>
> Our sexuality is complex because it involves physical, psychological, emotional, and political factors.[48]

---

[42] Comella, 207.

[43] Comella, 207. Comella quotes Laura Scharf from *National Organization for Women* (NOW), New York Chapter, Conference Proceedings, Women's Sexuality Conference: To Explore, Define and Celebrate Our Own Sexuality (New York City, 1974).

[44] Gerhard, "Politicizing Pleasure", 81-116, "Desires and Their Discontents", 117-148; Juffer, "The Mainstreaming of Masturbation?", 69-103. See also Christine Sarrimo, *När det personliga blev politiskt* (Stockholm/Stehag: Brutus Östlings Bokförlag Symposion, 2000), 24-31, 83-98.

[45] *Our Bodies, Ourselves,* 1973[71]; Davis, 2002, 223-247; Hallgren, 341-346.

[46] *Our Bodies, Ourselves,* 2.

[47] *Ibid.*, 3.

[48] *Ibid.*, 23.

The *Dirty Diaries* call for participants echoes this articulation of the importance of "learning to define our sexuality *on our own terms* [my emphasis]." Even more evidently, *Our Bodies, Ourselves'* articulation of the empowering experience of sharing thoughts and feelings with other women in the context of a supportive group, but also publicly, is invoked in the case of *The Queer X Show*. During the summer of 2009 a group of seven American and European women toured throughout Europe in a mini-van.[49] Making stops in Berlin, Paris, Copenhagen, Stockholm and other cities, they put up their burlesque performance *The Queer X Show* and spent time together with local queer, feminist and lesbian communities. The tour was documented by the filmmaker Emilie Jouvet and resulted in two films, *Too Much Pussy: Feminist Sluts in the Queer X Show* (2010) and *Much More Pussy* (2010). I attended the show when they performed in Stockholm during the Pride Festival in 2009. I also followed the blog they wrote throughout the tour.[50] On 3 August 2009 performance artist and dancer Mad Kate posted an entry where she described feelings of joy, gratitude and safety in being part of this collaboration: "I got the sense that I was entering a space in which I could share my mistakes and bad ideas with women who honestly wanted to help me make a better show."[51] In a vein echoing *Our Bodies, Ourselves*, she continues:

> What I appreciate most about this tour so far is the privilege and comfort of being surrounded by incredibly wonderful queer women; our ability to have these amazing conversations and not to feel like any of my opinions or feelings are wrong or illegitimate. [---]
> I am familiar with a school of thought that believes sexual desire is superfluous, that these are the things that can and should be repressed and reconsidered, or that sexual freedom is luxury or even childish. But I can't agree; freedom to express one's self sexually is tied into every freedom of expression of the body, from speech to basic needs like eating and sleeping. When we don't have the rope around us we suddenly realize just how much easier we can breathe.[52]

In her blog entry, Mad Kate also describes how the participants in the show, at an early stage of the tour, examine their cervixes together: "Already a level of comfort established between us; a clear message also about the type of women that we would be together – open, sexual, naked, raw, unafraid."[53] In *The Queer X Show* the practice of cervix examination was also performed

---

[49] The performers in the show were Mad Kate, Sadie Lune, Judy Minx, Wendy Delorme, Madison Young, DJ Metzgerei. The tour was documented by Emilie Jouvet.
[50] Mad Kate, "27 July 2009," The Queer X Show blog, http://queerxshow.wordpress.com/2009/08/03/27-july-2009/ (accessed 2010-03-13).
[51] Ibid.
[52] Ibid.
[53] Ibid.

on stage by the sex educator and performer Sadie Lune. As Gerhard points out, the discourse on sexual pleasure as the key to liberation in second wave feminism involved a new perspective on women's bodies and sexual organs, not least the clitoris, which was regarded as a "distinctively feminist body part" and came to signify authenticity and liberation.[54] Women's sexual organs, including clitoris and cervix and menstruation and masturbation were celebrated in consciousness-raising groups and literature, as well as in the artwork of Judy Chicago and the films of Barbara Hammer and Anne Severson.[55] Within this discourse and not least through the worldwide circulation of *Our Bodies, Ourselves*, women were encouraged to learn more about their sexual organs. Self-examination with speculum and hand-mirror and genital self-portraiture were practiced as feminist methods for heightening women's sense of autonomy and control over their bodies.[56] The practice of cervix examination would later be made famous in Annie Sprinkle's "Public Cervix Announcements" in the 1990s, where she invited members of the audience to her show *Post Porn Modernist* to look at her cervix through a speculum.[57] In the case of *The Queer X Show*, explicit reference was made to 1980s sex radicals such as Sprinkle as well as Candida Royalle and Carol Queen. However, both Sprinkle and *The Queer X Show* belong to the longer legacy of sexual consciousness-raising both on and off stage.[58]

---

[54] Gerhard 6, 7, 104-107. Two influential texts in this perspective were Anne Koed's article "The Myth of the Vaginal Orgasm," in *Notes From the First Years*, ed. Shulamith Firestone (New York, 1968) and Ti-Grace Atkinson, "The Institution of Sexual Intercourse," in *Notes from the Second Year*, ed. Shulamith Firestone (New York, 1970). See also Hallgren, 323-327. Highly influential was also Betty Dodson's Bodysex Workshops and book *Liberating Masturbation: A Meditation on Self Love* (Bodysex Designs, 1974). See Juffer, 69-70; Comella, 206.

[55] Hammer, *Dyketactics* (1974), *Menses* (1974), *Women I Love* (1976) and *Multiple Orgasm* (1976); Severson, *Near the Big Chakra* (1972); Valie Export: *Mann & Frau & Animal*, 1973. See Scott McDonald, Anne Severson and Yvonne Rainer, "Two Interviews: Demystifying the Female Body: Anne Severson 'Near the Big Chakra.' Yvonne Rainer: 'Privilege'," *Film Quarterly*, 45: 1 (Autumn 1991): 18-32; Richard Dyer with Julianne Pidduck, "Lesbian/Woman: Lesbian Cultural Feminist Film," in *Now You See It: Studies in Lesbian and Gay Film*, Second Edition (London & New York: Routledge, 2003[90]), 169-200.

[56] See Hallgren, 352, 357; and Ebba Witt-Brattström, *Å alla kära systrar!* (Stockholm: Norstedts, 2010), 104-108. See also Williams, 1990, 260. Williams discusses how the main character in *Three Daughters* (Candida Royalle, 1986) "[looks] at drawings and [investigates] her own genitals with a mirror."

[57] Gabrielle Cody, "Introduction: Sacred Bazoombas," in *Hardcore from the Heart: The Pleasures, Profits and Politics of Sex in Performance*, by Annie Sprinkle and Gabrielle Cody (New York: Continuum, 2001), 1-19.

[58] "Too Much Pussy ! Feminist Sluts in The Queer X Show, un road-movie documentaire entre filles," published 2010-03-02,
http://www.facebook.com/?ref=logo#!/note.php?note_id=334096238387&id=119867167658 &ref=mf (accessed 2010-03-09).

*The Queer X Show tour. Photograph by Mad Kate. Courtesy of the artist.*

Reading *Dirty Diaries* and *The Queer X Show* in relation to *Our Bodies, Ourselves* disrupts conceptualizations of the queer, feminist and lesbian past as a matter of displacement and generational conflict. The emphasis on sexual self-determination and pleasure, on coming together in supportive groups as well as sharing intimate experience and knowledge in public (through books, films, performances and blogs) ties contemporary queer, feminist and lesbian pornography to second wave feminism.[59] Nevertheless, insistence on and celebration of female sexual pleasure in second wave feminism was not without contest. The legacy of sexual consciousness-raising is not a unified but a conflicting and multi-layered one. Gerhard points out that while the conceptualization of sexual pleasure as a key to liberation united women in the early 1970s it also led to the intense debates that would be called the Sex Wars.[60] If the women's movement, as de Lauretis argues, is made up by both affirmation and critique, critique has also taken the shape of conflicts between feminists. Queer, feminist and lesbian pornography embodies these conflicts as they have been played out in debates about sexuality and pornography.

---

[59] See also Anu Koivunen, "Confessions of a Free Woman: Telling Feminist Stories in Postfeminist Media Culture," *Journal of Aesthetics & Culture*, 1 (2009), http://www.aestheticsandculture.net/index.php/jac/article/view/4644 (accessed 2011-11-17); Sowards and Renegar, 2004, 535-552.

[60] Gerhard, 149-153, 183-195.

# Politicizing pornography

> In the search for a lady machismo the rules are simple; pin her on her back for ten seconds and triumph. Methods are free, only limited to your own compassion.
>
> But like in relationships, even simple rules means different things for different players, and for every fight or relation, the rules are made up in the playing. The game becomes the construction and deconstruction of convention, striving to stay on top causing as little hurt as possible, for you and your opponent or partner.
>
> However, this is not a tragedy nor drama. This is a violent yet tender comedy of five women finding the limit of their own empathy, pain and physical strength. It is a futile sadomasochistic venture that leaves us in a burlesque dance of willpower, enticing us to explore the macho violence within female sexuality. Do we really want to win the game? What are we actually fighting for?[61]

In the *Dirty Diaries* short *On Your Back Woman!*, made anonymously under the pseudonym Wolf Madame, five women wrestle in pairs in different bedrooms. The action is in slow motion, focusing on the movements and emotions of the game. Both the short and its presentation in the *Dirty Diaries* DVD booklet thematize power struggles between women. I propose a reading of the film as an illustration of the internal tensions and fights that characterize queer, feminist and lesbian activism and history. In this presentation the notions of compassion, empathy and aiming at causing as little hurt as possible, all evoke questions about how the interpretive community of queer, feminist and lesbian pornography as, in Lynne Pearce's words, a "site of struggle," may still be safe for its players.[62] Gerhard contends that the second wave feminist construction of pleasure as the common goal for women's liberation both brought women together and became the seed of much conflict and debate. Discussions about differences between women complicated the notion of one common goal for all women's liberation. As Gerhard points out, the subject of the radical feminist fight for sexual freedom was largely constructed as "white, university educated and middle-class," but still as "representative of all women."[63] In anthologies such as *This Bridge Called my Back* (1981) and *All the Women Are White, All the Blacks Are Men, But Some of Us Are Brave* (1982) and in bell hooks' *Ain't I a Woman* (1981), black feminists insisted on discussing the fight for the right to sexual pleasure also in relation to "a history of sexual exploitation and violently racist denial of [black women's] privacy and bodily integrity."[64] In her account

---

[61] Wolf Madame, "On Your Back Woman," *Dirty Diaries* DVD booklet, 2009.
[62] Pearce, 1997, 212.
[63] Gerhard, 9.
[64] Gerhard, 103. Cherrie Moraga, Gloria Anzaldúa, ed., *This Bridge Called My Back: Writings by Radical Women of Color* (Persephone Press, 1981); Gloria T. Hull, Patricia Bell Scott

Gerhard contends that third wave feminism grew out of "minority feminists' critiques of white feminism" and "understand[s] that identity is forged through *competing* identifications, and thus [...] embrace contradiction [emphasis in original]."[65]

*On Your Back Woman! (Wolf Madame, 2009). Courtesy of the filmmaker.*

Importantly, however, while aiming precisely at diversity and at representations emanating from many different filmmakers, *Dirty Diaries* was also critiqued for lacking variation of bodies represented in the film. In an article about *Dirty Diaries* in the Swedish queer feminist cultural magazine *FUL*, Nasim Aghili finds that: "If the majority of the bodies and stories in the collection depict young, blonde, chalk white, alert bodies in normative positions, feminist knowledge has been lost along the way."[66] In Mia Engberg's response to this critique in the same article, she reflects on

---

and Barbara Smith, *All the Women Are White, All the Blacks Are Men, but Some of Us Are Brave: Black Women's Studies* (New York: The Feminist Press, 1982); bell hooks, *Ain't I a Woman: Black Women and Feminism* (Boston: South End Press, 1981).
[65] Gerhard, 4. See also Sowards and Renegar, 2004, 535-552; and Juhasz, 2001, 8. Juhasz defines third-wave feminism as insisting "that theories of gender, race, or sexuality wrought from identity – often first understood in isolation from each other – must be inter*r*elated [emphasis in original]."
[66] Aghili, 15. My translation from Swedish.

the difficulties in actualizing the aim at diversity, for instance in regard to age, and especially within the frames of a one-year production process:

> It was very difficult to find someone from another generation who wanted to participate, both as performers and directors. It turned out a rather small homogeneous group where the majority knew each other. I am 38 and I am probably the oldest. So it is people who go to Mejan and Konstfack [art colleges in Stockholm] and people who write. A kind of young, queer feminist, urban, white group one could say. Who is about 25-30.[67]

This discussion reiterates questions about social differences between women raised in second wave feminism. Thus, if the ongoing concern with sexual consciousness-raising disrupts understandings of the queer, feminist and lesbian past in terms of a clear-cut and linear development from one generation to the next, the debate about who *Dirty Diaries* represents similarly illustrates that the concern with differences is also ongoing, rather than obsolete or solved in third wave feminism. In her discussion Hemmings warns precisely that a decade-specific conceptualization of the feminist past risks marginalizing "racial and sexual critique of feminism" as "a necessary but temporary stage in the movement towards a more generalized notion of difference."[68] Hence, despite ongoing discussions at the *Dirty Diaries* meetings about diversity and about who the project should represent, the film also testifies to the need for continued critical awareness and development of specific strategies for representing other than "young, blonde, chalk white, alert bodies."[69]

As one of the few films in the collection representing both black and white bodies of different sizes, *On Your Back Woman!* also raises questions about differences and about how, as it is put in the DVD booklet, "rules means different things for different players." These questions also apply to how the individual shorts in the *Dirty Diaries* collection all interpret and express the concept of feminist pornography differently. This implies that the different shorts reiterate the queer, feminist and lesbian past in different ways. Yet, they all manifest the tension between affirmation and critique that de Lauretis defines as characteristic of the women's movement, including women's film. *Dirty Diaries* is a distinct example of how queer, feminist and lesbian pornography incorporates heterogeneous political and aesthetic legacies. Queer, feminist and lesbian pornography builds on second wave feminism's emphasis on sexual pleasure and self-determination, but the conflicts that this led to are likewise formative of this film culture, especially as it emerged at the peak of the Sex Wars. *On Your Back Woman!* evokes this history and these struggles, not least in its resonance with the magazine titles

---

[67] Mia Engberg interviewed by Aghili, 17. My translation from Swedish.
[68] Hemmings, 116.
[69] For instance at *Dirty Diaries* meeting, 2008-09-18.

*Off Our Backs* and *On Our Backs*, as they represent anti-porn and sex radical positions respectively.[70] In Freeman's terms, *On Your Back Woman!*, as well as the other shorts in *Dirty Diaries,* "[register] on their very surface" both the legacy of sexual consciousness-raising and the legacy of the Sex Wars.[71]

## Legacies of Sex Wars

Marit Östberg's *Dirty Diaries* film *Authority* further explores violent power struggles between women. The film features lesbian BDSM role-play between a graffiti artist and a policewoman. The "graffiti girl" gets caught by the policewoman in a restricted area where she is spraying something on the wall. After a chase scene into a deserted building the graffiti girl overpowers the policewoman and ties her to a chair. She kicks the chair with the policewoman on it until it falls. Then, after a while, she lifts the chair up again and unties the ropes. Now, the policewoman chooses to stay and allows the power play to continue. "In *Authority* sex is a dirty game, it's a threat, a promise. It's to be inside the limits of another person," Marit Östberg writes in the DVD booklet.[72] *Authority* was the second film Marit Östberg made for *Dirty Diaries*, after one of the performers from the first film she made, *Uniform* (2008), withdrew her participation. *Uniform* had a similar story to *Authority* but featured four performers, two controllers and two fare dodgers in the Stockholm subway. After a short chase scene the two controllers are overpowered and dominated by the other two women in two sex scenes set in a deserted train track area. One of the controller women is tied with her hands behind her back and placed over a low street lamp. The other woman penetrates her anally wearing red skin gloves, occasionally forcing her fingers into the woman's mouth and pulling her hair. At our third *Dirty Diaries* meeting in December 2008, also in Mia Engberg's workspace, we watch and discuss the film and Mia Engberg, considering the film in relation to notions of female sexuality as inherently softer, says that:

> I'm very happy to have this kind of hard stuff in the compilation ... because I think it's a problem that... lesbian erotica and also feminist erotica... always have to be soft and I think that's one of the ... oppressions or prejudice ... against female sexuality that it has to be so soft and it always has to involve love and falling in love ... I'm very proud to present this piece.[73]

Marit Östberg's two shorts produced for *Dirty Diaries* and the discussion at this meeting evoke the extensive sexuality debates between feminists associ-

---

[70] *Off Our Backs* (1970-2008); *On Our Backs* (1984-2006).
[71] Freeman, 63.
[72] Marit Östberg, "Authority," *Dirty Diaries* DVD booklet, 2009.
[73] *Dirty Diaries* meeting, 2008-12-16.

ated with the Sex Wars. Mia Engberg's critique of notions of female sexuality as "soft" echoes the sex radical critique of a construction of female sexuality as non-violent in cultural feminism.[74] This critique was also articulated in the paper *On Our Backs* and in the emergence of commercially available lesbian sex videos through companies with names such as Blush Entertainment, Tigress Productions, Lavender Blue Productions and Fatale Media in the early 1980s. As pointed out by a number of scholars, *On Our Backs* (run by the same women as Fatale Media), was an obvious response to the feminist anti-porn paper *Off Our Backs*.[75] *Dirty Diaries* and the discussions about Marit Östberg's films illustrate how queer, feminist and lesbian pornography articulates what has been described as wars between feminists over the meanings of sexual representations.

In 1979 B. Ruby Rich observed that, over a decade after Carolee Schneemann's autobiographical sexual exploration in *Fuses* (1965) and with the exception of lesbian films by Jan Oxenberg and Barbara Hammer, "an impasse over the whole issue of sexuality seems to prevail" in women's films.[76] She commented on how "some women have begun to feel that such a counterthrust does not substantially alter the problem, and that even control of one's own image does not necessarily influence the perception of its nudity or sexual meaning."[77] When I interviewed Barbara Hammer in Stockholm in June 2010 I brought up this observation and asked her about the reception of her sexually explicit lesbian films. She answered that her films have always caused debates among women.[78] Once when she was screening her film *Superdyke* at a women's center someone wrote "fascist" on the poster.[79] She said that these debates regarded both the nudity in her films as well as her experimental style. Rather than belonging to a supportive community of feminist filmmakers, Hammer contended that she has mostly worked alone and that she sees herself as a "lesbian maverick."[80] Similarly, in her account of avant-garde women filmmakers, Lauren Rabinovitz comments on how *Fuses* was excluded from the First International Festival of Women's Films and on how Schneemann's "self-proclaimed interest in creating 'sensory arenas' and her detailed, graphic depiction of various sexual acts seemed to

---

[74] Gerhard, 153-173; Hallgren, 275-420; Isaksson, 181-187.

[75] Arlene Stein, "The Year of the Lustful Lesbian," in *Shameless: Sexual Dissidence in American Culture* (New York & London: New York University Press, 2006), 44; Heather Butler, 2004, 178; Hunter, 2006, 15-28; Conway, 1997, 94; Straayer, 1996, 184-232.

[76] Rich, 114. Jan Oxenberg, *Home Movie* (1972), *Comedy In Six Unnatural Acts* (1975).

[77] Rich, 112.

[78] Interview with Barbara Hammer, Stockholm, 2010-06-11. See also Barbara Hammer, *Hammer! Making Movies Out of Sex and Life* (New York City: The Feminist Press, 2010), 100-118.

[79] Interview with Barbara Hammer, Stockholm, 2010-06-11. See also Ingrid Ryberg, "Flattaktik," *FLM*, 9/10 (2010): 16-17.

[80] Interview with Barbara Hammer, Stockholm, 2010-06-11.

keep her outside of critical discourse and practice being built-up around groups of feminist filmmakers in the early 1970s."[81] These examples indicate that the opening up of public space for consciousness-raising around sexuality in second wave feminism was not without debate and controversy, and that the feminist (film) movement did not always provide a supportive and affirmative space. In a conversation between Comella and the sex educator and activist Carol Queen they also comment on how some women in protest walked out from sex educator Betty Dodson's explicit vulva slide show at the NOW conference in 1973.[82]

In their respective accounts of US anti-porn feminism, Gerhard and Carolyn Bronstein describe how the second wave feminist movement increasingly came to focus on questions of sexual exploitation, danger and violence.[83] Over the course of the 1970s and through publications such as the paper *Off Our Backs,* Susan Brownmiller's *Against Our Will: Men, Women, and Rape* (1975), the anthology *Take Back the Night: Women on Pornography* and Andrea Dworkin's *Pornography: Men Possessing Women,* and organizations such as WAVAW (Women Against Violence Against Women, formed in 1976), the radical feminist critique of sexual liberation and sexist media representations grew into a critique of pornography more specifically, as naturalizing male domination and violence against women.[84] Interrelated with anti-porn feminism was the development of cultural feminism as a direction in second wave feminism focusing on women's difference from men and not least on female sexuality as radically different from male sexuality.[85] According to Gerhard, this lead to "a new sexual prescription," where "[t]ruly feminist sex was antiphallic, antirole-playing, and fundamentally egalitarian."[86] Women's sexual freedom was defined as "freedom from violent male sexuality."[87] Critique of violent male sexuality also came to be directed at lesbian sexual subcultures engaged in S/M, dildo penetration and butch-femme roles.[88] By the time of the famous Barnard Conference on

---

[81] Lauren Rabinovitz, *Points of Resistance: Women, Power & Politics in the New York Avant-garde Cinema, 1943-71* (Urbana & Chicago: University of Illinois Press, 1991), 192. See also Rich, 21-28.

[82] Carol Queen, interviewed by Lynn Comella, "The Necessary Revolution: Sex-Positive Feminism in the Post-Barnard Era," *The Communication Review*, 11 (2008): 282. Se also Gerhard, 150f.

[83] Gerhard, 173; Bronstein, 127-172.

[84] Susan Brownmiller, *Against Our Will: Men, Women and Rape* (New York: Simon & Schuster, 1975); Laura Lederer, ed., *Take Back the Night: Women on Pornography* (New York: William Morrow, 1980); Dworkin, 1981. See also Arnberg, 2010, 241-247.

[85] Hallgren, 308-327. Hallgren accounts for how these ideas developed in Swedish lesbian feminism.

[86] Gerhard, 152.

[87] Gerhard, 184.

[88] Carol S. Vance, "More Danger, More Pleasure: A Decade after the Barnard Conference," in *Pleasure and Danger*, ed. Vance, 1992, xxi; Bronstein, 303-305; Williams, 1993, 248.

Women and Sexuality in 1982 these conflicts were brought into the open. Anti-porn feminists accused the conference organizers, who aimed at discussing sexuality both in terms of "pleasure and danger," for promoting anti-feminist practices.[89] In their chronicle of the Sex Wars, Lisa Duggan and Nan D. Hunter write: "We were ultimately shocked to find ourselves defending our activist communities – of sex workers, of butch-fem dykes, of lesbian sadomasochists – against political attacks, launched *by feminists* [emphasis in original]."[90] Gerhard comments on how Dorothy Allison from the group the Lesbian Sex Mafia in her conference workshop paper strategically adopted anti-porn concepts of danger and safety in addressing the "repression of difference within feminism:"[91]

> Even within the community of my friends and lovers, I have never felt safe. I have never been safe and that is only partly because everyone else is as fearful as I am. None of us is safe, because we have never made each other safe… We have addressed violence and exploitation and heterosexual assumption without establishing first the understanding that for each of us desire is unique and necessary and simply terrifying.[92]

It was in this heated debate climate that the paper *On Our Backs* and the companies Femme Productions, Tigress Productions and Fatale Media were established a few years after the Barnard Conference. Hence, discussions about these productions also testify to the tensions that they emerged from, tensions that arise from the pull between affirmation and critique, pleasure and danger, safety and threat. Femme Productions was established by Candida Royalle and a number of other female porn actresses such as Annie Sprinkle.[93] Carol Queen finds that the company "while a reaction to anti-porn feminist rhetoric, was also an attempt, on a really feminist level, to take the

---

[89] Heather Love, "The GLQ Archive: Diary of a Conference on Sexuality, 1982," *GLQ*, 17: 1 (2011): 49-50; Comella, 203-205; Gerhard 150f.
[90] Duggan and Hunter, 5. Emphasis in original.
[91] Gerhard, 190, 9.
[92] Dorothy Allison, "Public Silence, Private Terror," in *Pleasure and Danger*, Vance, ed., 1992, 107. Quoted in Gerhard, 190. See also Vance, 1992, xxxv. In her introduction to *Pleasure and Danger* ten years after the Barnard Conference Vance also underscores the multidimensional significations of safety: "We want a safe space to think and speak within our own movement about experiences that are exhilarating and fearful; to explore desire in all its forms; to be welcomed without having to be the same; to celebrate pleasure as well as hurt, confusion, and damage. We want the safety to fantasize and explore, as well as to theorize sexuality. We want safe places to walk and work and live, an end to governments and laws which see women's sexuality as an invitation and justification for abuse, or demand renunciation of sexuality as the price of protection. We want a safe space where no woman is forced to choose between pleasure or safety."
[93] Williams, 1999, 149f.

means of production and put it into the hands of women."[94] Invoking the tension between affirmation and critique, she clarifies:

> So those women had a role in the industry that was being heavily critiqued by other feminists and had both their own role to continue and maybe to rehabilitate, depending on how they thought about it; they also knew that they had a perspective they could bring because they were already familiar with the conventions of porn.[95]

Lesbian pornography, according to Queen, while also produced by some women with background in the porn industry, came out more as do-it-yourself productions and as critique of anti-porn feminism.[96] In these productions the tension between affirmation and critique is also played out. For instance, the Fatale Media production *Suburban Dykes* from 1990 opens with a declaration echoing the second wave feminist emphasis on sexual self-determination, pleasure and consciousness-raising:

> Since 1984, Fatale's production of lesbian erotic videos provides a hitherto absent service for the lesbian community. As women and as homosexuals, lesbians deserve to have available to them quality sexual entertainment materials.
> These materials reflect the feminist right for control over our bodies, thereby promoting female sexual autonomy. Fatale is part of the socio-sexual movement fostering healthy sexual expression, and of women beginning to create erotic materials for ourselves.[97]

In the film, a lesbian couple in a suburban house with a jacuzzi contact a lesbian escort service through an add in *On Our Backs*. The butch who visits them educates these women in questions both about butch identity and dildos and about safer sex. As such, the film articulates a sex radical emphasis on sexuality not defined by radical feminist notions of antiphallic sex.[98] In the small amount of research on lesbian pornography it has been discussed as a critique both of anti-porn and cultural feminism and of mainstream pornography.[99] It has been discussed as directly addressing anti-porn and radical feminist conceptualizations of female sexuality in its explicit representations of lesbian sex practices such as S/M, butch/femme role-play and dildo penetration.[100] In 1992 Terralee Bensinger, for instance, critically discussed the

---

[94] Carol Queen interviewed by Lynn Comella, "The Necessary Revolution," 2008, 285.
[95] Queen, 2008, 286.
[96] Queen, 2008, 285-286. See also "The Evolution of Erotica," TV Series: *Lesbian Sex and Sexuality* 1:3 (2007-).
[97] *Suburban Dykes* (Fatale Media, 1990).
[98] See also Williams, 1993, 254-25.
[99] Bensinger, 1992, 73-76; Conway, 1997.
[100] Heather Butler, 45-46: Straayer, 214-217. Film examples include Tigress Productions' *Erotic In Nature* (1985) and Fatale Media's *Clips* (1988) and *Suburban Dykes* (1990).

notion of a unified feminist community promoted by cultural feminism where lesbians had to downplay their sexuality to fit in the movement.[101] She found that "there is a local urgency inside the lesbian community to re-invest a presently sanitized sexuality and to reconsider pornography while changing the setting of the debates altogether."[102] In 1996 Mary T. Conway similarly problematized US cultural feminism's arguing away of the vaginal orgasm and the penis in favor of clitoral orgasm. She found that "denying penetration was equated with a denial of phallic power."[103] In *Safe Is Desire* (Fatale Media, 1993) Conway saw a different understanding of the dildo and penetration, where "instead of the woman being perpetually available to the man, the dildo, newly independent of a male body and its time-bound logic, is perpetually available to the lesbian."[104] In this vein and arguing with both anti-porn feminism and mainstream porn, Cherry Smyth, in 1990, stated that:

> It is the 'butch/top's' aim in lesbian sex to give the 'femme/bottom' complete satisfaction, while the penis is often the only satisfied genital in heterosexual porn, made explicit by the come shot. In lesbian porn the presence of the dildo can subvert the potency of the penis by reasserting women's sexual sufficiency and proving that the woman lover is more powerful than the male rival.[105]

The legacy of the Sex Wars and debates about "anti-feminist sex practices" is played out in queer, feminist and lesbian pornography's representations of BDSM, penetration, fisting and butch and trans characters. This legacy is echoed in the presentation of Wolf Madame's *On Your Back Woman!* as an exploration of "the macho violence within female sexuality," as well as in

---

[101] Bensinger, 1992, 69-93. See also Cvetkovich, 2003, 4, 66. Cvetkovich (4) discusses contemporary lesbian public sex cultures as rooted in "a butch-femme culture that preceded the 1970s women's movement." See also Sue Ellen Case, "Toward a Butch-Femme Aesthetic [1988-89]," in *The Lesbian and Gay Studies Reader*, ed. Henry Abelove, Michèle Aina Barale and David M. Halperin (New York & London: Routledge, 1993), 294-306.

[102] Bensinger, 70.

[103] Conway, "Inhabiting the Phallus: Reading Safe Is Desire," *Camera Obscura*, 13: 2 38 (1996): 143. For more on these debates, see Judith Butler, "The Lesbian Phallus and the Morphological Imaginary [1993]," in *The Judith Butler Reader*, by Judith Butler and Sara Salih (Oxford: Blackwell, 2004), 138- 180; Elizabeth Grosz, "Lesbian Fetishism?", *differences*, 3 (Summer 1991), 39-54; Heather Findlay, "Freud's 'Fetishism' and the Lesbian Dildo Debates," in *Out In Culture, Gay, Lesbian, and Queer Essays on Popular Culture*, ed. Corey K Creekmur and Alexander Doty (London: Cassell, 1995), 328-342; June L. Reich, "Genderfuck: The Law of the Dildo [1992]," in *Camp: Queer Aesthetics and the Performing Subject: A Reader*, ed. Fabio Cleto (Edinburgh: Edinburgh University Press, 1999), 254-265; Wallenberg, 2008, 207-227; De Lauretis, 1994, 112-114. See also Straayer, 203, who stresses the difference between representations of lesbian sexuality and actual lesbian sexuality. She argues that "it is intellectually unsound to suggest a linear progression from antipenetration to dildo trespassing."

[104] Conway, 151.

[105] Smyth, 157.

Marit Östberg's films *Authority* and *Uniform*. Similarly invoking sex radical critique of anti-porn and cultural feminist notions of female sexuality, the female-to-male trans man Kael, in the opening interviews with the performers in Emilie Jouvet's film *One Night Stand* (2006), reflects over his participation in the project:

> I was pleased to be there with my transsexual body, its physical reality and to show female ejaculation. I'm quite proud. I'm glad there is fist fucking and a bit of power relation. I support this project, making a lesbian film. It was something the lesbian community was lacking. There are not only men, women, heterosexuals and gays – there are also trannies. The queer community is much more diverse, and I wanted to represent the trannies.

The highlighting of female ejaculation in this interview also resonates with how this feature, since the Fatale Media production *Clips* (1988) has become part of the repertoire of how to represent orgasms in queer, feminist and lesbian pornography.[106] This common feature challenges Linda Williams' discussions about the invisibility of female sexual pleasure and the dilemma this faces porn filmmakers with.[107] In her analysis of the videos of the production company SIR Video, Ragan Rhyne argues that lesbian porn appropriates "conventions like the money shot, the meat shot, and the narrative format of mainstream porn, vacating these codes of their phallocentric language and reclaiming them for lesbian sexuality."[108] These features differ from representations produced in heterosexual women's pornography from Candida Royalle and onwards. As early as 1993 Eithne Johnson noticed how lesbian pornography focuses more explicitly on genitals and orgasm than the films of Royalle.[109] She contended that "[s]ince these movies are made by and for lesbians, their production strategies do not need to resolve the genre's problem of portraying both male and female sexual narratives."[110]

---

[106] Deborah Sundahl a.k.a. Fanny Fatale who performs in *Clips* has since produced numerous explicit instruction films on the topic of female ejaculation, including titles such as *How to Female Ejaculate* (1992) and *Female Ejaculation: The Workshop* (2008). See Ingrid Ryberg, "Maximizing Visibility," *Film International*, 6: 6 (2008), 72-79; Rhyne 2007, 45; Straayer, 203; Smyth, 156. Film examples include *Pornographlics* (Dirty Pillows Inc, 2003) and *The Crash Pad* (Shine Louise Houston, 2005).

[107] Williams, 1999, 32, 50, 94. However, in her latest book, *Screening Sex*, Williams (2008, 320) admits having now discovered, through looking at websites dedicated to the female orgasm, that "the absence" and "nothing-to-see" of female orgasm she once built her argument on is actually "quite visible as an involuntary spasm." See also Eithne Johnson, "Loving Yourself: The Specular Scene in Sexual Self-Help Advice for Women," in *Collecting Visible Evidence*, ed. Jane M. Gaines and Michael Renov (Minneapolis & London: University of Minnesota Press, 1999), 231-3; Straayer, 1996, 244-52.

[108] Rhyne, 2007, 45.

[109] Eithne Johnson, "Excess and Ecstasy: Constructing Female Pleasure in Porn Movies," *The Velvet Light Trap*, 32 (Fall 1993), 30-49.

[110] Johnson, 1993, 40. See also Stein, 2006, 47, 58.

Hence, within the category queer, feminist and lesbian pornography different and sometimes contradictory visual features and strategies intertwine, not least in regard to genital display. Again I want to highlight how this political and aesthetic heterogeneity emanates from the tension between affirmation and critique.

## Re-vision of porn and sexpert tradition

> Porn is not just the naked act of fucking. Sadly enough this rarely holds true in what can be labeled pornography today. The overemphasizing in close-ups on genitals, usually female, and the excessive focus on male ejaculation as the fanfare of sexual intimacy is the signature of almost all pornographic produce today. Fantasy and sensualism has had to take the backseat leaving little but no room for the very imagination, which has the power to arouse and transport both body and soul into total bliss. Through our sexual fantasies, through that which lies hidden within can we better understand what turns us on. *Red Like Cherry* elaborates on detail, not for the sake of detail, but as a tension-builder and carrier of desire and want.
>
> Sometimes what you don't see is better for getting-off than what you see.[111]

Tora Mårtens' film *Red Like Cherry* in the *Dirty Diaries* collection is an experimental collage of a sexual meeting between a man and a woman. Editing together footage from a beach, a shower and a bed it superimposes glimpses of bodies, sand, water and sheets accompanied by a soundtrack of breathing and moaning. The film echoes Schneemann's *Fuses* and raises questions about what Laura U. Marks calls "video erotics," as will be discussed more in chapter 6. In her statement in the *Dirty Diaries* DVD booklet, Mårtens positions her film in opposition to porn conventions such as close-ups on female genitals and male ejaculation. As such *Red Like Cherry* reactivates a discussion about what Williams calls "feminine re-vision" of porn, for instance in the work of Candida Royalle.[112] This discussion is also characterized by a tension between affirmation of women's sexuality and critique of the phallicism of pornography.

Williams' feminist critique of porn consists in pointing out the phallocentrism that the pornographic will to knowledge builds on. In her view, hardcore pornography is not phallic only because it shows penises, but because it presumes to possess the truth about sex, through a focus on what is assumed to be visible and measurable proof of pleasure.[113] Therefore, she argues, a challenge to this model cannot be performed by way of including more imagery of women's genitals while discarding the penis. The solution is not

---

[111] Tora Mårtens, "Red Like Cherry," *Dirty Diaries* DVD booklet, 2009.
[112] Williams, 1999, 246-264.
[113] Ibid., 267.

simply to replace the penis with the vulva.[114] Williams calls for a more thorough reconsideration of the pornographic narrative and questions display of female genital pleasure in accordance with the principle of maximum visibility. Rather than setting up an alternative organ for fetishistic worship, the goal should be "to dismantle the hierarchy of norm and deviation and so create a plurality of pleasures accepting of difference."[115] Williams opposes the notion of revision with a notion of re-vision, where the former as a modification or cleaned up act simply adds and subtracts images and organs (exchanging penises with vulvas), and the latter more deeply involves a change in narrative from an "entirely different, woman's point of view."[116] In contrast to an exclusive focus on visual evidence of organ pleasure alone, she foregrounds scenes in Candida Royalle's films in which actors perform "pleasurably" for each other, where the heterosexual number does not necessarily have the sole goal that the male organ should perform, and where "[f]oreplay, afterplay and all the possible measuring distinctions of stages, amounts of arousal, and degrees of intensity blur."[117] She furthermore suggests that through such re-vision porn for women might function as a form of "education of desire" and "sexual self-discovery," "for a group that traditionally has lacked, as Jessica Benjamin puts it, 'a desire of one's own'."[118] She finds that Royalle's films illustrate Benjamin's contention that women's sexual subjectivity requires "a self-discovery associated with discovering one's inside – an inside that can only be known, however, through a trajectory that also takes one to the exciting outside."[119] Hence, Williams proposes a model of feminist pornography based both on critique of maximum visibility and on affirmation of women's sexual self-discovery.

In her talk at the Pornfilmfestival Berlin in 2009, and with reference to Nancy Friday, Candida Royalle herself contends that when Femme Productions was started the aim was to focus on female sexual pleasure and fantasies:

> I wanted to give women permission to explore their sexuality, to get comfortable with it, to delight in it, celebrate it and movies that they could feel good about their sexuality in watching… And I chose to make it explicit because I think that explicit sex and our genitals are part of sex and when you don't show it, in a way you're saying 'oh it's all beautiful and lovely – except for that'… and I didn't want to perpetuate that. I wanted to create a new vision.[120]

---

[114] Ibid., 260.
[115] Ibid., 102.
[116] Ibid., 246.
[117] Ibid., 251, 261.
[118] Ibid., 264.
[119] Ibid., 262.
[120] Candida Royalle presentation Pornfilmfestival Berlin, 2009-10-22.

In her films Royalle therefore has developed specific principles for altering porn conventions seen as marginalizing women's pleasure, such as the male come shot. Similar questions about how to emphasize female pleasure and fantasies are brought up in British filmmaker Petra Joy's "porn from a female perspective," evident in her statement that:

> The focus of my erotic films is female pleasure. I would like to empower the women who appear and who view my films to experience their own personal pleasures away from the stereotypes of female sexuality in mainstream porn. Most porn is done by men for men, expressing male desires. No wonder these films do not turn women on. I feel the need to create an alternative to the flood of images that reduce women to their genitals.[121]

In her films Joy has chosen to avoid porn conventions, such as "forced fellatio, extreme anal sex and cum shot into the woman's face."[122] In affirming a female perspective on sexuality, Joy, as well as Anna Span, also a British feminist porn filmmaker, forwards the need to cast "attractive" and "good looking" men as objects for the female audience's gaze.[123] Similarly, an ongoing discussion within *Dirty Diaries* concerned the possibility to objectify and sexualize the male body instead of again placing women's bodies in the focus of the gaze.[124] At one point Mia Engberg even sent out an email explicitly requesting heterosexual films:

> We still have a lack in hetero-stories! I want to see at least some real cocks in our collection. Or am I just old-fashioned? Or is it impossible to make feminist hetero-porn? I don't want to believe that. So hereby I send out a request: Do you know anyone who can make a hetero-contribution to *Dirty Diaries*? Or do you want to make one? Get back to me immediately because it is urgent.[125]

In the end Mia Engberg felt content about the balance between heterosexual and lesbian shorts in the collection.[126] One film answering this call was Elin Magnusson's film *Skin*, featuring a heterosexual couple who slowly releases each other's bodies from an extra layer of "skin" made out of body stockings. In Jennifer Rainsford's *For the Liberation of Men* an old woman fantasizes about three young masturbating men wearing wigs and lace tights. The camera closely follows the contours of their legs and crotches. With Johnson these films can be read as engaged in "resolving" problems of "male and

---

[121] Petra Joy, "Sensuality, Creativity and Respect/Humor/Inspiration," About Petra, Petra Joy website, http://www.petrajoy.com/vision.asp (accessed 2011-11-18).
[122] Ibid.
[123] Petra Joy website, http://www.petrajoy.com/vision.asp (accessed 2011-11-18); Anna Span talk at Malmö högskola, 2009-09-07.
[124] *Dirty Diaries* meeting, 2008-12-16.
[125] Email from Mia Engberg, 2008-11-11. My translation from Swedish.
[126] *Dirty Diaries* meeting 2008-12-16.

female sexual narratives."[127] As suggested above, films from lesbian companies such as Fatale Media and SIR Video rather engage in "resolving" problems of lesbian invisibility in cultural and anti-porn feminism as well as in culture at large. Importantly, therefore, lesbian pornography's visual strategies relate not only to porn conventions of maximum visibility. I propose that these varying strategies also arise from the "sexpert" tradition that grew out of second wave feminism's insistence on sexual pleasure, empowerment and consciousness-raising and therefore also complicate accounts of heterosexual women's and lesbian pornography as separate categories.[128]

In an article on sexual self-help advice for women, Johnson argues that community-based sexpert advice by, for instance, Carol Queen, Betty Dodson and Annie Sprinkle, should be distinguished from clinical sex instruction videos and pornography.[129] She highlights how female genital display and female masturbation in these films result in "counteraestethic signifying practices" that can be traced through "feminist health care documentaries, women's experimental films, and female masturbation films."[130] In contrast to the "analytic exhibitionism" in professional sex instruction videos, "the reflexive exhibitionism" in sexpert videos "works to integrate the interior and exterior genitals into a synthetically unified body image."[131]

The notion of queer, feminist and lesbian pornography as education, also forwarded by Williams, as well as by Heather Butler in her account of what she prefers to call dyke porn, ties in with second-wave consciousness-raising and knowledge production emanating from women's own experiences.[132] It also often regards questions of safer sex education, as attention to risks and exposure to sexually transmitted diseases was heightened during the 1980s AIDS epidemic.[133] Fatale Media films such as *Suburban Dykes* (1990) and *Safe is Desire* (1993) explicitly address lesbians' exposure to HIV and gloves, condoms and dental dams feature prominently in these and other

---

[127] Johnson, 1999, 40.
[128] Comella, 207.
[129] Johnson, 1999, 216.
[130] Johnson, 1999, 219.
[131] Johnson, 1999, 220, 224.
[132] Butler, 2004, 190. See also Rhyne, 42.
[133] Robin Gorna, "Delightful Visions: From anti-porn to eroticizing safer sex," in *Sex Exposed*, ed. Segal and McIntosh, 1993, 169-183; Juffer, 139-140. Manuela Kay, one of the organizers of Pornfilmfestival Berlin, editor of the German lesbian magazine *L-Mag* and producer of the German lesbian porn film *Airport* (1994) also underscored the connection between lesbian pornography and safe sex education when I interviewed her in Berlin 2008-10-26. Kay describes her experiences of producing and traveling around with a graphic film about lesbian safe sex in the early 1990s. She says what she found out then was that lesbians in Germany at the time lacked basic knowledge about safe sex and different lesbian sex practices, but also that they were reluctant to look at explicit material of lesbian sex and women's bodies and genitals. The production of *Airport* grew out of these experiences.

films.[134] The tradition of safer sex education is evident also in *Dirty Diaries* through the inclusion of sex toys, lube and condoms, for instance in *Fruitcake*. When we watch a rough cut of the film at our *Dirty Diaries* meeting in September 2008, Mia Engberg comments on how safe sex is central to queer, feminist and lesbian porn and how it is played out jokingly in this film in a sequence depicting anal penetration with a rose with a condom on it. One of the directors of the film, Ester Martin Bergsmark, contends that it is important to try to make the use of condoms sexy.[135]

The tension between understandings of genital display as educating and affirming female embodiment and sexuality, on the one hand, and as signifying problematic porn conventions, on the other, is played out in Mia Engberg's first feminist porn film, the lesbian short *Selma & Sofie* (2002). In the behind-the-scenes documentary to *Selma & Sofie*, *Bitch & Butch* (2003), Mia Engberg flips through the pages of a feminist anatomy book with detailed sketches displaying female genitals, that Mia Engberg finds incomparable to the sex education provided in schools. She points out to the documentary camera how the clitoris gets erect both on the outside and inside of the body. The lack of visibility, and under-representation of female sexuality in sex and anatomy education is here suggested as one motivation for making *Selma & Sofie*. However, in the actual film, the scenery is obscure, the lighting is soft and non-frontal and the film features few close-ups of genitals. According to assistant director Kajsa Åman their strategy was to make everything differently from what they saw in mainstream pornography.[136] Thus, if the need for more accurate sex education and visibility of female genitals and pleasure motivates Mia Engberg in the documentary, the actual film goes the other direction as it dismisses porn aesthetics and the principle of maximum visibility. *Selma & Sofie* as well as Mia Engberg's formulations in the opening quote to this chapter also reiterates discussions that have characterized women's cinema as it grew out of the second wave feminist movement.

## Politics as aesthetics

In Mia Engberg's short *Come Together* (2006) six women consecutively turn on, look and smile to the camera. Some wave. Some look shy. They all seem

---

[134] *Suburban Dykes* contains quotes such as: "Never fuck without gloves;" "Our bodily fluids will keep a safe distance from each other" and "Hope you're not like those other dykes who think they can't get AIDS." *Safe is Desire* contains quotes like, "Girl, this is the 90s, safe sex is one of the big issues of our time – get with it!"
[135] *Dirty Diaries* meeting, 2008-09-18.
[136] Kajsa Åman, panel discussion "Feminist Pornography: How To Make Non-Heteronormative Pornography," moderated by me at Stockholm Pride, 2006-08-04. This also regards the fact that the film was shot on 35mm film.

to be in their different homes, in the bathroom, in the bed, against a wall. Small details in the background give the sense of domestic private space. The soundtrack is an upbeat disco tune. The image is shaky and pixely. They hold the mobile phone camera themselves, pointing it at their faces. Soon there is a shift in mode. The music fades. Their breathing becomes heavier, their faces concentrated, their eyes shady and unfocused, the camera movements less steady. Some start moaning. Then the editing moves faster between their faces and the music escalates again. A woman in a bathtub twitches and screams in climax. Another woman breathes forcefully through her nose, makes a roaring sound and looks intensely at the camera.

*Come Together (Mia Engberg, 2006). Courtesy of the filmmaker.*

*Come Together*, where these six women film their own faces while masturbating, is included as bonus material on the *Dirty Diaries* DVD, but was made a few years earlier as part of a competition program called "Mobile Movies" at Stockholm International Film Festival sponsored by Nokia with their latest mobile phone model.[137] In the DVD booklet Mia Engberg describes how the film stirred strong reactions when it was published online: "Hell, they look ugly. They could've least put on some

---

[137] i.e. Nokia N93.

makeup."[138] Mia Engberg's response to these comments was the decision to make *Dirty Diaries*, "more films in the same genre, to open their eyes."[139] To her, the reactions proved that "we are still stuck in the old notion that a woman's sexuality should above all please the eye of the spectator – not herself."[140] She relates this to the fact that "[t]hrough the history of the art the image of the woman has been created by men to please the male gaze."[141] Throughout the production of *Dirty Diaries* there are recurring references to the notion of the male gaze as signifying the dominant forms of representing gender and sexuality in media, where women, as Mia Engberg puts it in the DVD booklet are reduced to stereotypes "suiting the patriarchal system: the whore, the wife, the mother, the muse."[142] *Come Together* challenges this gaze. The spectator is denied visual access to the women's bodies and genitals and is instead faced with the women looking back at the camera, returning the gaze and confronting the spectator's voyeurism. The film posits the women themselves as the filmmakers in control of the camera's gaze, manifesting their pleasure as it is expressed in the private reality of their homes.

## Avant-garde or documentary?

*Come Together* invokes the legacy of second-wave cultural critique and production in a number of ways, evident not least in Mia Engberg's common-sense use of the notion of the male gaze. While the notion of the male gaze as an everyday expression in the context of *Dirty Diaries* does not entirely correspond with Laura Mulvey's psychoanalytic model of classical Hollywood cinema's male scopophilia, *Come Together* nevertheless resonates with Mulvey's call for feminist deconstructive film practice and celebration of increasingly accessible film technology.[143] Mulvey argues that the goal for feminist film must be to break down the codes of representation of classical cinema in order to destroy voyeurism and male pleasure. In classical narrative film women can only be spectacles of the male gaze. Feminist avant-garde films such as Mulvey's own *Riddles of the Sphinx* (1977) and Sally Potter's *Thriller* (1979), through discontinuity editing and breaking the 180-degree rule, aimed at the spectator's "passionate detachment" and critical thinking.[144] In its non-narrative self-reflexive mode, calling attention to the gaze and reversing voyeurism, I suggest *Come Together* can be read in relation to this tradition of avant-garde feminist filmmaking. Furthermore, the

---

[138] Mia Engberg, "What is feminist porn?" *Dirty Diaries* DVD booklet, 2009.
[139] Ibid.
[140] Ibid.
[141] Ibid.
[142] Ibid.
[143] Mulvey, 1975, 7f.
[144] Mulvey, 1975, 18.

negative reactions to the film that Mia Engberg accounts for can be taken precisely as proof that the film destroys male visual pleasure.[145]

While Mia Engberg's use of the notion of the male gaze – besides testifying to the vast influence of Mulvey's work – does invite a relation to Mulvey and the avant-garde feminist film practice articulated in the 1970s, it also echoes second wave feminist cultural critique of objectifying, sexualized and stereotypical images of women in media more broadly. "We're not used to see women's sexual pleasure," Mia Engberg comments on the negative reactions to *Come Together* and opens up for a reading of the film, not as a breaking down of cinematic pleasure, but as a representation of what women actually look like when they have their orgasms. The intimacy and everydayness of the domestic spaces, the amateur documentary style of the film and natural appearance of the performers (although some quite obviously do wear makeup) invoke the demand for more truthful and authentic representations of women forwarded in the images-of-women-critique of the 1970s. In this vein Marjorie Rosen's *Popcorn Venus* (1973) and Molly Haskell's *From Reverence to Rape* (1974) critiqued the sexist, degrading and artificial roles assigned to women in popular cinema and called for realistic representations of real women's lives and experiences.[146] "[S]howing real women on the screen is, itself, revolutionary, conditioned as we are to the idealized, fantasy images of the commercial cinema," E. Ann Kaplan wrote in 1975.[147] In this vein, feminist documentaries such as *Growing Up Female* (Jim Klein and Julia Reichert, 1971) and *Janie's Janie* (Geri Ashur, 1971) sought to capture less stereotypical "images of women in their particular social, racial and class contexts."[148] The contrast between stereotypical and real representations characterizes not least discussions about lesbians on film. In 1981 Edith Becker, Michelle Citron, Julia Lesage and B. Ruby Rich contended that "[l]esbians are nearly invisible in mainstream cinematic history, except as evil or negative-example characters."[149] They furthermore stated that:

---

[145] See also Teresa de Lauretis, "Guerilla in the Midst: Women's Cinema in the 80s [1989]," in *Queer Screen: A Screen Reader*, ed. Jackie Stacey and Sarah Street (London & New York, 2007b), 28.

[146] Doane, Mellencamp, Williams, "Feminist Film Criticism," in *Re-vision*, ed. Doane, Mellencamp, Williams, 1984, 5.

[147] Kaplan, "Women's Happytime Commune," *Jump Cut*, 9 (1975), http://www.ejumpcut.org/archive/onlinessays/JC09folder/WomensHappytmCom.html (accessed 2011-11-16).

[148] Doane, Mellencamp, Williams, 1984, 7.

[149] Edith Becker, Michelle Citron, Julia Lesage and B. Ruby Rich, "Introduction to Special Section: Lesbians and Film," *Jump Cut: A Review of Contemporary Media*, 24-25 (March 1981), http://www.ejumpcut.org/archive/onlinessays/JC24-25folder/LesbiansAndFilm.html (accessed 2011-04-04). See also Tamsin Wilton, "Introduction: On invisibility and mortality," in *Immortal, Invisible: Lesbians and the Moving Image*, ed. Tamsin Wilton (London & New York: Routledge, 1995), 1-19.

Ironically, then, the most explicit vision of lesbianism has been left to pornography, where the lesbian loses her menace and becomes a turn on. [---] As long as lesbianism remains a component of pornography made by and for men, that will affect the 'positive image' of lesbianism. This is because lesbian sexuality will be received by most sectors of the dominant society as pornography.[150]

Therefore, they concluded that "[i]t is impossible to underestimate the need for films to affirm all aspects of lesbian identity, given the virulent hostility against lesbians in our society."[151] These examples illustrate de Lauretis' contention that the pull between affirmation and critique in the women's movement also gave rise to two different types of film work:

[O]ne called for immediate documentation for purposes of political activism, consciousness raising, self-expression, or the search for 'positive images' of woman; the other insisted on rigorous, formal work on the medium – or, better, the cinematic apparatus, understood as a social technology – in order to analyze and disengage the ideological codes embedded in representation.[152]

In Mia Engberg's *Selma & Sofie* along with the behind the scenes documentary *Bitch & Butch,* the aim to represent real women beyond stereotypes is explicitly pronounced. Mia Engberg then argued that in contrast to male heterosexual porn which is all about "silicon tits and fake nails,"[153] she wanted "to come closer to woman's true sexuality."[154] By casting a real life lesbian couple she wanted the sex to feel more authentic. In queer, feminist and lesbian pornography such notions of real and authentic women and lesbians and real and authentic sex are recurrently mobilized, also in accounts by research subjects in this project. In her discussion about lesbian sexual representations, Straayer's comments on how the reception of lesbian pornography within the American lesbian community in the 1980s was characterized by "reality-checking," where "[v]iewers looked for a visual representation of themselves."[155] For instance, a sex scene in *Erotic in Nature* (Christen Lee Rothermund, 1985) where two women are "air-fucking," as Straayer puts it, meaning that "the femme crouches on her hands and knees with the

---

[150] Becker, Citron, Lesage and Rich, 1981. See also Hallgren, 155-159. Hallgren accounts for how lesbian feminists in Sweden in the 1970s opposed notions of lesbianism as pornography.
[151] Becker, Citron, Lesage and Rich, 1981. See also Hammer, "Lesbian Filmmaking: Self-Birthing [1981]," in *Hammer!*, 2010, 99-104.
[152] De Lauretis, 2007a, 26. See also Kuhn, 1994, 125-190; Rich, "In the Name of Feminist Film Criticism [1978]," 62-84; Doane, Mellencamp, Williams, 8.
[153] Mia Engberg, interviewed by Mary Mårtenson, "'Jag är så trött på gubbporren'," *Aftonbladet*, 2001-11-28, http://www.aftonbladet.se/vss/kvinna/story/0,2789,109691,00.html (accessed 2006-06-09).
[154] *Bitch & Butch* (Mia Engberg 2003).
[155] Straayer, 213.

butch 'dry-humping' her from behind," was much debated.[156] In 2004 Heather Butler engaged in the debate around this particular film and critiqued the improbability of the action that she found is not giving a "fulfilling representation of a sex act."[157] Discussions about authenticity also interrelate with the questions of visibility and education discussed above. For instance, sex educator and Fatale Media co-worker Deborah Sundahl conceptualizes lesbian pornography as a critique of mainstream porn as well as a matter of making visible real women and real lesbians, as well as real orgasms and real love-making:

> Female orgasm itself has rarely been portrayed realistically in the majority of adult films. Fatale Media was started in direct response to the desire to show real women having real orgasms, as well as real lesbians making real lesbian love. *Clips* was the first Fatale Video to show me ejaculating on film.[158]

Queer, feminist and lesbian pornography rests on a "documentary impulse," characteristic of pornography as such, as Christian Hansen, Catherine Needham and Bill Nichols point out.[159] However, in the case of queer, feminist and lesbian pornography this impulse entails more than the fact that "people actually [have] sex" in front of the camera, as Richard Dyer puts it.[160] It also entails questions about authenticity as this notion is mobilized throughout debates about women's cinema. Rhyne points out that "[r]ealism remains a crucial trope in lesbian porn however the realism increasingly indexes the performers' sexuality and desire rather than simply meeting the realist requirements of the larger porn genre."[161] The documentary dimension of queer, feminist and lesbian pornography is especially evident in the common inclusion of interviews and behind-the-scenes material where performers reflect over their participation in the film, for instance in *Bathroom Sluts* (Fatale Media, 1991), *One Night Stand* (Emilie Jouvet, 2006) and *Trans Entities: The Nasty Love of Papi and Wil* (Morty Diamond, 2006).

As my reading of *Come Together* has suggested, features associated both with avant-garde and documentary feminist film practices intertwine in queer, feminist and lesbian pornography. Across this film culture's aesthetic and political heterogeneity the constitutive contradiction between affirmation

---

[156] Straayer, 214f.

[157] Butler, 2004, 177.

[158] Deborah Sundahl, "Fatale Media Newsletter August 2005," Fatale Media website, http://www.fatalemedia.com/newsletter/082005.html (accessed 2011-11-18).

[159] Christian Hansen, Catherine Needham and Bill Nichols, "Pornography, Ethnography, and the Discourse of Power," in *Representing Reality,* ed. Bill Nichols (Bloomington & Indianapolis: Indiana University Press, 1991), 211; Dyer, "Idol Thoughts: Orgasm and Self-Reflexivity in Gay Pornography [1994]," in *More Dirty Looks: Gender, Pornography and Power*, ed. Pamela Church Gibson (London: BFI, 2004), 102-109.

[160] Dyer, 2004, 109.

[161] Rhyne, 45.

and critique is echoed. *Come Together* serves as one example of how a number of issues in feminist film theory, as it emerged during second wave feminism, are rearticulated in this interpretive community as, in Kuhn's words, "a series of circles or spirals,"[162] and in Hemmings' words, "ongoing contests and relationships" constantly returned to.[163] As a hybrid film practice queer, feminist and lesbian pornography combines documentary, educational, experimental and narrative filmmaking.[164] As such it actualizes de Lauretis' description of how women's film "destabilizes the criteria by which film-critical categories have been set up."[165] In queer, feminist and lesbian pornography this includes definitional criteria for pornography, such as maximum visibility and scientia sexualis. In shifting the definition of women's cinema from a question of formal, stylistic and thematic markers to a matter of "the production of a feminist social vision" and "political critique [...] and the specific consciousness that women have developed to analyze the subject's relation to sociohistorical reality," de Lauretis also brings up the question of differences among and within women as these are addressed for instance in Lizzie Borden's *Born In Flames* (1983).[166] In her discussion the split or division in feminist film culture appears as "the very strength, the drive and productive heterogeneity of feminism."[167] Similarly, I contend that the driving force in queer, feminist and lesbian pornography is constituted in its heterogeneity and struggles as these nevertheless centers around the production of a social vision, or with Freeman, a "collective political fantasy" of a safe space for sexual empowerment.[168] In conclusion I will bring out more specifically how the political and aesthetic legacies of queer, feminist and lesbian pornography mobilize the figure of safe space.

## Sexual empowerment in private or public?

> I wanna expose myself to guys; old men, grown-ups, family fathers and other slobs. I'm totally serious. I don't wanna do it to take revenge on the patriar-

---

[162] Hemmings, 2005, 131.

[163] Kuhn, 1994, 193.

[164] See Alexandra Juhasz, "They Said We Were Trying to Show Reality – All I Want to Show Is My Video: The Politics of the Realist Feminist Documentary," in *Collecting Visible Evidence*, ed. Gaines and Renov, 1999, 190-215; Jane Gaines, "Women and Representation: Can We Enjoy Alternative Pleasure?" in *Issues in Feminist Film Criticism*, ed. Erens, 1990, 75-92; Julianne Pidduck, "New Queer Cinema and Experimental Video," in *New Queer Cinema: A Critical Reader*, ed. Michele Aron (Edinburgh: Edinburgh University Press, 2004), 80-97; José Esteban Muñoz, *Disidentifications: Queers of Color and the Performance of Politics* (Minneapolis, London: University of Minnesota Press 1999); Alison Butler, 2002, 19.

[165] De Lauretis, 2007b, 24.

[166] De Lauretis, 2007a, 29, 34.

[167] De Lauretis, 2007a, 35.

[168] Freeman, 65. See also Bensinger, 1992.

chy, even if my cunt is a weapon these days. I just wanna do it. I wanna treat you to some pussy. That turns me on. I'm a female flasher. Yep, female exhibitionists are pretty unusual. I mean it's fucked up, but maybe it's not so strange, since as a woman you're in a physical disadvantage. What if somebody gets a hard-on and wants to rape you while you're sitting there on a park bench jacking off!

I've tried to find porn films with women flashers. There's none, and once again, it's fucked up. I'll probably make my own porn film soon. Meanwhile, the gay porn films remain my favourites, where evidently straight men fuck each other. Hihi, even gays believe that the actors are gay. No, relax, it's only straight men getting paid a little extra.

Back to the flashing, I've decided simply to expose myself where it's safe and where nobody can interrupt me. Obviously I wouldn't just jack off in the park like some male moron. Nope, I choose smart places. I have two favourite spots; balconies facing courtyards with hundreds of windows and on shore in front of passing ferries and boats. I mean, who's gonna jump in and stop me?! I'm gonna find some like-minded and put together a group. But no guy exhibitionists can join, because you're all disgusting and because we girls are taking out a patent on being gross in public. The only body part guys are allowed to show in public is male boobs. Cause I Love male boobs. Bye![169]

*Flasher Girl on Tour (Joanna Rytel, 2009). Courtesy of the filmmaker.*

---

[169] Joanna Rytel, "Flasher Girl On Tour," *Dirty Diaries* dvd-booklet.

In Joanna Rytel's *Dirty Diaries* film *Flasher Girl On Tour* she plays the role of a female flasher and exposes herself in various public spaces in Paris, such as in the Metro, in a park and from a hotel balcony. She is often filmed from behind so that the film spectator does not see what she reveals to the public. Instead there are occasional subjective shots where Rytel holds the camera and directs the gaze at men, at "male boobs" and at a waiter's bottom. Just as other short in *Dirty Diaries*, *Flasher Girl on Tour* reiterates discussions about sexual objectification as these emanated through second wave feminism's politicizing of sexuality. In her film these discussions are played out in relation to questions about the sexualization of the public sphere. In its attack on and appropriation of male dominated public sexualized spaces such as the red-light district Pigalle, Rytel's film ties in with a tradition of feminist performance art and intervention in public spaces, also emanating from second wave feminism. *Flasher Girl on Tour* echoes, for instance, Valie Export's performance *Genital Panik* (later re-enacted also by Martina Abramovic), where Export exposed her genitals in a cinema theater as a comment to women's role in cinema. Rytel's film, I propose, echoes second wave feminism's opening up of public space for female sexuality, but it also builds on the feminist critique of the sexualized public sphere.

Similarly, this tension between affirming women as sexual subjects in the public and simultaneously problematizing gendered power structures in the sexualized public is played out in Åsa Sandzén's *Dirty Diaries* short *Dildoman*. *Dildoman* is an animation set in a strip club where the female strippers subvert the action by using one of the male visitors as a dildo. Just as in Rytel's film, male dominated sexual space is appropriated for women's sexual pleasure and male pleasure is literally destroyed as the "dildoman" is crushed and dies when the woman orgasms. Pella Kågerman's *Dirty Diaries* film *Body Contact*, a mockumentary about an amateur porn film shooting staged by two women and a man that they pick up on an Internet dating site, stages a reclaiming of the sexualized public space of the Internet. When the man arrives to the apartment he is at first reluctant, but eventually allows them to film the sex, performing what he believes are good porn positions. The film focuses on the awkwardness and mundaneness of the casual amateur porn-shooting scenario. At one point the woman filming the sex scene asks the woman in the scene if she is okay. In all of these three *Dirty Diaries* films gendered power relations in the sexualized public are put at stake. The women become the perpetrators and men are used and objectified for their purposes. However, these films all also acknowledge and problematize women and men's different conditions for participating in the sexualized public sphere. In her presentation in the DVD booklet Rytel crucially asks: "What if somebody gets a hard-on and wants to rape you while you're sitting there on a park bench jacking off!" She continues: "I've decided simply to expose myself where it's safe."

# Välkommen på disputationsfest!

17 februari 19-01 på Judy's, Närkesgatan

På scen: Oni Ayhun & Mar Ritt (http://www.oniayhun.com/)

DJs: Sunny & Kjell, electriCAT, Über, Grizzlybear

Välkomstdrink och tilltugg – Bar till självkostnadspris

O.S.A. senast 10/2: doktoringrid@gmail.com
Bidrag till lokalhyra och artister: 100 kronor sätts in på Catharina Lofts konto i Handelsbanken: clearnr 6117 kontonr 504 139762
Glöm inte att ange ditt namn vid insättning!

Tal och andra uppträdanden anmäls till Fox Loft: doktoringrid@gmail.com/tfnnr 0730293232

Disputationsakten äger rum 10.00, F-salen, Filmhuset, Borgvägen 5. Då försvarar jag min avhandling *Imagining Safe Space. The Politics of Queer, Feminist and Lesbian Pornography*
Opponent: Prof. Patricia White

Varmt välkommen!/Ingrid

In her discussion about Candida Royalle's films, Williams emphasizes that these narratives create safe and exciting places where women can enact their desires without fear of punishment or guilt. Building on the psychoanalytical thinking of Jessica Benjamin, Williams underscores the idea of combining safety with excitement in order to allow for women to become autonomous sexual agents, to discover their own sexual subjectivity instead of being "receptacles for the desires of male subjects."[170] In Williams' discussion, as well as in the films of Rytel, Sandzén and Kågerman the public is a place both for sexual pleasure and of danger, again reflecting the legacy of queer, feminist and lesbian sexuality debates. In queer activism and theory, emerging also partly through the Sex Wars, the reclaiming of public space, rather than confining non-normative sexuality to the closet, home or private sphere, is a central concern.[171] However, it has also been pointed out that discussions about public sex cultures often rest on and presume a notion of the modern male white subject, while neglecting how other social subjects historically have not possessed the same urban mobility.[172]

In her work on lesbianism, space and cinema, Lee Wallace critiques what she calls a "sexual and political hyperbole" attached to gay public sex culture that renders lesbian domestic culture asexual.[173] Referencing Vivian Sobchack's discussion about Bakhtin's concept of chronotope, Wallace proposes this concept as particularly useful for considering "the relation between textual representations of lesbianism and the sexual cultures with which those texts are historically contemporaneous."[174] She describes how lesbianism has predominantly been represented through the chronotopes of the bar and the college, well represented in ethnographic work on lesbian culture, as well as through their more fictionalized counterparts, the prison and the classroom. She highlights the apartment as a new "post-Stonewall" chronotope in lesbian feature films. She argues that the apartment is a space where the assumed dichotomy between the bar space, as associated with public sex and sexual dissent, and the college space, as associated with education, assimilation and privacy is disrupted. As a flexible space in relation to publicity and privacy, the apartment "[refits] the contradictions between [lesbian cultural] aspiration and [sexual] dissidence and thus can provide the fictional setting for lesbian narratives that are simultaneously socially smooth and sexually rough."[175] Wallace, thus disrupts binary oppositions that

---

[170] Williams, 1999, 262.

[171] Lauren Berlant and Elizabeth Freeman, "Queer Nationality," in *The Queen of America Goes to Washington City*, by Lauren Berlant, 1997, 145-173; Warner and Berlant, 1998.

[172] Ahmed, 2004, 151-153, 163f; Halberstam, 2005, 12-17.

[173] Lee Wallace, *Lesbianism, Cinema, Space: The Sexual Life of Apartments* (New York & London: Routledge 2009), 133.

[174] Wallace, 3.

[175] Wallace, 133-134. See also Kelly Hankin, *The Girls in the Back Room: Looking at the Lesbian Bar* (Minneapolis & London: University of Minnesota Press, 2002).

also structure linear narratives of the queer, feminist and lesbian past. Therefore her discussion about cinematic space is useful in historicizing queer, feminist and lesbian porn film culture.

In queer, feminist and lesbian pornography Wallace's chronotopes of bar, prison, college, classroom and, not least apartment are all present.[176] In Shine Louise Houston's *Crash Pad* film (2005) and *Series* (2008-), the apartment is staged precisely as a flexible space in relation to publicity and privacy. The Crash Pad is an apartment for casual sex where those who have the key can go for play dates or chance encounters. The early Fatale Media production *Suburban Dykes* (1990) also reclaims domestic space as sexual space when the film's bored lesbian couple calls a lesbian phone sex and escort service and gets a visit from a butch lesbian to spice up their sex life.[177] My own *Dirty Diaries* film *Phone Fuck* is set in the flexible spaces of two apartments, interconnected and sexualized through a phone sex call. *Phone Fuck* features two women's sexual encounter over the phone, while both are masturbating in their separate apartments. The private spaces of the two women's apartments and their respective sexual pleasures are shared between them in a mutual fantasy – but also publicly – through mobile phone technology. Similarly, the women in *Come Together*, in their different domestic locations nevertheless "come together" in the sense that they share the mobile phone camera and are edited together in the cinematic space of the film, but their individual masturbation scenes are also shared publicly, as "dirty diaries." As commented on already, Marit Östberg's short for the collection, *Authority*, is set in public spaces and echoes queer activist reclaimings of the public sphere. Importantly, through their public circulation, these "diaries" all disrupt the dichotomy between private and public and embody the legacy of second wave feminism's sexual consciousness-raising in small groups, but also shared in public.

Queer, feminist and lesbian pornography builds on the legacy of discussions about pleasure and danger, assimilation and dissent in terms of space. Importantly, its problematization of questions of power relations and safety pertains also to the domestic space and to the space shared by sexual partners. In *Safe is Desire*, a date between two women ends up in an argument about whether or not they should use safer sex products. As the woman who does not want to practice safe sex leaves the other woman's apartment she

---

[176] For instance, bar/nightclub: *Safe Is Desire*, prison: *River Rock Women's Prison* (Kathryn Annelle, 2010), college: *After School Special* (Fatale Media, 2001), classroom: *Phineas Slipped* (Keri Oakie, 2003). Similar to the apartment, another cross-over space in queer, feminist and lesbian porn is the sex shop/book store, which forms the backdrop of for instance *Special Delivery* and *Bend Over Boyfriend 2*. Just as the apartment, this space bridges dichotomies in between urban dissident public subculture and education.

[177] Juffer, 199. Juffer argues in regard to Femme Productions videos' circulation in video stores and catalogs that "[i]t is possible that domestication will encourage a movement between public and private spheres."

tells her that she will lock the door behind her. The other woman replies: "Thanks, but right now my personal safety is not threatened by a stranger." Safe space is here evoked as a space in between sexual partners, involving negotiations and trust.[178] Elin Magnusson's *Dirty Diaries* film *Skin* also thematizes such negotiation around safety and trust. The film features a heterosexual couple wearing body stockings that they cut each other out from.[179] In her presentation of the film Magnusson writes:

> In a room on the seventh floor in a cold city, two people are waking up. They hug each other hard, still, it's not enough to be able to forget where one body starts and the other ends. Neither of them has a sex or a face and they both wear more layers of skin than they ought to. Old disappointments and badly healed wounds have turned them into this. The hardened skin makes them ask for help to remember the sensation of heat. With a pair of scissors they ask each other for permission to expose, rip up and get in.
> This is an inquiry to get rid of what's been long since dead. It's surgery. Something forgotten turns into a memory that later transforms into fingers, and finally a hand. Hair begins to smell and the sweat is pouring.
> In close-ups about closeness we see the longing for something new. Art meets porn in a ripping horniness without censorship.[180]

Similarly to *On Your Back Woman!*, *Skin* raises questions about power struggles in relationships and about not harming each other. In Marit Östberg's film *Authority,* trust is also emphasized as a crucial aspect of BDSM role-play. In other films featuring BDSM, such as the early Fatale Media production *Shadows* and the trans porn film *Trans Entities*, participants' negotiations of boundaries and safe words and discussions about the content of the role-play is included in the films.

These examples all demonstrate how the figure of safe space is mobilized in queer, feminist and lesbian pornography's blurring of boundaries between public and private space. They also bring up questions about the relationship between the real space of queer, feminist and lesbian cultures and the fantasy spaces constructed within these. This relationship is evoked in Mia Engberg's reflections about authenticity and fantasy in the opening quote to this chapter, in Wallace's remarks about lesbian chronotopes as both ethnographic and fictionalized spaces, and across this film culture's legacy of documentary and sex educational filmmaking. This relationship between spaces on and off screen will be further discussed in the following three chapters. The ethnographic spaces of queer, feminist and lesbian porn exhibition and reception will be in the focus of the next chapter. The constitutive

---

[178] Williams, 1999, 260.
[179] *Skin* also echoes Yoko Ono's *Cut Piece* (1965). Halberstam, 2008, 150, discusses Ono's performance in terms of "radical passivity," refusal and anti-sociality. In talks about her film Magnusson has often underscored that in *Skin*, the woman is the one in control of the action.
[180] Elin Magnusson, "Skin," *Dirty Diaries* DVD booklet, 2009.

tension between affirmation and critique of this interpretive community as a site of struggle will there be reframed as a tension between notions of intimate and counter public.

# 4. Affirmation and critique: reception contexts and situations

On a May evening in 2008 I press the small bell to Club LASH, a monthly members-only kinky, fetish and S/M club for women and transsexual people located in Scandinavian Leather Men's basement space on a quiet street in Södermalm in Stockholm. There is a buzz and the rather unnoticeable doors unlock. A friend and colleague who will be my assistant for the evening and I enter and walk down the sloping floor to the entrance and bar areas where this evening's crew busily gets everything in order. We are both regular visitors to Club LASH. We make sure the crew, many of whom we know from before, are aware that we are present as researchers this evening. I pin an information sheet on a notice board in the entrance area. This night's theme is the annual event Bad Birds Ball. There will be performances and a "bad bird" ball queen will be chosen. A DJ is getting installed in the small booth above the dance floor and a designer is unpacking leather skirts and corsets that she will be displaying and selling in one part of the bar area. In the bar area there is also a small monitor attached close to the ceiling where lesbian porn will be screened. This is why we are here. As the one permanent site where lesbian porn is regularly screened in Stockholm, I have decided to make Club LASH the starting point for my fieldwork. I have brought questionnaires in both Swedish and English, asking questions about consumer habits and asking for further participation in the project. We decide to make the entrance area our main spot for handing out the questionnaires. When the club opens we start asking the arriving visitors to fill out the questionnaires. People are both slightly embarrassed and amused, but generally positive to the project and to participating. At an early stage of the evening filling out questionnaires dominates the activities engaged in at the club.

This chapter looks closer at some of the different sites where queer, feminist and lesbian porn is circulated, the practices of participation in these spaces and the embodied experiences articulated in these contexts. The results from the questionnaires at Club LASH, as well as Pornfilmfestival Berlin, where the same questionnaire was run in October 2008, demonstrate that while the home is the most common place of lesbian porn consumption, a club or a festival is the second most common context.¹ The questionnaires also indicate that while watching by oneself is most common, watching together with others is as common as watching together with one other person. Importantly then, the questionnaires indicate that queer, feminist and lesbian porn spectatorship is not only a matter of individual, private or isolated consumption. Chapter 3 historicized the production of queer, feminist and lesbian pornography and demonstrated how its political and aesthetic legacies revolve around the figure of a safe space for sexual empowerment. This chapter focuses on the reception of queer, feminist and lesbian pornography and discusses how its meanings are shaped by the different contexts where it circulates and how the figure of safe space is mobilized within these. It accounts in particular for some of the many reception sites, practices and situations of *Dirty Diaries* and the meanings and experiences that have been articulated within these. As such the chapter follows Jane Juffer's insistence on analyzing how particular sites of production, distribution and consumption and specific conditions of access and agency within these shape the meanings and uses of porn.² Juffer argues that:

> To understand access, we must have a theory of agency, with agency defined as the relationship between the individual subject and the different forces that enable and constrict her movement between sites where sexually explicit materials are available and back to the home, where it is consumed. Feminists, both antipornography and anticensorship, have failed to produce a theory of agency in relation to pornography precisely because the discussions have been dislocated, occurring at a highly generalized level far removed from the conditions of everyday life.³

The porn consumption discussed in this chapter, however, takes place more in public than in the home. The chapter shows how different sites and practices of distribution and consumption produce different conditions of access and agency for different viewing subjects in the reception situation. Building on Miriam Hansen's discussion about film as a public sphere and spectatorship as shaped by both the "theater" and the "film" experience, both by "the situation of reception" and by the "world on screen," the chapter discusses queer, feminist and lesbian pornography as an alternative public sphere where, just as in Hansen's discussion about early cinema, alternative understandings of gender and sexuality are produced, circulated and practiced.⁴ The previous chapter argued that throughout its political and aesthetic legacies this interpretive community is invested in constructing a safe space for sexual empowerment. In this chapter the tension between affirmation and

---

¹ By the time I ran the questionnaire I used the categorization "lesbian pornography." See chapter 2 for more on this.
² Juffer, 8.
³ Ibid.
⁴ Hansen, 1991, 93.

critique that is played out in this politics of constructing safe space is conceptualized as a tension between the notions of counter public and intimate public. I examine how, on the one hand, queer, feminist and lesbian pornography functions as a space for affirmation and recognition. On the other hand, it functions as a public platform for critique and challenging of dominant notions of gender and sexuality. As such, this interpretive community actualizes trajectories both at the level of subjectivity, where its participants are affirmed and empowered affectively, and at the level of the public sphere, where queer, feminist and lesbian pornography claims and gains increased accessibility and visibility. The chapter argues that in queer, feminist and lesbian pornography these trajectories are intertwined.

## An affective scene for recognition

One of the participants in the questionnaire at Club LASH who also signs up for further participation is Jennifer, who chooses to participate anonymously in the research. She is a 35-year old lesbian and a cultural producer who has been an active member of Club LASH since 2000. I meet her on a Tuesday evening in November 2008 in a seminar room at the Department of Cinema Studies in Stockholm. It is a strange place for talking about porn and sexuality, not least because this part of Filmhuset (the "Film house"), where the department is located, is more or less a construction site at this time. A thin layer of dust covers the tables. Nevertheless, our conversation is open and free flowing. I have known Jennifer for many years, from Club LASH and other queer, feminist and lesbian contexts in Stockholm. I ask her how she first came into contact with lesbian pornography and what lesbian porn means to her.[5] Jennifer describes how she, after working some years in the porn industry, felt that her sexuality was "destroyed" and "broken down" and in need of being "rebuilt." "I had a lot of complexes, really bad self-esteem," she says. She came out as a lesbian and got involved in Club LASH where she also learned about lesbian porn. She watched films at the club but also borrowed them to view at home. She stresses how important the films were for her at this time in her life, both as a means of learning about lesbian sexuality and discovering her own desires and "preferences," but also in helping her accept and affirm her body and sexuality, in daring to become more confident and uninhibited. She admired the girls in the films and wanted to be like them:

---

[5] By this time I used the categorization "lesbian pornography" in the interviews. Research subjects often commented on this terminology and its relation to representations of lesbians in mainstream heterosexual porn. Both Jennifer and another research subject stressed that they preferred to call it "flatporr," roughly translatable to "dyke porn."

> The good films... yes, it is really different compared to... and I've watched a lot of mainstream [porn]. I can't say that I get a better self-esteem as a woman from watching that. But the thing is that I do, I did, from these lesbian films. They were strong proud girls who liked their bodies even if they were not perfect, they were natural. They did not even seem to bother very much about how they looked. And they seemed to enjoy it for real. And they were uninhibited, they just let themselves go. That impressed me, so they were role models. I just: wow! I also want to become like that in bed.[6]

Jennifer's account resonates with several other research subjects' accounts. For instance, Flora Schanda, a 26 year-old literature student and, as she calls herself, "queer BDSM activist and lesbian sex positive activist," who I interview in Berlin during the Pornfilmfestival in 2008, talks about the importance of seeing identities that she can relate to represented in film.[7] "I get a feeling that there is a place for my gender and sexual identity – that it can be desired and that there is a good way of representing it, a sexy way," she says. She finds that this is "empowering" and gives her a "higher sexual self-esteem." Both Jennifer's and Flora's accounts invoke Linda Williams' suggestion that porn for women may function as an arena for sexual self-discovery, as well as discussions about lesbian pornography as a vehicle for sexual affirmation, recognition and education in research addressing lesbian pornography.[8] In 1997 Becki L. Ross found that:

> Erotic images validate our sexuality as one healthy, meaningful, and empowering part of our lives as lesbians (and gay men). Sexually explicit images produced by and for lesbians challenge the barrier of sexual fear, inhibition, ignorance, and shame by unapologetically foregrounding lesbian desire, and thus expanding the realm of knowable human sexual expression.[9]

In Lisa Henderson's words lesbian pornography "brings lesbian desire above ground, affirming its legitimacy and encouraging lesbian women to find and embrace what pleases them sexually."[10] In this vein, Cherry Smyth also wrote in 1990 that:

> Lesbian sexuality has been repressed, rendered invisible and impotent by society. By watching porn, we can on some level recognize ourselves, defend our right to express our sexuality and assert our desire. It includes us in a subcultural system of coded sexual styles, gestures and icons which affirms our sense of belonging.[11]

---

[6] Interview with Jennifer, Stockholm, 2008-11-04. My translation from Swedish.
[7] Interview with Flora Schanda, Berlin, 2008-10-27.
[8] Williams, 1999, 259-264; Henderson 178; Heather Butler, 2004, 190; Rhyne, 42.
[9] Ross, 300.
[10] Henderson, 1992, 178. Henderson here discusses *On Our Backs*.
[11] Smyth 1990: 154. See also Lisa Henderson "Simple Pleasures: Lesbian Community and Go Fish," *Signs: Journal of Women in Culture and Society*, 25:1 (1999): 37-64.

However, Juffer problematizes a notion of porn as liberation and transgression as it was articulated in the pro-sex literature of the 1980s and 1990s. She critiques the "belief in the transformative power of representation and interpretation as fairly isolated practices" and a conceptualization of transgression as placeless individual reader agency and subversion in an undifferentiated public sphere.[12] She points out how, for instance, the feminist celebrations of Annie Sprinkle (by for instance Williams and Straayer) often disregard the conditions for and contexts of women's porn consumption: "Williams and Straayer both suggest that it is through the reading/viewing of individual texts, such as Sprinkle's performances, that women may, like Sprinkle, liberate themselves into a world of polymorphous, orgasmic sexuality freed of material boundaries."[13] She argues that an individual viewer's ability to interpret and transgress codes and conditions in order to arrive at a state of pleasure does not transform the conditions of access that define women's consumption of porn. What is illuminated in Jennifer's account is precisely that her empowering experiences of lesbian porn take place within a specific context providing specific conditions for her consumption. Club LASH, where she first learns about lesbian porn, is a place designed for sexual exploration and play and informed by BDSM principles of safety and consent. Jennifer contrasts this context with the porn industry where she used to work:

> I was 19 years old when I started to work in those places [the porn industry] and I had not even discovered my sexuality then. I did not know myself what I was, I was rather confused over all and this thing with BDSM – it was just bloody chaos everything... But at LASH I could discover it, explore and develop this in a protected environment. If you compare it was really like coming to an oasis with safe and warm atmosphere and acceptance and there was love [laughs]. Which, if you compare with the porn industry where you only – there was no love, it was just cold, cold and hard.[14]

In research on queer, lesbian and transgender public sex and BDSM cultures, the notion of safety as a precondition for sexual exploration is crucial. In an analysis of a lesbian/queer bathhouse event in Toronto, Corie Hammers highlights the centrality of constructing a space that is simultaneously perceived as sexual and safe, informed by "feminist principles of sexual exploration and sexual liberation"[15] and by principles of "consent, respect, and

---

[12] Juffer, 15.
[13] Juffer, 16.
[14] Interview with Jennifer, Stockholm, 2008-11-04. My translation from Swedish.
[15] Corie Hammers, "An Examination of Lesbian/Queer Bathhouse Culture and the Social Organization of (Im)Personal Sex," *Journal of Contemporary Ethnography*, 38:3 (2009): 312.

confidentiality."[16] In Robin Bauer's work on "dyke/trans" BDSM communities, safe space and consent are also highlighted as general standards and characteristics.[17] In his study, people engage in BDSM in order to "explore and get to know one's own boundaries or push/transgress them, or both, within a framework of negotiated consent."[18] Underground sites of sexual culture, such as sex dungeons and BDSM clubs, have been conceptualized both as symbols or effects of discrimination and marginalization, and as sites of potential empowerment and resistance. In Phil Hubbard's summary of these discussions, he notes that "[i]f cities contain sites of sexual confinement, these spaces are also potentially sites of sexual liberation."[19] With reference to Linda McDowell he argues that geographies of sexual citizenship may also "provide spaces for sexual experimentation among 'counter-public' groups."[20] Queer, feminist and lesbian porn film culture intersects with such sites of public sex and BDSM culture where safety is understood as a precondition for sexual empowerment, evident not least in the case of Club LASH. In Jennifer's account the club provides the necessary conditions for her access to lesbian porn as well as for her enhanced agency in exploring her own sexuality.

## Relying on safe space

As pointed out in chapter 3, the figure of queer, feminist and lesbian porn as a safe space for sexual empowerment is imagined throughout this film culture. It is played out not least in many films' inclusion of safer sex instructions and of interview material with the performers where principles of safety and consent as guiding the production are emphasized. In line with this investment in the figure of safe space throughout this interpretive community, Jennifer's account articulates an understanding of the films she watched at Club LASH as "fair." In contrast to the porn industry in large she talks about how performers in what she calls "real lesbian porn" are real lesbians and bisexual women and participate out of their own free will, for political reasons and have influence over the production.

---

[16] Hammers, 311. See also Catherine Jean Nash and Alison Bain, "'Reclaiming Raunch'? Spatializing Queer Identities at Toronto Women's Bathhouse Events," *Social & Cultural Geography*, 8:1 (2007): 47-62.

[17] Robin Bauer, "Transgressive and Transformative Gendered Sexual Practices and White Privileges: The Case of the Dyke/Trans BDSM Communities," *Women's Studies Quarterly*, 36: 3-4 (2008): 233-253.

[18] Bauer, 234.

[19] Phil Hubbard, "Sex Zones: Intimacy, Citizenship and Public Space," *Sexualities*, 4:1 (2001): 60.

[20] Hubbard, 60; Linda McDowell, "City Life and Difference," in *Unsettling Cities*, ed. John Allen, Doreen Massey and Michael Pryke (London: Routledge, 1999), 143-160.

> It was differently made… I think good porn… then the performers should like what they do, it's that simple. They should be horny for real. They should do it primarily because they like it, not primarily for the money… And then they should have something to say. They should have influence over the production… You should know that it has been fair and – when it is lesbians who do – these are small companies. It is not possible to compare with the big big porn machinery… the porn industry… This is an entirely different thing and then it feels much better to watch, then it is much easier to take pleasure – if you know that it is real and that it is made with a good intention and a much better message than in mainstream porn.[21]

Jennifer's articulation of how performers in lesbian pornography are "horny for real" unlike the stereotype "Barbie dolls" in mainstream porn echoes how notions of "real" and "authentic" are played out in this film culture, as accounted for in chapter 3. These notions also recur in other research interviews. For instance, Rosa Danner, a researcher and activist who I interview over Skype the month after the Pornfilmfestival Berlin in 2008, writes that she prefers films that have "more feeling" and are "more authentic" than the "industrialized stereotypes in mainstream porn."[22] In both her and Jennifer's accounts, notions of "real" and "authentic" become a precondition for a pleasurable experience of the film. With Juffer, these notions provide conditions of access. In her discussion, pornographic texts themselves function as sites "where issues of access are partially determined."[23] While women may well find pleasure in a variety of texts, "texts that specifically target women will more likely function to increase access because of how they often circulate in a manner that legitimates women's sexual pleasures, in turn helping to create the times and spaces in which to exercise those pleasures."[24] Juffer further claims that "women who make porn will more likely increase the many conditions of access that contribute to the 'environment' in which women feel comfortable watching porn."[25] In this sense the pro-sex literature that Juffer critiques is, on the other hand, also central in contributing to the legitimacy of queer, feminist and lesbian porn consumption. In Jennifer's case the "fairness" she perceives in the films, together with the "protected environment" of Club LASH, provide also a "mental" space, as Juffer puts it, for pleasure and sexual agency.[26]

Similarly, Iris Segundo, a 22 year-old student and freelancer who attended the Pornfilmfestival Berlin 2008 as assistant of the short *Passion for Football* (*Passión our el Futbol*, Rut Suso & Maria Pavón, Spain, 2006), told me in an interview that if performers in a porn film do not have safe sex,

---

[21] Interview with Jennifer, Stockholm, 2008-11-04. My translation from Swedish.
[22] Interview over Skype with Rosa Danner, 2008-11-25.
[23] Juffer, 23.
[24] Juffer, 56.
[25] Juffer, 175.
[26] Juffer, 71f.

she cannot take pleasure in the film.[27] Access to sexual pleasure, in these examples, is a matter of conditions provided both at specific sites and by the films and other texts circulating in this interpretive community, both by the "theater" and the "film" experience, in Hansen's terms. These examples again invoke Williams' discussion about how the legitimacy of Candida Royalle's films "enable women to create for themselves the safe space in which they can engage in sex without guilt or fear."[28] She suggests that "the mixture of safety with excitement [...] may be just what is needed *for* excitement."[29] In chapter 5 the "mental" and embodied space of the film experience will be discussed more in depth.

In Jennifer's account lesbian pornography became an arena for a safe and contained exploration of her own desires and sexuality. Her story demonstrates that sexual liberation, becoming more confident and uninhibited, rather than a matter of placeless individual reader agency, is conditioned by this interpretive community's investment in a politics of constructing safe space for sexual empowerment. As a "collective political fantasy" of safe space and played out in different reception sites, practices and situations, queer, feminist and lesbian pornography becomes a space that conditions and shapes certain film experiences.[30] This space is the space of queer, feminist and lesbian pornography as an intimate public.

The accounts of Jennifer and other research subjects, as well as the centrality of notions of belonging, inclusion, legitimizing, valorizing and affirmation in lesbian porn discourse, invoke Lauren Berlant's discussion about intimate publics as places of "recognition and reflection," where a particular group's claimed core interests and desires are circulated.[31] Intimate publics express "the sensational, embodied experience of living as a certain kind of being in the world."[32] An intimate public is "a porous, affective scene of identification among strangers that promises a certain experience of belonging and provides a complex of consolation, confirmation, discipline, and discussion about how to live as an *x* [emphasis in original]."[33] Thus, rather than organized by political aspirations, Berlant contends that intimate publics are organized by a promise of affective recognition and social belonging for a group who is expected to share "a worldview and emotional knowledge that they have derived from broadly common historical experience."[34] Therefore, she questions the political potential of intimate publics. Berlant both stresses and complicates the relation between transformed subjectivity and

---

[27] Interview with Iris Segundo, Berlin, 2008-10-26.
[28] Williams, 1999, 264.
[29] Ibid.
[30] Freeman, 65.
[31] Berlant, 2008, viii.
[32] Ibid.
[33] Ibid.
[34] Berlant, 2008, viii.

social change, between feelings of investment and agency.[35] She develops the notion of intimate public partly in dialogue with the notion of counter public that she claims overemphasizes politics. I argue that these two notions are intertwined in queer, feminist and lesbian pornography, where activism is both a matter of feelings of affirmation, empowerment and liberation and of reformulating and publicly challenging dominant notions of gender and sexuality.[36] The dynamic and intertwined relation between intimate and counter public trajectories in queer, feminist and lesbian pornography also sets the figure of safe space in motion.

## Claiming public space

In an article published on the Swedish political debate website *Newsmill* in the week of the premiere of *Dirty Diaries* in August 2009, the director Marit Östberg argued in favor of "more horny women in public."[37]

> Feminist porn wants people to be horny, wants to encourage people to feel sexy and to be sexual objects, but decide for themselves how, why and for whom. Once you have that power it is much easier to decide when you DO NOT want to be sexual. [---] *Dirty diaries* is an important project because we need to create more images of desire, ways of having sex and different ways of screaming out our horniness. We need more portraits of sexy fantasies. With the film *Authority* in *Dirty Diaries* I want to celebrate all the proud, shameless, horny and queer bodies that paint their dreams over the public sphere.[38]

Through Marit Östberg's and other *Dirty Diaries* filmmakers' debate articles and participation in the media around the time of the release, as well as through the film's wide circulation in Sweden as well as abroad, *Dirty Diaries* gained far more publicity and attention than Swedish short films usually do.[39] As discussed in chapter 3, a number of films in the collection, such as *Flasher Girl on Tour* and *Dildoman*, also enact a reclaiming of public space. In Marit Östberg's short *Authority* a graffiti girl enters a restricted area and is

---

[35] Berlant, 2008, 12.

[36] See also Bobo, 59-60; and Berlant and Freeman, "Queer Nationality," in *The Queen of America Goes to Washington City*, by Lauren Berlant, 1997, 167-173.

[37] Marit Östberg, "Vi behöver fler kåta kvinnor i offentligheten," *Newsmill*, 2009-08-27, http://www.newsmill.se/artikel/2009/08/27/vi-behover-fler-kata-kvinnor-i-offentligheten?page=1 (accessed 2010-06-21). My translation from Swedish.

[38] Ibid.

[39] "Mest lästa på DN.se 2009," *DN.se*, 2009-12-31, http://www.dn.se/nyheter/mest-lasta-pa-dnse-2009 (accessed 2011-10-13). Sofia Curman and Maria Ringborg, "Porr för feminister?" *DN.se Kultur&Nöje*, 2009-08-28, http://www.dn.se/kultur-noje/film-tv/porr-for-feminister-1.940378 (accessed 2010-06-17); Conan O'Brien, The Tonight Show, 10 September 2009, NBC.

caught by a policewoman. In both *Authority* and Marit Östberg's first short for *Dirty Diaries*, *Uniform*, lesbian sexual role-play is set in public spaces. As thematized in Mia Engberg's short *Come Together*, where a number of women film their own faces while masturbating, *Dirty Diaries* appropriates the male dominated space of filmmaking and cinematic representation, and, by using mobile phone cameras, claims means of production for sharing and circulating in public women's self-represented sexual pleasure. *Come Together* self-reflexively raises questions about who controls what pictures surround us, and how publicity through new media technologies can be made differently. As such, the short invokes Michael Warner's reading of a photograph of a group of drag queens in 1950s and 1960s New Jersey.[40] The photograph depicts the drag queens together in a domestic space. They are all equipped with cameras, pointing them at each other and taking pictures, including of the person who took this photograph. Warner contends that "[t]he private setting protects them from an environment of stigma, but clearly their aspiration is to a different kind of publicness," and that cameras in this photograph "create publicly circulating images, making possible a different style of embodiment, a new sociality and solidarity."[41]

Following Warner's, as well as Nancy Fraser's and Iris Marion Young's discussions about counter publics, queer, feminist and lesbian porn film culture can be understood as a counter public sphere where non-dominant discourses on sexuality and gender circulate.[42] Fraser defines what she calls "subaltern counterpublics" as "parallel discursive arenas where members of subordinated social groups invent and circulate counterdiscourses, which in turn permit them to formulate oppositional interpretations of their identities, interests, and needs."[43] These arenas, Fraser contends, function both as "spaces of withdrawal and regroupment" and as "training grounds for agitational activities directed toward wider publics."[44] Similarly, Young argues that in feminist counter publics, women are encouraged "to speak for themselves, from their own experience" and "form images and interests with which to speak to a larger public that ignores or distorts women's concerns."[45] In Warner's development of the concept he stresses that counter publics are in conflict with the dominant public and its modes of address and, as in the drag queen photograph, attempts to create "rival modes of

---

[40] Warner, "Introduction" to *Publics and Counterpublics* (New York: Zone Books, 2002b), 13f.
[41] Warner, 2002b, 13f.
[42] Fraser, "Rethinking the Public Sphere," 1990; Young, "Unruly Categories," *New Left Review*, 1/222 (March-April 1997), http://www.newleftreview.org/?page=artivle&view=1899 (accessed 2010-08-25).
[43] Fraser, 1990, 67.
[44] Fraser, 1990, 68.
[45] Young, 1997, 8-9.

publicness."[46] As Hubbard demonstrates, in much theory on sexual minorities, activism and the public sphere there is an imagined trajectory from the margins to inclusion, participation and visibility as sexual citizens in the public sphere.[47] For instance, Nancy Duncan argues that "significant social change requires organized action in the public sphere and access to various resources, including the media, rather than individualistic, privatized action."[48] Occupying the public sphere has been a crucial strategy not least in queer activism, summarized in Queer Nation's slogan: "We're here we're queer, get used to it!"[49] Queer subcultures but also LGBTQ film festivals, films and television productions, such as *Queer As Folk* and *Shortbus* (John Cameron Mitchell, 2006), have been discussed in terms of counter publics.[50] These discussions about counter publicity resonate with Hansen's contention that "the cinema can, at certain junctures, function as a matrix for challenging social positions of identity and otherness and as a catalyst for new forms of community and solidarity."[51]

This trajectory towards participation and visibility in the public sphere also describes the expanding public visibility of queer, feminist and lesbian porn, not least in the cases of *Dirty Diaries* and Pornfilmfestival Berlin. Such visibility was also actualized in *The Queer X Show*, where a number of sex radical performers and activists toured in Europe during the summer of 2009. In Emilie Jouvet's *Too Much Pussy: Feminist Sluts in the Queer X Show* and *Much More Pussy*, the two films documenting *The Queer X Show* tour, there are a number of scenes where the performers in the show claim public space, not only on stage, but also for sexual role-play, for instance at a cemetery, and for promoting the show.

In one sequence, three of the women walk towards the camera, down a street at night in Paris and start taking off their clothes, announcing that "this is a live street strip show." Queer, feminist and lesbian porn's participation and visibility in the public sphere builds on the second wave feminist opening up of public space for sexual consciousness-raising and empowerment, as well as on queer activism's public manifestations, evident in the explicit reference to another Queer Nation slogan in the punk soundtrack to *Too*

---

[46] Warner, 2002b 14; and 2002a, 86.

[47] Hubbard, 2001, 61.

[48] Nancy Duncan, "Renegotiating Gender and Sexuality in Public and Private Spaces," in *Bodyspace: Destabilizing Geographies of Gender and Sexuality*, ed. Nancy Duncan (London & New York, 1996), 138.

[49] The slogan was used during the Pride march in New York 1990. See for instance Berlant and Freeman, "Queer Nationality," 1997; Rosenberg, 2002, 34-39.

[50] Nick Davis, "The View from the *Shortbus*, or All Those Fucking Movies," *GLQ*, 14:4 (2008): 623-637; Suzanne Fraser, "Poetic World-Making: Queer as Folk, Counterpublic Speech and the 'Reader'," *Sexualities*, 9 (2006): 152-170; White, Rich, Clarke and Fung, "Queer Publicity," *GLQ*, 5:1 (1999): 73-93.

[51] Hansen, "Early Cinema, Late Cinema: Transformations of the Public Sphere [1993]," in *Viewing Positions*, ed. Williams, 1997, 146.

*Much Pussy* and *Much More Pussy*, declaring that "every time we fuck we win!"[52] This participation and visibility in public also relates queer, feminist and lesbian pornography to contemporary discussions about the sexualization of the public sphere and blurred boundaries between private and public, not least through new media technologies.

As pointed out in chapter 1, *Dirty Diaries* reactivates a discussion about third wave, or what Wencke Mühleisen calls Nordic new feminism, and its relation to mainstream sexualization.[53] Third wave feminism is sometimes described as altering 1970s consciousness-raising and the idea that the personal is political into narcissistic striptease and questions of lifestyle and consumer rights and citizenship.[54] Angela McRobbie problematizes how a notion of women's consumption of and taking pleasure in sex entertainment as a sign of feminist success interrelates with "a triumphant neo-liberal popular culture [defining] and [organizing] a sexual world."[55] She instead calls for analysis of how "popular feminism is absorbed into a more commercial sex industry, making it more acceptable since it now seems to be a totally women-friendly phenomenon."[56] Mühleisen critiques a binary opposition between regarding sexualization as either liberating or repressive. This "stands in the way of an understanding of the potential, the problems, and the paradoxes concerning mainstream sexualization."[57] She sees in Nordic new feminism a participation in mainstream sexualization as a claiming of accessibility to feminist discourse in the public sphere. The wide distribution and reception of *Dirty Diaries* demonstrates precisely some of the potential, problems and paradoxes involved in claiming public accessibility for queer, feminist and lesbian pornography.

---

[52] From the leaflet "Queers Read This" distributed at pride march in NY, June 1990. Published in Rosenberg, 2002, 168.

[53] Mühleisen, "Mainstream Sexualization and the Potential for Nordic *New Feminism*," *NORA*, 15: 2-3 (2007): 172-189.

[54] Rebecca Munford, "BUST-ing the Third Wave: Barbies, Blowjobs and Girlie Feminism," in *Mainstreaming Sex,* ed. Attwood, 2009, 183-197; Kaarina Nikunen, "Cosmo Girls Talk: Blurring Boundaries of Porn and Sex," in *Pornification*, ed. Paasonen, Nikunen, Saarenmaa, 2007, 73-85; Angela McRobbie, *The Aftermath of Feminism*, 2009; Koivunen, "Confessions of a Free Woman," *Journal of Aesthetics & Culture*, 1 (2009), http://www.aestheticsandculture.net/index.php/jac/article/view/4644 (accessed 2011-11-17); Sowards and Renegar, 2004.

[55] Angela McRobbie, "Pornographic Permutations," *The Communication Review*, 11 (2008): 230.

[56] McRobbie, 230. See also Lisa Henderson, "Slow Love," *The Communication Review*, 11 (2008): 219-224.

[57] Mühleisen, 2007, 184.

## *Dirty Diaries*: public circulation and shifting address

In her presentation of the project at our first *Dirty Diaries* meeting at Café Copacabana in June 2008, Mia Engberg talks about how the film is planned to be distributed and consumed. She emphasizes that, while her previous film *Selma & Sofie* was shot on 35mm film and had a theatrical release, *Dirty Diaries* is primarily produced for DVD consumption at home:

> This is not the kind of film you see in the cinema. You should be able to get turned on. That is something private. Everybody says that women do not like pornography. Maybe women do like pornography but they do not dare showing it because we are brought up in a certain way. So you should be able to buy this and have it at home and watch it with your partner or alone.[58]

When the DVD is released a bit over a year later it comes in a white paper box depicting only a white drop pouring from the top and the letters DIRTY DIARIES in black. Besides the DVD case and the disc, the box also contains a booklet in thick ground paper with portraits of the filmmakers and presentations of the individual shorts. When Mia Engberg hands out the DVDs at our fifth *Dirty Diaries* meeting in August 2009, she explains that she wanted the DVD to be something you can buy in art spaces and be able to put in your bookshelf: "nice, simple and a bit secret."[59]

*Dirty Diaries DVD box.*

---

[58] *Dirty Diaries* meeting, 2008-06-12. My translation from Swedish.
[59] *Dirty Diaries* meeting, 2009-08-25.

As such, *Dirty Diaries* actualizes Juffer's contention that women's erotica's aesthetic address is one crucial condition for providing access and as such functions as one of the "forces that enable and constrict her [the individual subject's] movement between sites where sexually explicit materials are available and back to the home, where it is consumed."[60] The intent at being consumed and kept primarily at the home also aligns *Dirty Diaries* with Juffer's as well as Williams' discussions about the new conditions for porn consumption that video provided women with.[61] However, the *Dirty Diaries* DVD box is also wrapped in a plastic film and a loose sheet with thumbnail pictures showing explicit sexual action from the films was attached to the back. Mia Engberg contends that this was a compromise deal between her and the distribution company Njutafilms, a company specialized in "cult film, classics, children's film, documentary, quality erotic and art house film."[62] She describes how the distributor "thinks we are so uncommercial and arty that he almost started crying blood when he saw the cover – no tits, no nice girls" and how he worried that nobody would buy a DVD box where you do not even understand what is inside.[63] The sheet with the thumbnail pictures was attached in order to show that the film depicts naked bodies. Similarly, while Mia Engberg produced a poster featuring the same image of a white drop as the DVD box, Njutafilms produced a poster featuring a (restaged) film still from *Authority* where one woman sits on the face of another and pulls down her panties over the other woman's face.

These negotiations and compromises between Mia Engberg and Njutafilms testify to *Dirty Diaries'* belonging to different contexts of production, distribution and consumption. Through its financial support from the Swedish Film Institute and distribution through Njutafilms the film belongs both to a context of Swedish "quality" short film production and to a context of underground cinephilia.[64] Furthermore, the film's wide circulation has also resulted in different marketing strategies and framings of the project, as well as in many different discussions and reactions. Thus, while produced primarily for DVD consumption and while it had a limited theatrical release of only three screenings (including the premiere) at Bio Rio in Stockholm, *Dirty Diaries* has screened vastly in different exhibition contexts in Sweden as well as abroad. The shorts have circulated between prestigious short film

---

[60] Juffer, 8. See also Jane Gaines, 1990, 182.

[61] Juffer, 172-175; Williams, 1999, 229-264.

[62] "Om Njutafilms," Njutafilms website, http://www.njutafilms.nu/ (accessed 2011-11-19).

[63] *Dirty Diaries* meeting, 2009-08-25. My translation from Swedish.

[64] See discussion in chapter 1. See also Nick Davis, 629. In an article about *Shortbus* (John Cameron Mitchell, 2006) as belonging to a counter public consisting of explicit sexual art house films, Nick Davis points out that these often depend on the national and capitalist structures that they also critique, "not just as fundamental objects of contestation but for financing and circulation, especially in countries like Canada, France, and Great Britain, where state monies often feed the budget of these heretical texts."

festivals such as Clermont-Ferrand in France, documentary film festivals such as CPH:dox in Copenhagen, alternative erotic film festivals such as MIX NYC in New York and Perv Filmfestival in Sydney, do-it-yourself festivals such as FilmIdyll in Stockholm, Ladyfest in Zagreb and Genderbenderfestival in Bologna, as well as in museum and conference contexts.[65]

In these many different distribution and exhibition contexts *Dirty Diaries* has been marketed and discussed in a number of different ways. For instance, when the film in June 2010 had its theatrical release in 15 cinemas throughout France, distributed by the company KMBO, it was marketed with a poster of a bare-breasted woman resembling "Marianne" of the French revolution.[66] In reviews in several major papers and film journals *Dirty Diaries* was discussed, mainly in positive terms, in relation to mainstream and amateur porn, as well as to underground and experimental cinema.[67] When the film was screened at Paris Porn Film Fest, the French version of Pornfilmfestival Berlin, a "Porn studies day" at the School for Advanced Studies of Social Sciences preceded the festival.[68] One of the attending filmmakers from *Dirty Diaries* observed that the discussions at the Porn Film Fest formed part of a subcultural discourse on post porn whereas the broader public interest seemed more concerned with mainstream porn.[69] *Dirty Diaries* testifies to Hansen's as well as Juffer's emphasis on how different reception sites, practices and situations shape different meanings, not least as the film's address changed in different contexts. My own participation in and observations from a number of different situations of reception further demonstrate how a wide range of different meanings and experiences of *Dirty Diaries* were shaped and articulated in different contexts. Within these the figure of safe space was also mobilized in different ways. In the following I account for three examples.

---

[65] See appendix for a list of *Dirty Diaries* screenings.
[66] The first version of this poster featured a female Che Guevara with naked breasts, but was exchanged to Marianne, due to copyright issues.
[67] *Premiere*, June 2010; *Cahiers du Cinema*, June 2010; *Libération*, 2010-06-30; *Le Monde*, 2010-06-30.
[68] Paris Porn Film Fest website, http://parispornfilmfest.com (accessed 2010-08-03).
[69] Email received from Jennifer Rainsford, 2010-07-27.

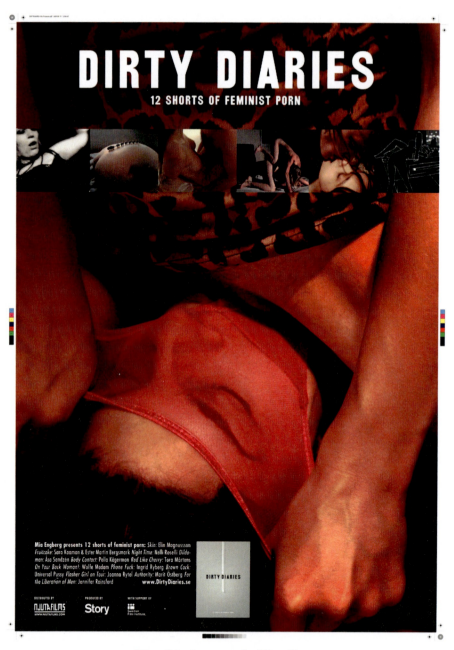

*Dirty Diaries poster by Njutafilms.*

*French Dirty Diaries poster by KMBO.*

## Cinemateket, Stockholm, 17 November 2009

In November 2009, the Swedish cinematheque, Cinemateket, which forms part of the Swedish Film Institute, screened *Dirty Diaries* in the theater Klarabiografen in Kulturhuset (The Culture Center) in Stockholm. I was invited to give a short introduction before the film. When I arrived I was struck by the line outside the movie theater: it consisted to a considerable extent of single, middle-aged men in trench coats. I exchanged some amused comments with the staff of Cinemateket on how well this fulfilled the stereotypical image of traditional porn audiences.[70] The director of Cinemateket, Lova Hagerfors pointed out that this demographic segment is also a well-represented category among Cinemateket's members as such. She was also very pleased that a lot of young women had become members in order to get tickets to the screening this evening. This was only the fourth public screening of *Dirty Diaries* in Stockholm since the release and it was soon sold out. Inside the theater it took some time before the seats were filled. Single seats in between the middle-aged men in trench coats remained unoccupied for a while. Eventually, the audience settled down and I was introduced and invited to give my short introduction. In my talk I commented on how unusual it was to screen porn in movie theaters nowadays, in contrast to the situation during the so-called "golden age of porn."[71] Several of the middle-aged men in the audience nodded knowingly. The rest of my introduction stressed that *Dirty Diaries* and the concept of feminist porn implied a critique against conventional representations of sexuality and gender. During this part I felt instead as if I addressed the young women in the audience. I became very aware that I talked to an audience with many different frames of reference.

During the screening the audience was quieter compared to other screenings where, in particular, the animation *Dildoman* and the mockumentary *Body Contact,* as the forth and fifth films in order after sexually explicit and detailed images in *Skin*, *Fruitcake* and *Night Time*, have produced loud and relieved laughter. There was no time assigned to questions after the film and very few audience members came up to me as I waited in the foyer afterwards in case anyone would want to give comments or ask anything. My general impression from this screening was that the audience was friendly and interested, but also reserved and modest. It seemed not to be an audience accustomed to queer, feminist and lesbian porn or to public screenings of porn as such. I interpreted the quiet and reserved response as a result of unfamiliarity with this film culture and perhaps as insecurity about how to

---

[70] Williams, 1999, 99. Williams refers to this stereotype as "the raincoat brigade – furtive, middle-aged men who went to see the exploitation fare, the beaver films, and whatever else was becoming legal on the big screen in the late sixties and early seventies, and so named for their presumed masturbatory activity under raincoats."

[71] Larsson, 2007, 99. Larsson claims that the concept of the golden age of porn can describe both an American and a Swedish context.

properly react to and think about the films. I also understood the withheld response in relation to the specific setting of this evening's screening: Cinemateket as an extension of the Swedish Film Institute and the objective to promote "quality" film, as well as Klarabiografen in Kulturhuset, a prominent cultural institution in Stockholm.

## Hamburg International Short Film Festival, 1-7 June 2010

At Hamburg International Short Film Festival in June 2010, *Dirty Diaries* was screened as a special programme.[72] When I arrived at the festival center the afternoon before the first out of two screenings, the first thing I saw was a notice announcing that the screening was sold out. The audience at that night's screening in the small theater B-Movie was young and seemed cheerful and excited. People were drinking beer and talking during the screening. Afterwards I announced that I was interested in audience comments, but nobody spontaneously came up to me. I approached a group of women in the small theater bar who seemed to be discussing the film. They expressed many mixed feelings about the film. In particular, they discussed the film in relation to representations of lesbians. They felt one problem with the shorts was that they reproduced stereotypical images of lesbians as "shorthaired" and "masculine."[73] This would only add to the audience's prejudice against lesbians. At the same time they found some of the films "sexy" and "hot," although they hesitated to call it pornography. One of the women found that the films were almost "too real" and "intimate." As such, these women engaged in major discussions that make up this interpretive community, regarding notions such as positive and negative images and authenticity, as highlighted in chapter 3.

Two nights later the film screened in the festival's largest theater Metropolis where it also gathered the largest audience of the festival.[74] Because of the large size of the theater it was hard to pinpoint the general response during the screening. The Q&A in which I and two other filmmakers from the project participated was dominated by men defining what they considered to be pornography and objecting to the feminist purposes of the project. Not many women took part of these discussions, but afterwards many of the women in the audience stayed and shared their predominantly very positive experiences of the films and thoughts on the topic of feminist porn with us. In the large mixed-audience theater the practice of ending the screening with a Q&A did not seem to produce favorable conditions for women's agency

---

[72] According to Hamburg International Short Film Festival's website the festival has an audience of around 14 000 and screens 400 films,
http://festival.shortfilm.com/index.php?id=festivalnews&L=1 (accessed 2011-10-21).
[73] *Dirty Diaries* screening, Hamburg Short Film Festival at B-Movie, 2010-06-03.
[74] *Dirty Diaries* screening, Hamburg Short Film Festival at Metropolis, 2010-06-05.

and public participation. However, this "theater" experience did not seem to prevent a positive "film" experience, in Hansen's terms. Furthermore, as one of the festival's "special programmes" *Dirty Diaries* was given attention in the festival nightclub, where the organizers had set up a "darkroom," in "honor of" *Dirty Diaries*, as one of the festival directors jokingly told us. Made provisionally out of thin plywood with "glory holes" and set up right next to the bar, it seemed more of a joke than designed for actual sexual encounters. However, along with the inclusion of *Dirty Diaries* in the festival as such, it also suggested a blurring of boundaries between underground sex cultures and "overground" publicity in the present sexualized public sphere.

## Malmö högskola, 7 September 2009

An open lecture at Malmö University, Malmö högskola, an evening in September 2009, the week after the release of *Dirty Diaries,* serves as a third example of how different sites, practices and situations shape different meanings and experiences of queer, feminist and lesbian porn. The "Shift lectures" are a series of lectures aiming at identifying and providing perspectives on current phenomena. For the lecture "Dirty Diaries and female porn" the organizers invited the well-established British porn director Anna Span, the porn researcher Mariah Larsson, and Joanna Rytel and me from *Dirty Diaries*. We each gave a short presentation. Span showed clips from her films and Rytel and I our *Dirty Diaries* films, *Flasher Girl on Tour* and *Phone Fuck*. The audience in the lecture hall, which consisted largely of students and young people, were given the opportunity to ask questions after each presentation. The dark large auditorium, the spotlights and our headset microphones made the space seem somewhat anonymous and the audience hard to get a clear sense of, but in general the atmosphere was respectful and interested.

The lecture was also broadcasted directly on Malmö högskola's website where people could participate in a chat and ask questions through the web moderator. When I read the chat log a few weeks after the lecture I realized that this online and interactive ambition had failed, partly because of the low quality of image and sound that many participants in the chat complained about, but mainly because the chat quickly turned into a forum for aggressive sexist and racist remarks such as: "feminist porn, I guess that means there is an ugly hairy auntie who sleeps with immigrants."[75] Another excerpt reads:

    lolboll: why couldn't they have made animal porn instead?

---

[75] Chat log received by email from project coordinator Evelina Mildner Lindén, 2009-10-06. [My translation from Swedish.]

> lolboll: 350 thousand to buy horses and shit for[76]
> K: lolboll: that would have been liberated for real
> Karl-Bengt: feminist animal porn
> Rimjob: batik witches fucked by horses :)
> K: to bongo drums, on möllan[77]
> K: in multiculti bitches dresses
> Rimjob: feces squirting like confetti

Set up as an occasion for discussion and analysis in an academic context, the particular reception site(s), practices and situation of the "Shift lecture" resulted in the most disturbing responses out of all the *Dirty Diaries* screenings I attended over the course of almost one year.[78] Rather than reflecting on the content in the lectures or the films, the participants in this web discussion seemed to be triggered more by the topic of feminism and pornography as such, by each other and by the opportunity to publicly articulate racist, homophobic and sexist sentiments.[79] The discussion was largely formulated as a reaction, or protest, precisely to the fact that we who participated in this lecture were given public space and visibility for feminist discussions: "back in the days bitches like this were drilled in the head, now they're on TV shouting all the time." While *Dirty Diaries*' wide circulation through different distribution and consumption contexts demonstrates how queer, feminist and lesbian pornography as a counter public claims and provides visibility, accessibility and publicity for counter discourses on sexuality and gender, the chat log from Malmö högskola also demonstrates that a trajectory from margins to public and mainstream sexualization is not without "paradoxes and problems," in Mühleisen's words, including, most crucially, putting the figure of safe space at stake.

## Intertwining intimate and counter public trajectories

Hubbard rejects the "conceptualization of public space as representing a democratic space where marginalized groups can seek to oppose oppressive aspects of heteronormality," and the idea that "having free access to public space represents the achievement of full citizenship."[80] He problematizes the trajectory from marginalization to public visibility and asks whether it is not

---

[76] "350 thousand" refers to the amount of money that *Dirty Diaries* was first supported with from the Swedish Film Institute.

[77] "Möllan" refers to an area in Malmö, Möllevången, known for its ethnic diversity.

[78] Mia Engberg received hateful emails already during the production phase. For a discussion about gender, sexuality and the Internet, see Janne Bromseth and Jenny Sundén, "Queering Internet Studies: Intersections of Gender and Sexuality," in *The Handbook of Internet Studies*, ed. Robert Burnett, Mia Consalvo, and Charles Ess (Blackwell Publishing, 2010), 270-299.

[79] See Sara Ahmed, "Affective Economies," *Social Text* 79, 22: 2 (2004): 117-139.

[80] Hubbard, 63.

more privacy rather than publicity that dissident sexualities need.[81] The wide circulation of *Dirty Diaries* in different contexts illustrates Mühleisen's contention that feminist accessibility and participation in mainstream sexualization involve potential as well as problems and paradoxes. Public visibility and participation expand and increase access to this film culture and thus the potential for providing a new "experiential horizon," in Hansen's words, for viewers who may not have come across this film culture otherwise.[82] However, it also runs the risk of delimiting conditions for agency, such as during the Q&A at Metropolis in Hamburg, where women did not participate in the public discussion to the same extent that men did. At Cinemateket in Stockholm members of the younger, female part of the audience seemed hesitant to sit down in between the single middle-aged men in the theater. In Malmö the online participation and accessibility of this film culture opened up for hateful assaults. My own embodied experiences in different situations of screening and discussing *Dirty Diaries* have at times felt more as exposure than as participating in affirming and protected environments. I have found myself in situations that made me question the very point of addressing other audiences than the ones that this film culture aims at empowering, audiences that cannot relate to queer, feminist and lesbian activist cultures and where my position could only be one of defense.[83] These experiences, however, have also formed a crucial part of the research material and have prompted analysis. Without denying or diminishing the privilege of my position as a researcher participating in a most interesting and exciting project and being invited to talk about this at a number of occasions, I find that my own experiences of exposure in these situations has laid important ground for this chapter's conceptualization of queer, feminist and lesbian pornography as embodying a tension between counter public challenging and intimate public affirmation. This tension has been actualized also in Marit Östberg's interview accounts of her experiences of participating in this film culture as director and performer, debater and consciousness-raising group organizer, in Berlin and in Sweden.

## "I wanted to use my body in my queer activism"

Questions of public participation, safety and exposure form a large part of the seven interviews I made with Marit Östberg, from the beginning of her involvement in this film culture and over the course of almost three years

---

[81] Hubbard, 64. See also Peggy Phelan, *Unmarked: The Politics of Performance* (London & New York: Routledge, 1993); Beverley Skeggs, "Matter out of place: visibility and sexualities in leisure spaces," *Leisure Studies,* 18 (1999): 213-232.

[82] Hansen, 1991, 117.

[83] This refers in particular to a panel discussion on "Sex in Media" at Publicistklubben Malmö, 2009-09-28.

where she directed three films and performed in three, of which one was her own *Dirty Diaries* film *Authority*.[84] Her case illustrates that participation in this interpretive community often involves a number of different practices and activities, blurring the boundaries between cultural producers, activists and audiences. Marit Östberg and I know each other and have shared an interest in queer, feminist and lesbian porn for many years. The interviews I made with her often took the form of conversations and comparisons of our different experiences and reflections of this film culture. As such, Marit Östberg has contributed greatly to the theorizing of the issues in this chapter. Her shifting experiences and conceptualizations of queer, feminist and lesbian pornography during these years illustrate the complex dynamic and interrelatedness of the two trajectories of intimate public recognition and counter public visibility. In her accounts these trajectories are intertwined from the beginning.

When I first interview Marit Östberg over Skype in August 2008, shortly after she has moved to Berlin from Stockholm, she has just, for the first time, participated as a performer in a film directed by Emilie Jouvet. She describes how she finds Jouvet's *One Night Stand* to be one of the best "dyke porn films" and when Jouvet asked her if she wanted to perform in her new film she decided to do so.[85] She had then just decided to make a film of her own for *Dirty Diaries* and was in a period where she "thought a lot about [her] own participation in film." She describes her decision to perform in Jouvet's film as a matter both of breaking a cultural dichotomy and of changing her own personal way of feeling in relation to sex.

> I think it is interesting to break the dichotomy filmmaker-porn actress (that as filmmaker I am not just a viewing eye). But also… there is so much prejudice precisely with being a porn actress – I wanted to break with my own prudishness in some sense.[86]

In her account "prejudice" is linked to her own sense of "prudishness." She further explains:

> I think lesbian/queer porn is very important, to show different sexualities and different forms of shooting/representing sexualities and bodies. I think Emilie Jouvet does this in a good way and I decided that I wanted to use my body in my queer activism (just as I write, walk in demonstrations and will make my

---

[84] During these years Marit Östberg directed the films *Uniform* (2008) and *Authority* (2009) for *Dirty Diaries* and later *Share* (2010). She performed in *Authority* and in a film by Emilie Jouvet during the summer of 2008, a project that was later cancelled. She also performed in Cheryl Dunye's feature *Mommy Is Coming* (2012). In October 2011 she completed a new film, *Sisterhood*.
[85] Interview with Marit Östberg over Skype, 2008-08-11. My translation from Swedish.
[86] Ibid.

own film). Another reason was personal – that I wanted to work with my relation to guilt and shame and sexuality and publicity.[87]

Marit Östberg also explains that the audience she imagines for her performance in Jouvet's film is her own queer community and that it is important "to make 'alternative' sexualities visible to us." In line with other research subjects' accounts, she finds it "important that 'those like me' can identify with bodies and sexuality" and "to expand the world and understandings of sexuality." This entails "affirming lust, create curiosity and wanting to explore sexuality." "I think that it is empowering," she writes. Furthermore, she describes how during the filming she "felt safe" and to her surprise felt that the camera "became a part of the sex" and that she liked it, "the thought of being horny and full of lust for others." She describes the camera as "a 'kind' eye – an eye that wanted me to take pleasure." I ask her to clarify her thoughts about this "kind eye," and she writes: "The good eye I guess I mean is the room where sexuality like mine is allowed to take up space, is affirmed and explodes room. Explodes narrow understandings of sexuality." I ask if there is also "an evil eye" that "limits the sexual expression" and Marit Östberg answers: "Yes maybe, for me there has been sorrow in my sexuality, taboos, limitations. Fear. So unnecessary that people walk around feeling like that when it so fantastic. To show lust is a most important thing." Her articulation of feelings of safety, of being affirmed and allowed to take up space with her sexuality, in contrast to feelings of sorrow, shame and fear, resonates with Jennifer's and other research subjects' accounts and again invokes Berlant's description of intimate publics as places for consolation, recognition and reflection. Her account also invokes Fraser's definition of counter publics as arenas for formulating "oppositional interpretations" and Warner's discussion about "rival modes of publicness." Marit Östberg discusses her personal experiences of affirmation and empowerment – also in the particular situation of her own performance in Jouvet's film – in relation to a wider context of "narrow understandings of sexuality."

The struggle to overcome guilt and shame and the interrelatedness of personal development and public activism are recurring questions throughout our conversations. In October 2009 we do our fifth interview in Berlin where we will both have our *Dirty Diaries* films screened at the Pornfilmfestival. I interview Marit Östberg in her small flat a few blocks from the festival theater the afternoon before our films will be screened. Marit Östberg, who has recently shot, but not yet edited the film *Share*, contends that making porn also as director is important to her own sexuality and that her thoughts about sex have developed also by being close to other bodies who "lived out their sexuality without guilt and shame."[88] She talks about how this "room" allows

---

[87] Ibid.
[88] Interview with Marit Östberg, Berlin, 2009-10-24. My translation from Swedish.

her to "develop as a human being" and about how sexuality becomes a kind of "energy" because it is about "lust." She explains: "It means a lot to me to be in this room because… I have been so much of an activist… in my days and never before found this kind of room where like the driving force is lust." When we meet this time it has been a couple of months since the release of *Dirty Diaries* and from my own experiences of representing the project in several different contexts during these months I am interested in discussing how the film culture is shaped differently in different contexts and what it means to make this sexual culture public. Marit Östberg talks about a column she is about to write for the Swedish paper *Kom Ut* ("Come Out") where she will articulate her ideas about performing in porn in relation to "the assumption that showing your body and sexuality would be the most exposing thing you could do." "For me, to write a text is much more exposing than to show my body," she says. She talks about the differences between the Swedish queer activist context, which she describes as "academic" and the queer activist context she finds in Berlin. She finds that the Swedish context "talks about the body the whole time but there is a very strong taboo in showing your sexuality and your body. What is important is to show your thoughts and your intellect."[89] Marit Östberg states that to her at this point: "the most political and subversive in all of this is not those thoughts but precisely to let go." If Berlant contends that intimate publics often lack political aspirations, Marit Östberg's account, on the other hand raises questions about how activism may lack "lust" and "energy." The interrelation between the trajectories of intimate and counter publics here also involves a negotiation between body and intellect. Marit Östberg's accounts articulate a tension between, on the one hand, lust and body, and on the other hand, activism and intellect, but also a struggle to overcome this tension.

Nevertheless, if at this point Marit Östberg wrote in her column for *Kom Ut* that: "to have sex in front of a camera does not equal exposing all you have," some months later she found herself overwhelmed with guilt and shame as she sat in the audience during the screening of her film *Authority* and three other *Dirty Diaries* films at London Lesbian and Gay Film Festival in March 2010.[90] I see her at the short film festival in Hamburg a few months later. We settle down for an interview (our sixth) at a café outside the film festival center the afternoon before the main screening of *Dirty Diaries*. She describes how during the screening in London she felt as if she was no

---

[89] She gives an example from an article she has published in the Swedish magazine *Ottar* where she writes about performing in her own film. She had written that she performed in her own film, not just because it was difficult to find performers and not just because she was an exhibitionist, but also because she wanted to question who stands behind and who stands in front of the camera. When the article is published it says: "I am not performing in the film because it is difficult to find performers, I am not because I am an exhibitionist. I play in the film because I want to question who stands behind and who stands in front of the camera."
[90] Marit Östberg, "Hjälteporr," *Kom ut*, 3 (2009), 45.

longer as strong as she had felt when she decided to make the film and perform in it herself and as she felt when writing articles about this experience at *Newsmill*, in *Kom Ut* and in other papers.[91] She felt as if she had made a choice that implied that she had "excluded" herself from other opportunities in life, that she would be excluded from everything she had built up before, such as possibly continuing an academic career.[92] She also felt she could no longer see the difference between the porn she was involved in and the larger sexualization of the public sphere. She describes how around this same time, she also started to google herself and realized that the search results for her name included "just a lot of naked bodies." Marit Östberg relates this experience of crisis to a depression related to other factors in her life. She says that this made her feel not strong enough to "separate all the roles I had taken – the performer, the filmmaker and the debater… I could not carry them all." Importantly, her feelings of shame and crisis were not related to the reception site or situation. On the contrary, she emphasizes that the atmosphere at the festival and in the movie theater was "supportive" and that she got a very positive response from people coming up afterwards telling her that they "loved" her film. Returning to Berlin after this experience Marit Östberg decided to call together a group of "other queer porn performers" with a similar "activist background" as herself. She describes this as a feminist base group where they share and discuss their different experiences in order to help and empower each other:

> It means… a lot to have a context where you… do not feel alone and where you do not have to be strong the whole time, [where] you can bring out your threatening clouds and… difficult situations you've been in, but also to have this political ground to stand on together and build something together.[93]

The last two times I interview Marit Östberg, both times in my apartment in Stockholm, in September 2010 and June 2011, she further reflects on the "risks" involved in a wider public accessibility of this film culture and of losing the link to the subculture. "There is actually a rather hard world out there, outside of our bubble… you have to protect yourself from that," she says.[94] She says that she has realized that the "politics," as well as the "self-critique" is what makes this film culture meaningful to her, not to "make porn for its own sake." She says that although, when she first got involved in this film culture, she was carried away by the empowering experiences of focusing on the body and on lust and "not having to be political," she has

---

[91] Marit Östberg, "Rätt att ge skattepengar till feministisk porr," *Aftonbladet*, 2009-09-05, http://www.aftonbladet.se/debatt/debattamnen/samhalle/article5741067.ab (accessed 2009-09-08); Marit Östberg, "Nu kör vi!", *Ottar*, 3 (2009): 20-23.
[92] Interview with Marit Östberg, Hamburg, 2010-06-05.
[93] Interview with Marit Östberg, Hamburg, 2010-06-05. My translation from Swedish.
[94] Interview with Marit Östberg, Stockholm, 2010-09-28. My translation from Swedish.

now realized that these are "not possible to separate." She also stresses how these experiences and especially the subcultural context and consciousness-raising group in Berlin have made her regain a new sense of strength. Marit Östberg's accounts illustrate both a counter public trajectory of activist participation and visibility in public, but also a reverse trajectory back to a small feminist base group, to an intimate context for recognition and affirmation. Throughout the all in all eight interviews I made with her the notions of intimate and counter public are evoked as well as intertwined.

\*\*\*

The examples discussed in this chapter, Jennifer's account of lesbian pornography in the context of Club LASH, *Dirty Diaries*' different distribution sites and marketing strategies, my own accounts of different reception situations and Marit Östberg's account of her practices of participation in this film culture over the course of three years, all testify to how the meanings of queer, feminist and lesbian pornography shift and are shaped differently in different contexts. While Jennifer's experience of lesbian porn took place within the context of Club LASH, *Dirty Diaries* has circulated in contexts that are much more accessible to the public, which has produced a range of different responses. Many of these contexts, such as the ones discussed above, are not, unlike Club LASH, Pornfilmfestival Berlin and a number of other contexts where *Dirty Diaries* has been screened, primarily set up for engaging in queer, feminist and lesbian sexual culture and activism. To some extent all of these screenings were characterized by a slightly awkward and hesitant, but still interested atmosphere. What also characterized these screenings was that participation was differentiated in the sense that the blurred boundaries between audience, activist and cultural producer were reinstalled, positing the audience as onlookers and filmmakers as debaters. Crucially, in Malmö högskola's chat forum participation implied something very different. These examples illustrate how accessibility in mainstream sexualization involves potential, as well as problems and paradoxes.

Furthermore, while the examples discussed in this chapter support Juffer's contention that different pornographic texts need to be discussed in relation to the specific sites where they circulate and not as a matter of individual reader agency and interpretation, they also raise questions precisely about how different readers produce different meanings of texts, depending on their different positions and practices of participation within this interpretive community, as well as on their individual backgrounds and histories. Participants' different positions and practices in these contexts, such as performing or being part of an audience, also provide different conditions for access and agency, and feelings of safety and exposure. As such, not only do different sites, practices and situations provide different conditions of access and agency, but also, different bodies are preconditioned in different and shifting ways. As an intimate public, queer, feminist and lesbian pornography bring together subjects sharing a certain "emotional knowledge" about "a certain kind of being in the world," as Berlant puts it. The "common historical experience" articulated in this interpretive community concerns a "core interest and desire" for a safe space for sexual empowerment. In Jennifer's case her background in the porn industry and sense of having "bad self-esteem" and "a lot of complexes" provided specific conditions for her experiences of lesbian pornography in the context of Club LASH. In Marit Östberg's account her understandings of her "identity, interests and needs," in Fraser's words, also changed and shifted over the years, not least through her involvement in queer, feminist and lesbian pornography. As such, different bodies shape different meanings of pornographic texts, but also, queer, feminist and lesbian pornography shape these bodies. The next chapter discusses these processes more in depth.

# 5. Carnal fantasizing: embodied spectatorship

When I attended the Pornfilmfestival Berlin in October 2010 I had a deeply ambiguous experience. I went to see the film *Much More Pussy* by the French director Emilie Jouvet.[1] *Much More Pussy* is the second film Jouvet made from the footage documenting the burlesque performance show *The Queer X Show*, where a group of seven sex radical women toured Europe in a mini-bus during the summer of 2009. While the first film *Too Much Pussy: Feminist Sluts in the Queer X Show* focuses on the performances and discussions between the women, the second film, *Much More Pussy*, focuses more on the sexual encounters that occurred during their tour, between the women in the show and other people that they met along the way. I had attended *The Queer X Show* when they performed in Stockholm during the Pride festival in August 2009 and was excited to see what Jouvet had made of the material. Together with a friend I settled down towards the front of the theater at Moviemento in the Kreuzberg district, the main location of the Pornfilmfestival Berlin. The theater soon became crowded. Jouvet, as well as some of the women from the show were also present. This was the first public screening of the film. A man sat down next to my friend and from the very start I noticed the unwelcome way he looked and smiled at her. My friend started to fidget about and held her arms tight around herself. I asked her if she wanted me to tell him to back off, she said: "no it's okay." Then the film started and I was absorbed by the tremendous force of these women's intimate interactions, by the intensity of their different experiences and thoughts on gender and sexuality that they share with each other and bring into sexual role-play and by the careful responsiveness and participative presence of Jouvet's camera. During these 90 minutes I had one of my most powerful film experiences within this film culture and at this festival that I had been participating in both as filmmaker and researcher since it was started in 2006. Afterwards, as I left the theater, I realized that I had not noticed any fidgeting indicating that my friend had still been uncomfortable during the screening. I did not get the chance to ask her then but in my mind I thought that perhaps it was not just that I had been completely overwhelmed by the film and unaware of what happened next to me. Perhaps the man stopped once the film started. Perhaps he lost his rude courage once he was confronted with the fierce women in the film, with the control they possessed

---

[1] *Much More Pussy*, screening at Pornfilmfestival Berlin, 2010-10-29.

over their sexualities and bodies. This was the fantasy I wanted to believe and chose to take with me from this experience when I returned to Sweden. Because if, as the film's punk soundtrack repeatedly declares, quoting Queer Nation's 1990 manifesto – "every time we fuck we win" – this man should not. Or was this man in fact the symbolic "winner" of the sexualized public sphere enabling this film festival? Most crucially, this experience directed attention to how different social subjects participate in the sexualized public on different terms.

As this example demonstrates, and as argued throughout chapter 4, experiences and meanings of queer, feminist and lesbian porn are not a matter of isolated acts of interpretation and reader agency, but are located in and shaped by specific sites, practices and situations. The meaning of queer, feminist and lesbian pornography is in Miriam Hansen's words shaped both by the theater experience and by the film experience. At play in my experience of *Much More Pussy* were, in Hansen's words, "multiple and dynamic transactions" between the space of the screen and the space of the theater, as well as between this film culture's function as both an intimate public and as a counter public.[2] As pointed out in chapter 4, queer, feminist and lesbian pornography both claims visibility and accessibility in the public for counter discourses on sexuality and gender, and provides affective affirmation and recognition. In my experience at the screening in Berlin these two functions clashed. The public sharing of an intimate project of sexual recognition, self-discovery and empowerment seemed to also play into the hands of dominant gender and sexual structures and result in women's exposure and unsafety.

While the previous chapter discussed how specific screening contexts shape different meanings and experiences of queer, feminist and lesbian porn, this chapter accounts more for the relation between films and viewers in this interpretive community and analyzes the embodied and psychic processes that this relation involves. It focuses on research subject's accounts of film experiences and discusses how queer, feminist and lesbian pornography shapes embodied subjectivities. I address this question through the work of Linda Williams, Vivian Sobchack and Teresa de Lauretis on embodied spectatorship and Sara Ahmed's work on queer orientations. I contend that as a collective political fantasy, queer, feminist and lesbian pornography has the potential to touch, shape and (re)orient its viewers and make new worlds imaginable and come into reach.

---

[2] Hansen, 1991, 118.

# Gendered and sexualized body experiences

A few months after the screening of *Much More Pussy* I emailed my friend in Berlin asking her what had really happened during the screening. She answered that the man had put his arm at the armrest, then slowly moved it closer to her body and touched her. She writes:

> The hand was there throughout the film, on the armrest. At some point I put his hand back at the armrest since it had landed on my side of it. The person did not seem to realize that he did something that made me feel uneasy. When I looked at him, he seemed to have the coziest time ever, seemed mostly happy that I looked at him.[3]

In her account of the history of moving-image sex, Williams argues that through public screenings of sexual images in American movie theaters since the 1960s, bodies have become "habituated to diverse qualities and kinds of sexual experiences" and that "sexual sensations previously viewed as private" become socially integrated.[4] She contends that "where sexual arousal was once deemed antithetical to all civilized public culture, now, through screening sex, our bodies are not simply shocked into states of arousal but habituated and opened up to this changing environment in newly socialized ways."[5] Referencing Hansen's discussion about Walter Benjamin's notion of innervation, of the body as a "porous interface between the organism and the world," Williams describes screening sex not just as a shock of modernity or eros but also as play, where "playing at sex, too, is a way of habituating our bodies to a newly sexualized world."[6]

> In Foucault's terms we are disciplined into new forms of socialized arousal in the company of others, but in (Hansen's understanding of) Benjamin's terms we are more than just disciplined; we may also learn to play at sex the way a child might play at being a windmill or a train by incorporating more subtle forms of psychic energy through motoric stimulation.[7]

According to Williams then, screening sex functions both as a technology disciplining and educating viewers into specific forms of arousal and desire and as a more open and undisciplined process and space for imagination. As pointed out in previous chapters, the interpretive community of queer, feminist and lesbian pornography is also made up by such discipline and play at sex, through the sexpert tradition as it is actualized in films, but also in workshops on fisting, bondage and safe sex at Pornfilmfestival Berlin. In her

---

[3] Email received 2011-02-17. My translation from Swedish.
[4] Williams, 2008, 18.
[5] Williams, 2008, 18.
[6] Williams, 2008, 18. Williams quotes Miriam Hansen's article, "Benjamin and Cinema: Not a One Way Street," *Critical Inquiry*, 25:2 (1999): 317.
[7] Williams, 2008, 18.

discussion about the feminist masturbation discourse of the 1970s, Jane Juffer similarly points out that the "'liberation' of the home as a site of masturbatory activity" also came with "its own set of regulatory codes," such as "a certain hierarchy of appropriate masturbatory activity and kinds of fantasy material."[8] Intimate publics, as Berlant also puts it, provide both consolation and discipline.[9]

My experience at the screening of *Much More Pussy* in Berlin highlights that discipline, habituation and "socialized arousal in the company of others" need to be understood in relation to the specific bodies involved and their location in gendered and sexual power structures, as these also intersect with class and race.[10] In this situation, socialized arousal and regulatory codes included sexual harassment. Thus, for different bodies to be "habituated and opened up" to sexualized environments has different meanings and implications and rules for play are differently conditioned. As Iris Marion Young puts it in her discussion about female body experience, "[t]o open her body in free, active, open extension and bold outward-directedness is for a women to invite objectification."[11] In Ann Cvetkovich's work on trauma, sexuality and lesbian public cultures, she stresses that vulnerability, openness and receptivity is both a risk and an effort. It is "a privilege that is often unavailable and harder to achieve than the conventional stereotype of women as sentimental would have it."[12]

Feminist phenomenologists have highlighted that how we live and feel our bodies is not unconditioned by gender. Rather, in de Lauretis' words, "the body is a gender symptom in that it bears the inscription of gender and speaks it back through the subject's very senses, through the perceptual apparatus that constitutes the bodily ego."[13] Building on the work of the sociologist Gesa Lindemann, de Lauretis discusses the process through which perception becomes gendered.[14] She analyzes the experience of a pre-op transsexual woman called Verena at a public women's toilet. When she hears another woman enter the toilet, Verena all of a sudden cannot pee out of fear that she will be perceived of as a man. When she hears the other woman peeing she relaxes and is again able to pee. De Lauretis describes this process as a negotiation between the image Verena has of her own body and her body as it feels, between the objectified body and the lived body.

---

[8] Juffer, 72.
[9] Berlant, 2008, viii.
[10] See Attwood, 2009, xxii.
[11] Iris Marion Young, "Throwing Like a Girl: A Phenomenology of Feminine Body Comportment, Motility, and Spatiality [1980]," in *On Female Body Experience: "Throwing Like a Girl" and Other Essays* (Oxford: Oxford University Press, 2005), 45.
[12] Cvetkovich, 69.
[13] Teresa de Lauretis, "Gender Symptoms, or, Peeing Like a Man," *Social Semiotics*, 9:2 (1999b), 264.
[14] De Lauretis, 1999b.

When the objectified body becomes dominant, Verena can only perceive of herself as a male body. In de Lauretis' analysis, Verena exemplifies how gender is inscribed in our bodies, how the sensory registers of perception implicate gender in the body as it feels. Similarly, Young demonstrates how historically given gender structures condition and precede "the action and consciousness of individual persons."[15] She describes feminine bodily existence as characterized by a "tension between transcendence and immanence, between subjectivity and being a mere object."[16] This negotiation between experiencing the body as an object and as capacity implies that "feminine movement exhibits an *ambiguous transcendence*, an *inhibited intentionality*, and a *discontinuous unity* with its surroundings [emphasis in original]."[17] In this sense, women who enter sexualized public space do so with specific sets of historical and bodily preconditions.

Relating this perspective to Juffer's emphasis on conditions of access and agency and on "the relation between the individual subject and the forces that enable and constrict her movement between sites where porn is available" implies that these conditions and forces are also implicated in the body of this subject.[18] As my example from Pornfilmfestival Berlin demonstrates, these forces are lived as embodied experience where certain bodies' agency and access, or, with Sara Ahmed, "extension" and "reach in space," are more enabled and others more constricted – as in the image of this man reaching past his side of the armrest to touch my friend squeezing her arms around herself.[19] Ahmed addresses how habitual actions and norms that are repeated over time and with force shape bodies and how bodies are gendered, sexualized and raced by how they extend into and are oriented in space.[20] Gender, for instance, "becomes naturalized as a property of bodies, objects, and spaces partly through the 'loop' of this repetition, which leads bodies in some directions more than others as if that direction came from within the body and explains which way it turns."[21] Thus, orientations operate simultaneously as effects and are lived and experienced as originary. In the situation in the theater in Berlin gender was performed precisely as habitual and naturalized actions. In her email my friend writes:

> Despite my 30 years I still have not learned to say no, that I'm in charge of my body and very easily could tell a man to stop if he crosses a boundary.

---

[15] Young, "Lived Body vs. Gender: Reflections on Social Structure [2002]," in *On Female Body Experience* 2005, 25.
[16] Young, 2005, 32.
[17] Young, 2005, 35.
[18] Juffer, 8.
[19] Ahmed, 2006.
[20] Ahmed, 2004, 145; Ahmed, 2006, 91, 5.
[21] Ahmed, 2006, 58.

> Words to mark boundaries are something I've often needed but not had access to. I have to struggle to dare saying no, it does not come naturally.[22]

My friend describes how she had arrived to this screening with the feeling that here she could feel bodily lose and free, that she would not have to be self-conscious about her body in this context. Her experience of unease, just as Marit Östberg's account of shame in the theater at the London Lesbian and Gay Film Festival and panic over finding pictures of naked bodies when googling herself, can be read with Ahmed's description of the feeling of disorientation as involving "becoming an object" and "losing one's place."[23] Referencing Frantz Fanon's black phenomenology and description of the hostility of the white gaze she contends that "disorientation is unevenly distributed: some bodies more than others have their involvement in the world called into crisis."[24] In her discussion about "bodies that are not extended by the skin of the social,"[25] Ahmed allows the term "queer" to slide between describing how non-white bodies can queer white spaces and referring "those who practice nonnormative sexualities."[26] The bodily feeling of disorientation can be "a violent feeling, and a feeling that is affected by violence, or shaped by violence directed toward the body."[27] The situation in the theater in Berlin, where my friend held her arms around herself and felt unable to tell the man to stop involved white bodies, but can be described with Ahmed's discussion about Fanon and about how disorientation may block action and accumulate stress and how "[b]odies can even take the shape of such stress."[28] In this sense, feelings of unsafety, threat and lack of agency are implicated in certain bodies: non-white bodies, women, queers.[29] Similarly, in her discussion about lesbian public cultures, Ann Cvetkovich discusses how "the normalization of sex and gender identities can be seen as a form of insidious trauma."[30]

De Lauretis points out that the implication of gender in the body occurs through the discursive construction of gender that film also participates in. Film, as she famously puts it, is a "technology of gender."[31] It participates in the ongoing discursive construction of gender, which has real and embodied implications for individual subjects as this construction is interactively reworked into self-representations. Emphasizing the embodied and real impli-

---

[22] Email received 2011-02-07. My translation from Swedish.
[23] Ahmed, 2006, 159, 160.
[24] Ibid., 159.
[25] Ibid., 139.
[26] Ibid., 161.
[27] Ibid., 160.
[28] Ahmed, 2006, 160.
[29] See also de Lauretis, "The Stubborn Drive: Foucault, Freud, Fanon," in *Freud's Drive*, 2010, 39-57.
[30] Cvetkovich, 46.
[31] De Lauretis, 1987.

cations of representations, de Lauretis argues that gender "becomes 'real', when that representation becomes a self-representation, is individually assumed as a form of one's social and subjective identity."[32] As social subjects we become "engendered" through an interactive subjugation to our society's gender system, to its technologies of gender, such as film, but also other representations.[33] As such, the discursive construction of gender is rooted in the experience of the body.[34] Film forms part of the process of engendering bodies and producing female body experience.

However, this also implies that film might play a role in the production of other experiences. As I demonstrated in chapter 4, queer, feminist and lesbian pornography is articulated within this interpretive community as contributing to processes of empowerment, improving self-esteem, getting rid of guilt and shame and becoming less inhibited. In the case of *Dirty Diaries*, discussions at meetings often revolved around how we as sexual subjects are gendered, how our desires and fantasies are shaped by representations, how we see others and ourselves "through the male gaze," but also about how we, through creating "our own explicit images," in Mia Engberg's words, can "liberate our own sexual fantasies from the commercial images that we see every day, burying their way into our subconscious."[35] Queer, feminist and lesbian pornography then raises questions not just about technologies of stress, shame, disorientation and inhibition, but also about how such gendered and sexualized body experiences can be changed and reshaped into feelings of self-esteem and empowerment. As Vivian Sobchack argues, it raises questions about how "the film's material conditions for providing access to the world [...] provide us actual and possible modes of becoming other than we are."[36]

## Carnal identification

> A festival is a completely different surrounding, with a lot of people. But then it can also be arousing... It can even be a turn on if it's really sexy and you think – how many of the other people will be aroused? ... Because sometimes you feel... the energy in the room changing... Especially... with *One Night Stand*, the first time I saw it the whole crowd, I think we all felt something was changing... slowly throughout the film, I don't know what happened but everybody left really flushed and like, it was a really different energy around. It was really funny to experience and sometimes you have that at festivals – the people just come in – "oh we're gonna watch a film" – and then they come

---

[32] De Lauretis, 1999b, 259f.
[33] De Lauretis, 1999b, 160.
[34] Patricia White, "Introduction: Thinking Feminist," in *Figures of Resistance*, 2007, 6.
[35] Mia Engberg, "What is Feminist Porn?", *Dirty Diaries* DVD booklet, 2009.
[36] Sobchack, 1992, 162.

out in a whole different state. And that's an added value of seeing it with other people… If all the people are comfortable with being there as well.[37]

I meet Marije Janssen, a 29 year-old organizer and writer specialized in sex worker rights, sexuality, gender, media and art, at a brunch place in Kreuzberg the Monday after the Pornfilmfestival Berlin in 2008, where we both have participated intensively during four days of screenings, workshops and performances. She will take the train back to Utrecht, where she lives, in a couple of hours. We start talking about Emilie Jouvet's film *One Night Stand*, which we both saw when it was screened at the first Pornfilmfestival Berlin in October 2006. Marije Janssen's positive recollection of this screening resonates with my own memory of it. It invokes Williams' discussion about screening sex as a matter of socially integrated sexual sensations in a very different way than the screening of Jouvet's film *Much More Pussy* in 2010. The difference between these two experiences again highlights the importance of locating discussions about spectatorship in relation to specific sites, practices and situations. Marije Janssen, who considers herself to be "mostly straight," further describes how surprised she was about the "strong physical sexual reaction" she had when watching *One Night Stand*. She did not expect to be sexually aroused but the film had a "raw energy" that made her discover "new desires:" "I was intrigued with my own feelings also of sexual arousement and attraction to these women and these kinds of sexuality – also with women that I wouldn't find particularly attractive, but this raw sexuality which was shown, that just did it for me."

This experience of *One Night Stand* challenged Marije Janssen's ideas about who and what turns her on when watching porn. She compares this with another film, the female-to-male trans porn film *Trans Entities: The Nasty Love of Papi and Wil* (Morty Diamond, 2006), where she experienced a similar "powerful energy" that aroused her. At the same time, she was also surprised about feeling attracted to trans persons: "I cannot identify and I'm not particularly attracted to them but it's the experience in the end that counts more than the body types." She talks about how she usually identifies with female characters in porn, as well as with the "more submissive characters," which corresponds with her role in her own BDSM practice. In her account of her physical reaction to *One Night Stand* and *Trans Entities*, her surprise originated from the difference she perceived between herself and the people in the film. The films did not represent persons that she would find attractive if she "saw them on the street," but they had a "powerfulness" and "energy" that made her aroused, and which has led her to become "more open" to explore new aspects of her sexuality. In Williams's words her body was habituated and "opened up" to these "diverse qualities and kinds of sex-

---

[37] Interview with Marije Janssen, Berlin, 2008-10-27.

ual experiences."[38] Williams also claims that viewers may find sexual pleasure in pornographies not directly addressed to them in accordance with gender or sexual identity. She finds that what she herself learned from writing *Hard Core* "was actually how easy it was to identify with diverse subject positions and to desire diverse objects."[39] She contends that:

> Rather than assume that each sexual predilection has its own kind of representative porno, it seems more apt to assume that pornographies are becoming part of the process by which spectators discipline themselves to enjoy different varieties of visual and visceral pleasure – pleasures that are both produced in the imagination and felt in the body.[40]

Marije Janssen's account of her experiences of *One Night Stand* and *Trans Entities* also invokes Sobchack's discussion about processes of identification in the film experience, not as engagement with or recognition of characters or subject positions, but "with the sense and sensibility of materiality itself."[41] Sobchack speaks of a "carnal identification with material subjectivity," where things on the screen are sensible in a "prepersonal, and global way," like the smell of fresh laundry in *Pretty Baby* (Louis Malle, 1978) and the taste of pork noodles in *Tampopo* (Juzo Itami, 1986).[42] In her main example she describes her sensual experience of watching *The Piano* (Jane Campion, 1993) and of how her own fingers made sense of the blurred opening shots of fingers held up against the sun before she could consciously recognize what she was watching. Even if the relation between the body and the cinematic representation is restricted in the sense that they do not touch each other the same way two unmediated bodies can touch each other, Sobchack argues that the cinesthetic subject's embodied film experience is both figural and literal. It is a sensual experience perceived both "as real" and "as if real," "a partially fulfilled sensory experience."[43] This sensual experience at the movies does not reduce but enhances the cinesthetic subject's sensual being. Since it is not possible to literally touch, smell or taste the figures on the screen, the cinesthetic subject will direct its attention towards its own subjective lived body: "[I] will reflexively turn toward my own carnal, sensual, and sensible being to touch myself touching, smell myself smelling, taste myself tasting, and, in sum, sense my own sensuality."[44] In her experience of *The Piano* Sobchack's sense of touch is thus intensified as she cannot touch the skin and clothes on the screen but direct her tactile intentions

---

[38] Williams, 2008, 18.
[39] Williams, "Second Thoughts on Hard-Core," in *More Dirty Looks,* ed. Church Gibson, 2004b, 171-172.
[40] Williams, 1999, 315.
[41] Sobchack, 2004, 65.
[42] Ibid.
[43] Sobchack, 2004, 76.
[44] Ibid., 77.

towards her own skin and "become not only the toucher but also the touched."[45]

However, whereas Sobchack underlines that the cinesthetic subject does not feel her or his own body in the film experience, Marije Janssen, on the other hand, is much more precise in her articulations. Sobchack contends that the viewer's intentions are aimed at the materiality in the film and therefore that the viewer's own body feels more diffuse, less literal. It is neither exactly the character Ada's woolen stockings nor her own silk blouse she feels on her skin when watching *The Piano*.[46] Contrarily, Marije Janssen's account of how she experiences the action in the film in her own body is more concrete. She describes how she usually "imagines" how it feels "physically." "If I see somebody go down on somebody else I will feel the same physical reaction in my self – so then it is a very strong identification," she explains.[47] When I ask her if this applies even if there is a practice that she does not have any experience of, she answers that this is a different kind of physical arousal, where she does not feel the exact same action in her own body; it is more "voyeuristic," as she puts it. She explains with the example of fisting: "Heavy fisting – I've never done, so I don't know how it feels. But mild fisting – I know how it feels, then I can feel it really in my own body. But with the really heavy stuff that I've never done I won't feel it because I don't know how it feels. But it will turn me on."

For Sobchack, carnal identification with the smell of fresh laundry and the taste of pork noodles are prepersonal and global experiences, which later ground more local identifications. Marije Janssen's account, however, highlights how the viewer's previous experiences and practices inform and affect how she or he experiences and feels the film in her or his own body. Here, not all bodily experiences are accessible or transferable to all viewing bodies. Her account raises questions about whether any viewer can experience the sensation of being "in the touching but also in the touched" and experience "the general erotic mattering and diffusions of [...] flesh" in relation to pornographic representations of various sexual practices.[48] Marije Janssen thinks that fisting is not "comparable to anything else," and that it is therefore "hard to imagine:" "I just don't know how it feels to have a fist in myself – which is really strong." This also raises questions about whether it is necessary to once have tasted or smelled pork noodles in order to experience this taste in the film experience of *Tampopo*. What kinds of experiences are available and can be shared between different bodies in the film experience?

---

[45] Ibid., 77.
[46] Ibid., 78.
[47] Interview with Marije Janssen, Berlin, 2008-10-27.
[48] Sobchack, 2004, 66.

*Publicity still, One Night Stand (Emilie Jouvet, 2006). Courtesy of the filmmaker.*

## Habituation to porn consumption

Similarly to Marije Janssen's distinction between physically feeling the same action represented on screen in her own body and enjoying it more "voyeuristically," other research subjects also reflect over their relation to queer, feminist and lesbian pornography in terms of "voyeurism."[49] In these accounts, the very act of screening and watching sexual images as a socially integrated practice, for example at the Pornfilmfestival Berlin, is a matter of "habituation," of opening up to and learning to play at being a porn spectator. Manuela Kay, one of the organizers of the Pornfilmfestival and the director of the lesbian porn film *Airport*, who I interviewed in Berlin in October 2008 and who also participated at a *Dirty Diaries* meeting in Stockholm in December 2008, described her experience of screening porn to lesbians in Germany. When she started traveling around with her sex instruction films and with *Airport* in the early 1990s she found that lesbians were not used to seeing lesbian sex on film and in public. She realized that it takes time for people to "digest" the experience of watching pornography.

> A lot of people… thought when they see their first porn in their life they will be so turned on and their sex life will change immediately or something. So they were totally disappointed… But funny enough later quite a few people that saw the film somewhere… they came to me and told me that… it took like a few days or weeks and some of the images kept coming back and then they have like an erotic experience like afterwards, because… they kind of… were so scared to let these pictures… actually… like to take them in properly, but they came back and then they would slowly like daring – once they were out of the public space also and in private they were able to digest it… and its like, well, actually some of these scenes and some of the images that are still in my head did turn me on but I didn't realize it when I watched the film.[50]

Manuela Kay finds that the audience at the Pornfilmfestival Berlin is very different to these lesbian audiences in the mid-1990s: "It is more like a party… everybody is laughing and flirting and it's a whole new sort of confidence." Her account highlights the question of habituation to the very practice of participating in screenings of sex. Mary T. Conway analyses how this question is also played out in the Fatale Media films *Bathroom Sluts* (1991) and *Safe is Desire* (1993) that she argues "anticipate, organize, produce, and mobilize the lesbian porn spectator."[51] Taking as her starting point the under-theorization of lesbian spectatorship in porn studies as well as in feminist film studies in large, she examines how the two films teach the lesbian viewer how to watch porn as well as create a place for the lesbian spectator in theory. According to her, the films thematize voyeurism and spectatorship by showing women looking at other women having sex, and by emphasizing a link between looking, pleasure and desire.[52] Similarly, Ragan Rhyne points

---

[49] Interview with Flora Schanda, Berlin, 2008-10-27; interview with Helene Delilah, Stockholm, 2008-11-25.
[50] Manuela Kay, *Dirty Diaries* meeting, 2008-12-16.
[51] Conway, 1997, 93.
[52] Conway, 1997, 104.

out how films from SIR Video thematize the act of buying porn videos.[53] As pointed out in chapter 4, Juffer also stresses the importance of, for instance, Femme Productions in producing "public legitimation of women watching adult videos."[54] This implies that not only do *Dirty Diaries* and Pornfilmfestival Berlin legitimize and create space for queer, feminist and lesbian porn spectatorship, but also that participation in this film culture is a matter of habituation to being a spectator and to enjoying "different varieties of pleasure."[55]

Marije Janssen's "carnal identification" with *One Night Stand* and *Trans Entities* demonstrates, on the one hand, that her engagement in the film is not determined by identification with characters and that her ability to be turned on by the film is not limited to practices she herself has experienced. On the other hand, her account also demonstrates that her identity and previous experiences do shape and determine what kind of sensual experiences are available to her in the viewing situation. Importantly, throughout my interview material it is also evident that not all audio-visual representations of sex are sexually exciting or result in an "involuntary mimicry of the bodies on screen," as Williams defines the notion of body genres.[56] For instance, one research subject tells me that she thinks it looks painful when she watches heterosexual porn.[57] One recurrent example is anal sex. For instance, in accounting more specifically for her embodied experiences of pornography, Jennifer tells me that she likes to take on "all different kinds of roles in identifying with pornography," just as she does in her own sex life and BDSM practice where she defines herself as "switch."[58] She likes watching all kinds of lesbian porn with "all kinds of women" and sexual practices, but anal sex is one exception. She explains that when she watches anal sex, she identifies only with "the one giving anal sex," since she in her own sex life, finds this role less unpleasant than "receiving." Jennifer also talks about how films can both turn her on and disgust her. She takes as one example *Belladonna's Fucking Girls 3* (Belladonna, 2006), a film she brings with her to the interview. The scene she chooses to play features fetish play between two women and Jennifer explains that she finds the women and the fetish objects very attractive. At a specific point she turns the film off – before the scene proceeds with anal penetration with large dildos. Jennifer says that it turns her off to watch some of the stuff they do in the film, like when "they fellate the dildos so deep that they throw up."[59]

---

[53] Rhyne, 2007.
[54] Juffer, 175.
[55] Williams, 2008, 18.
[56] Williams, 1991, 4; See also Paasonen, 2007.
[57] Interview with anonymous research subject, Stockholm, 2008-11-25.
[58] Interview with Jennifer, Stockholm, 2008-11-04.
[59] Interview with Jennifer, Stockholm, 2008-11-11.

These examples of how carnal identification in the film experience is shaped and conditioned not only by the cinesthetic subject's general ability to perceive the film corporeally, but also by different viewing subjects' personal histories and practices, demonstrate that spectatorial processes depend on "whose body" is watching.[60] As Sobchack herself puts it elsewhere, "[t]he essential body is always also a qualified body."[61] While the essential body provides the "ontological functions" and capacity to carnally identify with a film (regardless of this body's particular and specific modality), it is the particular qualified body (with its specific history and modality) that determines what kind of carnal identifications are accessible in the film experience.[62] Thus, the essential body refers to the very ability to corporeally and viscerally experience the film, while the qualified body conditions how this experience literally feels (for instance, if being turned on by fisting is also felt in the same parts of the viewer's body or not). Sobchack's ambiguity in regard to whether differently qualified bodies experience the same "general erotic mattering" of flesh in the same images highlights the necessity to situate these discussions in relation to specific bodies and situations. In the theater in Moviemento in Berlin, during the screening of *Much More Pussy* in October 2010, I, my friend and the man next to her were all conditioned to different experiences, not just because of what literally happened in this situation of reception (both in the theater and on screen), but also because of how we, as three different social subjects, three differently qualified bodies, have access to different embodied experiences. As de Lauretis argues, spectatorial processes are inseparable from the social, racial, cultural, and personal history of each spectator, as well as from its surrounding discourses, practices, and representations.[63]

## Queer, feminist and lesbian porn as fantasy

> I really appreciate porn and for me it does not matter if it is man-woman, man-man, woman-woman. I have enough fantasy. If I feel like enjoying porn, I don't care about the constellations. But a lot of porn is really really bad in different ways and if lesbian porn also has bad qualities then it does not work for me.[64]

Chris is a 51 year-old lesbian who signs up for participation in the research project through the questionnaires at Club LASH and participates anony-

---

[60] Sobchack, 1992, 143-163.
[61] Sobchack, 1992, 144.
[62] Ibid.
[63] De Lauretis, 1995, 75.
[64] Interview with Chris, Stockholm, 2008-11-06.

mously in the project. She has a background in coaching and philosophical studies. I interview her both individually and together with Jennifer at the Department of Cinema Studies in November 2008. Chris talks about how she enjoys watching "hetero porn" and "gay porn." She thinks that she is "good at imagining" how it feels even if it is not lesbian pornography. It has to do with what "appears to be pleasurable" and with how the "horniness in the film is contagious." She finds that she has the ability to "translate" what happens in the film to her own body, and that this translation is possible even if it represents practices that she herself does not have any experience of, for instance when the biological sex of the bodies in the film differ from her own. She says: "It is very difficult for me to imagine myself as a gay male, but it works just as well. It does not seem to be particularly dependent on me being one of them, but this heat, and, what should I say, close-up on sex stuff – that works as pornography for me."[65]

Chris's account resonates with Marije Janssen's in the sense that arousal is not dependent on "being one of them." She highlights two aspects that she thinks condition whether she is turned on or not by porn. There is something in the "pornographic image as such," in close-ups on for instance penetration, "as a symbol for lust," which turns her on. Secondly, she says that if the "horniness" in the film is "zipless" and "straight forward" enough, if "lust takes over," it will "infect" her. She takes as examples *The Postman Always Rings Twice* (Bob Rafelson, 1981), and Erica Jong's novel *Fear of Flying* that she also invokes in her use of Jong's famous concept of the "zipless fuck." However, while she takes these influential narratives as examples, Chris also states that a coherent storyline is not a necessary quality for turning her on. Chris's reflections about what works and does not work for her in pornography and about how pornographic representations are translated to her own body invokes de Lauretis' discussion about film as fantasy.

Similar to her theory of film as a technology of gender, de Lauretis develops the concept of "sexual structuring" in order to theorize the "under construction" character of subjectivity and sexuality as constituted through this "dynamic and interactive process."[66] She stresses that "neither the body nor the subject is prior to the process of sexuation; both come into being in that continuous and life-long process in which the subject is, as it were, permanently under construction."[67] Central to the concept of sexual structuring is the psychoanalytic notion of fantasy as the field where sexuality is constituted. Building on Laplanche's and Pontalis' readings of Freud, de Lauretis defines fantasy as "the dynamic grid through which external reality is adapted/reworked in psychic reality."[68] Subjectivity is constituted through

---

[65] Interview with Chris, Stockholm, 2008-11-06.
[66] De Lauretis, "Habit Changes [1994]," in *Figures of Resistance*, 2007, 205.
[67] De Lauretis, 2007a, 205.
[68] De Lauretis, 2008, 17.

the ongoing process of adapting, translating and reworking "enigmatic messages" both from the unconscious as well as from culture. A such, "[f]antasy is the psychic mechanism that structures subjectivity by reworking or translating social representations into subjective representations and self-representations."[69] Moreover, rearticulated to film spectatorship, the concept of fantasy implies that the spectator does not simply identify with the protagonist or with any specific role or character in the film. Fantasy is not the object of desire but functions as the narrative scenario, mise-en-scène, and structuring scene of desire.

Read from this perspective, Chris's experience of arousal when watching gay male porn is not dependent on identification with the characters, on "being one of them," but on how she translates these representations into subjective representations. The "ziplessness" of the narrative scenario and the mise-en-scène of "close-up on sex stuff" works as fantasy for her. Penetration as "a symbol for lust" is, in this reading, one of the messages that Chris reworks into internal reality through the dynamic grid of fantasy.

However, in opposition to other feminists who apply Pontalis and Laplanche to discussions of film as fantasy, de Lauretis considers the idea that the spectator can choose and move in and out of any of the subject-positions inscribed in the film regardless of gender or sexual difference to be an oversimplification.[70] A public representation is not the same thing as a private fantasy. Ignoring the question of who produces the fantasy, of whose fantasy the film represents, leaves the theory of spectatorship with a universal subject unmarked by differences. In her reading of her own experience of Sheila McLaughlin's *She Must Be Seeing Things* (1987), de Lauretis contends that she does not identify with any of the women or roles since the film works as a fantasy for her, but that the subject of the film's fantasy is constructed as a lesbian subject and therefore the spectator is addressed in a lesbian subject-position. However, "such a position is not accessible to all viewers, not even lesbian-identified, because the film's fantasy may very well *not* be their own [emphasis in original]."[71]

Chris similarly articulates that just because it is lesbian pornography does not mean that it works for her. However, she finds it hard to put her finger on the dividing line between what works as pornography for her and what does not, between being "infected" by and able to "translate" what she sees or not. She says that sometimes there is a limit if she thinks the action between the performers is "strange," if they do something she cannot understand as pleasurable, or if the film evokes "ridicule." She mentions a lesbian porn film with "little combat broads" that she found ridiculous in their "naive political eagerness." Thus, despite being a lesbian film, this film did not

---

[69] De Lauretis, 1999a, 307.
[70] De Lauretis, 1995, 75; 1994, 139-142.
[71] De Lauretis, 1994, 142.

work as fantasy for her. Here Chris's account also reactivates debates over representations in lesbian porn discourse. For instance, and as commented upon in chapter 3, Heather Butler critiques the improbability of the sex scene between two women in *Erotic in Nature* (Tigress Productions, 1985) that she feels is not giving a "fulfilling representation of a sex act."[72] She finds it difficult to "ascertain what exactly the two are actually doing."[73] Straayer contends that lesbian audiences in the 1980s prioritized "reality-checking over fantasy experience."[74] Her contention that "[a]lthough pornography's generic otherworldliness encourages fantasy, its privileged verisimilitude implies realism," resonates with Juffer's discussion about the reconciliation of fantasy with reality in female erotica and raises questions about the relation between fantasy and reality in queer, feminist and lesbian porn film culture.[75]

## Identification vs. desire?

In a critical discussion of theories of female spectatorship, de Lauretis remarks that feminists have operated within a heterosexual framework, where female spectators can be active and desiring only through processes of masculinization, masquerade and transvestism.[76] In lesbian theories of spectatorship, for instance in Jackie Stacey's reading of *All About Eve* (Joseph L. Mankiewicz, 1950) and *Desperately Seeking Susan* (Susan Seidelman, 1985), lesbian desire is confused with identification, according to de Lauretis.[77] Homosexual lesbian desire is reduced to homosocial women-identified female bonding, to a wish to be like the other woman. This wish is devoid of sexual aim since desire is "swept under the rug" of sisterhood, female friendship and the mother-daughter bond.[78] However, while critical of the heterosexual desexualized notion of desire between women in film theory, de Lauretis also recognizes that spectatorial processes of identification and desire may co-exist: "[B]*oth* woman-identification *and* desire (*both* autoerotic and narcissistic drives, *and* female object-choice or object-love) may be simultaneous present [emphasis in original]."[79] Addressing de Lauretis critique, Stacey argues for the necessity to engage with actual audiences in order to further theorize female spectatorship beyond "masculinisation or narcissism."[80] Jennifer's account in chapter 4 highlights precisely the co-

---

[72] Heather Butler, 2004, 177.
[73] Ibid.
[74] Straayer, 214ff.
[75] Straayer, 213; Juffer, 136.
[76] De Lauretis, 1994, 116-123.
[77] Jackie Stacey, "Desperately Seeking Difference," *Screen*, 28: 1 (Winter 1987), 48-61.
[78] De Lauretis, 1994, 117.
[79] De Lauretis, 1994, 120.
[80] Stacey, 1994, 29.

existence of desire and identification. The women in the lesbian films she watched at Club LASH became role models for her at the same time as she found them desirable. In several interview accounts notions of recognition, reflection and identification are similarly tied to articulations of processes of getting a higher sexual self-esteem, becoming more uninhibited and sexually empowered. Here identification and desire are not opposed.

The question about the relation between sexually driven desire and desexualized identification is partly echoed also in Marit Östberg's contrasting between intellectualizing activism and bodily sexual practice and "letting go," in the previous chapter. Over the course of three years of participation in queer, feminist and lesbian porn film culture, she concludes that for her "the bodily" and "the political" are inseparable and that they are tied together not least through her "bonding" with others in the consciousness-raising group for queer porn performers and in her subcultural context in Berlin. With reference to de Lauretis, Sara Ahmed addresses the risk of "[underplaying] the sexual aspects of lesbianism," but highlights the interconnectedness between desire, identification and activism.[81]

> [W]e don't have to take the 'sex' out of lesbianism to argue that lesbian sociality tends toward other women in ways that are more than sexual, or even more than solely about desire. Lesbian bonds can involve orientations that are about shared struggles, common grounds, and mutual aspirations, as bonds that are created through the lived experiences of being 'off line' and 'out of line.' To be orientated sexually toward women as women affects other things that we can do.[82]

Marit Östberg's accounts of her personal development over the years that I interviewed her directs attention to the temporal dimension of spectatorship as an ongoing process of habituation and opening up to new environments and sensations. Thus, if the embodied film experience is shaped by the qualified body's "particular and specific modality," in its turn it also forms part of shaping this body onwards, after the screening.[83] Here, identification, bonding or activism may provide a safe condition for accessing and exploring desire, even if this desire is not immediately present or accessible in the actual viewing situation. In her critique de Lauretis still points out how *All About Eve, Desperately Seeking Susan* and *Black Widow* (Bob Rafelson, 1987) may offer "discursive consent" to engage in lesbian fantasies that are "*made safe* by the films' heterosexual narrative logic [emphasis in original]."[84] This again ties in with Williams' contention that "the mixture of safety with excitement [...] may be just what is needed *for* excitement [em-

---

[81] Ahmed, 2006, 103.
[82] Ibid.
[83] Sobchack, 1992, 144.
[84] De Lauretis, 1994, 121. See also Karen Hollinger, "Theorizing Mainstream Female Spectatorship: The Case of the Popular Lesbian Film," *Cinema Journal*, 37:2 (Winter 1998): 8.

phasis in original]."⁸⁵ In this sense, identification and desire are not isolated or static processes but ongoing and informing each other. In Williams' terms arousal and desire are questions of socialization and habituation, or as de Lauretis puts it, they are "under construction," as they form part of the processes of engendering and sexual structuring. I propose queer, feminist and lesbian pornography, as increasingly more accessible public fantasies, also forms part of this structuring and engendering, of the technologies of sex and gender.⁸⁶

De Lauretis conceptualizes the process of how bodies are shaped by the social as a process of semiosis. Building on C. S. Peirce she describes sexuality as "a particular instance of semiosis," a "process in which objects and bodies are displaced from external to internal or psychic reality […] through a chain of significate effects or interpretants, habits, and habit-changes."⁸⁷ This model then charts the trajectory between the social and the psyche with the body as the mediating link, a permeable surface where subjectivity is constituted through a:

> chain of interpretants, an ongoing series of semiotic mediations linking objects, signs, and events of the world to their 'significate effects' or, we might say, their meaning effects in the subject – a subject that can thus be said to be 'the place in which, the body in whom, the significate effect of the sign takes hold and is real-ized.'⁸⁸

Following this argument, identification with role models in queer, feminist and lesbian pornography may eventually, through this chain of interpretants, produce a significate effect of desire. Importantly, however, according to de Lauretis, this process is not intellectually controlled or structured only by willpower.⁸⁹ If Williams suggests that viewers "play at sex" and "discipline themselves to enjoy different varieties of visual and visceral pleasure," de Lauretis stresses how the ongoing process of sexual structuring, "overdetermined by both internal and external forces and constraints," is structured by different forms of fantasy: "conscious and unconscious; subjective, parental, and social; private and public."⁹⁰ As such, desire and fantasy are not coherent and do not always match politics or identities.⁹¹

---

⁸⁵ Williams, 1999, 264.

⁸⁶ See also de Lauretis, 1995, 68.

⁸⁷ De Lauretis, 2007a, 204.

⁸⁸ De Lauretis, 1999b, 265. De Lauretis here refers to and quotes her own discussion in *Alice Doesn't: Feminism, Semiotics, Cinema* (Bloomington & Indianapolis: Indiana University Press, 1984), 182-3.

⁸⁹ De Lauretis, "The Intractability of Desire [1999]," in *Figures of Resistance*, ed. White, 2007a, 219-222.

⁹⁰ De Lauretis, 2007a, 204.

⁹¹ See also White, 2007, 19f.

## Discipline and (politically incorrect) play

At our second *Dirty Diaries* meeting in September 2008, one of the filmmakers talks about how difficult she finds it to "bring feminism into your horniness."[92]

> I can feel that... my horniness... it is as if it has a determined way, like I already know before where it is going to go which is so damn boring... When I see images... I'm usually not turned on by the guys but by the... girls and like raw-stereotypes which... I know, just: but this does not feel okay, but... what should one do with that like sexuality or like that... feeling... that also like evokes some sort of shame and guilt. Is one to live that out in order to like then move on or should one just deny it or... I miss a debate about this in the feminist world. It cannot be just me... who is like radical feminist and like... is turned on by... silicone chicks.[93]

Throughout the production phase of *Dirty Diaries* the possibility for reshaping desires and fantasies is recurrently discussed, similarly to how Mia Engberg, in the DVD booklet, asks: "How do we liberate our own sexual fantasies from the commercial images that we see every day, burying their way into our subconscious?"[94] On the other hand, at this meeting she also critically comments on how women "censor" their own and other women's fantasies. This echoes how, in Juffer's terms, feminism also comes with "its own set of regulatory codes and hierarchies."[95] At this meeting in September 2008 Mia Engberg says:

> We do not have to tell each other what is wrong and what is right and what is nice and what is dirty. Maybe we can leave that phase now – in the feminist discussion – and that's also one point with this project. Maybe not all of us should make politically correct films... Maybe we should make like silicone breast films where you fuck – I don't know, whatever... What if I would make a film where you hear my voice say that I fantasize about being raped by a sleazy man and then I express that somehow in the images – then I've conquered that fear and have appropriated the image.[96]

In a similar vein, in the documentary *Too Much Pussy* from *The Queer X Show*, there is one scene from the mini-bus where the women discuss their fantasies and desires. The queer porn and performance artist and writer Wendy Delorme refers to an autobiographical book by the queer writer Michelle Tea where she describes how she as a young feminist goes to consciousness-raising groups in order to get rid of her rape fantasies. She tries masturbating while thinking about being on a boat on the ocean and feeling

---

[92] *Dirty Diaries* meeting, 2008-09-18.
[93] Ibid.
[94] Mia Engberg, *Dirty Diaries* DVD booklet, 2009.
[95] Juffer, 72.
[96] *Dirty Diaries* meeting, 2008-09-18.

the wind in her hair. However, as she gets close to orgasm her fantasy gets twisted. She lands on an island and a group of men jump from a tree and rape her as she comes. Delorme says that similarly, for her, whenever she tries not to fantasize about "something hardcore or degrading" it always "jumps" at her at the last minute. "At some point I had to make the conscious decision not to feel guilty about my fantasies. This is our duty also as feminists – not to guilt-trip ourselves and feel wrong about our desires," she argues. In the same scene porn actress and activist Judy Minx talks about BDSM as a way of "using things that hurt you in real life and power dynamics that hurt you in real life" in an empowering way. Highlighting the difference between fantasy and reality, Minx also says: "Just because a lot of women are into rape role-play or fantasies doesn't mean that actual rape is ever okay."

These examples reactivate Jane Gaines' critique of the feminist conceptualization of film as either oppression or pleasure and as pioneering "a new aesthetic based on refusal," where "the creation of a new language of desire was made contingent on the destruction of male pleasure."[97] Gaines argues that "politically correct practices and proper fantasies do not necessarily fuel [women's] passion."[98] These examples also evoke discussions about masochist fantasies as providing necessary preconditions enabling women to let themselves go and enjoy sexual representations.[99] Minx's account also echoes Elizabeth Freeman's discussion about Isaac Julien's *The Attendant* (1993), where she argues that "S/M relentlessly physicalizes the encounter with history and thereby contributes to a reparative criticism that takes up the materials of a traumatic past and remixes them in the interests of new possibilities for being and knowing."[100]

In de Lauretis' discussion, desire and fantasy, as forming part of the process of sexual structuring, cannot be reeducated, disciplined or regulated by willpower in accordance with the individual subject's politics. On the other hand, since the subject of fantasy is located in the "slide of meaning between the subjective and the social," the spectator's "own sociopolitical location and psycho-sexual configuration have much to do with whether or not the film can work for her as a scenario of desire."[101] De Lauretis argues that "[t]he work of unconscious fantasy, important as it is for our understanding of psychic contradiction and divisions in the social subject, cannot simply replace the complex intersections of conscious and unconscious processes in

---

[97] Gaines, "Can We Enjoy Alternative Pleasure?", 1990, 81.
[98] Gaines, 1990, 87.
[99] See Elizabeth Cowie, "Pornography and Fantasy: Psychoanalytic Perspectives," in *Sex Exposed*, ed. Segal and McIntosh, 1993, 132-152; and Williams, "Power, Pleasure, and Perversion: Sadomasochistic Film Pornography," in *Hard Core*, 1999, 184-228.
[100] Freeman, 144.
[101] De Lauretis, 1995, 64.

the subject of fantasy."[102] In accordance with this, many research subjects, rather than "playing at" all forms of screening sex, in Williams' words, articulate that not all pornographic texts work as a scenario of desire and that this is a question of politics and ethics. Jennifer explains that while it is possible for her to get turned on by mainstream porn, she prefers "real" lesbian porn because it feels better to know that it is a "fair" production without "antifeminist, homophobic or heteronormative messages."[103] Similarly, Chris says that for her there are some evident "no-nos," features that are "disgusting" and "turn-offs" in pornography. For instance she gets "furious" if she watches heterosexual porn where the "women appear to not enjoy it." "Angry and horny do not go together," she explains.[104]

Elaborating the question of whose fantasy the film represents, de Lauretis distinguishes between unconscious and conscious engagement in the fantasy scenario.[105] She forwards the process of secondarization, of the reworking of the unconscious fantasy into a form more acceptable to consciousness. Referring to a discussion by Judith Butler about the anti-porn feminist Andrea Dworkin, de Lauretis also differs between subjectivity and subjecthood.[106] While Butler claims that fantasy is a scene of the subject's fragmentation, de Lauretis points out that the threat of fragmentation through pornography's engaging of the unconscious fantasy activates secondarization. The subject of fantasy is then both unconscious and conscious, especially when confronted with a pornographic text, according to de Lauretis.[107] Opposing Dworkin's critique of pornography as "injurious and discriminatory action," Butler states that: "the effect of fantasy is not to force women to identify with a subordinate or debased position, but to provide the opportunity to identify with the entire scene of debasement, agents and recipients alike."[108] De Lauretis, on the other hand, stresses that Dworkin is neither the producer nor the subject of the pornographic fantasy, and that "the pornographic text is not her fantasy but a fantasy produced by others and which, as she sees it, seeks to interpellate her with a certain identification, to assign to her a place that she will not or cannot occupy."[109] Furthermore, she contends that Dworkin's feminist sociopolitical subjecthood, conscious, and based on a political and collective identity, resists and disapproves of the pornographic scenario, while at the same time her subjective and unconscious identification is fixed with the victim's position. This discussion raises questions

---

[102] De Lauretis, 1995, 82.
[103] Interview with Jennifer, Stockholm, 2008-11-04.
[104] Interview with Chris, Stockholm, 2008-11-06.
[105] De Lauretis, 1994, 143-148; 1995, 78-83.
[106] Judith Butler, "The Force of Fantasy: Feminism, Mapplethorpe, and Discursive Excess [1990]," in *Feminism and Pornography*, ed. Cornell, 2000, 487-508.
[107] De Lauretis, 1995, 79-80.
[108] Judith Butler, 2000, 497. Quoted by de Lauretis, 1995, 80.
[109] De Lauretis, 1995, 82.

about how queer, feminist and lesbian pornography as a collective political fantasy engages participants in this interpretive community and mobilizes both subjectivity and subjecthood.

At our *Dirty Diaries* meeting in December 2008, Marit Östberg's film *Uniform* became the subject of an animated discussion. In the film, two train ticket controllers catch two fare dodgers in the Stockholm subway. After a short chase scene the two controllers are overpowered by the other two women and dominated in two sex scenes set in a deserted train track area. One of the controller women is tied with her hands behind her back and placed over a low street lamp. The other woman penetrates her anally wearing red skin gloves, occasionally forcing her fingers into the other woman's mouth and pulling her hair. The dominated woman moans and after a while starts crying. In this version of the film, Mia Engberg has added bloopers at the end, short clips with behind-the-scenes material where one person in the cast checks with the crying woman if she is okay and she replies that she is. There is a long discussion about whether the bloopers function as a necessary reassurance for the viewers or if it takes the power out of the hard scene as if to excuse it. Manuela Kay, who participated in this meeting, finds that lesbian and feminist porn should not have to do this anymore, that "we're beyond that."[110] Mia Engberg is ambivalent about the question as she considers the film in relation to how "male porn is full of abuse," how almost all of her girlfriends "have been raped or risked being raped" and how, for her, it is "impossible to just take away all the history of like white male oppression [...] and just say that we can do whatever we want." She is concerned about how the film can be read as if someone is being raped, "and that's kind of the feminine destiny that we want to leave – don't we?" she laughs.[111] One of the filmmakers asks why we cannot identify with the aggressor instead of the victim. Someone else responds that her goal or idea of change is not to be in the man's position.

In these different reactions to the film it was evident that not everyone could identify with the aggressor's position, nor embrace the "entire scene of debasement, agents and recipients alike."[112] In my view, the discussion concerned whether the bloopers would provide "discursive consent," which could enable and make such a reading more acceptable and accessible instead of being overridden by concerns about whether or not the woman participated out of free will and about whether or not to reproduce rape scenarios on film. This discussion articulates precisely how both the subjective and

---

[110] Manuela Kay, *Dirty Diaries* meeting, 2008-12-16.
[111] Mia Engberg, *Dirty Diaries* meeting, 2008-12-16. After a screening of *Uniform* – without bloopers – at the Pornfilmfestival Berlin in October 2008, a couple of months prior to this meeting, one woman in the audience celebrated the fact that since she knew the film was a queer feminist production it allowed her to affirm and enjoy a rape fantasy.
[112] Judith Butler, 2000, 497.

the social, the conscious and the unconscious shape the reception and restrict the significations of the film and the individual viewers' "particular path through its multiple significations," as de Lauretis puts it.[113]

## "Every time we fuck we win"

My own path through the multiple significations of *Much More Pussy* at the screening in Berlin in October 2010 was shaped both by the theater experience and by the film experience, as well as by conscious and unconscious engagements with the scenario. Despite, or fueled by the fact that my friend was sexually harassed by the man next to her, the film worked as fantasy for me as I felt overwhelmed by its force and by the reworkings and negotiations around sexuality that was enacted in its scenarios. In their conversations as well as in their sexual role-plays these women negotiate and work through, in Ahmed's words, "the habitual actions and norms" that shape and press on their lives, bodies and desires. During their tour they also literally face the violence of these norms. In Paris one of their friends, a trans guy, is subject to hate crime after returning home from their show. In Malmö they participate in a ceremony for the murdered victims of a shooting attack against a gay youth center in Tel Aviv. The force that blew me away when I saw *Much More Pussy* was not the force of an instant or ultimate transformation of gender and sexual hierarchies or a construction of an alternative world beyond these hierarchies, but the force of a continuous resistance in the face of these hierarchies and violent norms. Here the figure of safe space is mobilized not so much as a matter of a safe world or a bubble inside the world, but of the safety of a public sphere where the unsafety of being queer, female or lesbian is continuously acknowledged, worked through and negotiated, where naturalized and habitual actions and directions are challenged and reformulated and where new actions and orientations shape new worlds and bodies. This implies that in the Queer Nation quote in the soundtrack to *Too Much Pussy* as well as *Much More Pussy*, the constant repetition of the phrase: "every time we fuck we win," temporality is crucial. In Ahmed's terms, it is through the loop of repetition that bodies take certain shape and are oriented in certain directions.[114]

According to Ahmed, disorientation occurs when "bodies inhabit spaces that do not extend their shape, or use objects that do not extend their reach," when bodies fail to line up, when they are out of place.[115] In such moments the world becomes "slantwise." Importantly, moments of disorientation may be unsettling as well as exciting and joyful. Rather than aiming at overcom-

---

[113] De Lauretis, 1995, 82.
[114] Ahmed, 2004, 145; Ahmed, 2006, 91, 5.
[115] Ahmed, 2006, 160.

ing or reorienting such moments, one might stay with them and "achieve a different orientation toward them."[116] Marit Östberg's account of her experience of personal crisis at the London Lesbian and Gay Film Festival in 2010 can be read with Ahmed as a feeling of disorientation and of losing her place or ground. Creating a consciousness-raising group for other queer porn performers in Berlin, where such experiences of crisis are shared and analyzed, could be understood as an achievement of a different orientation toward this disorienting moment. Marit Östberg talks about how she has gained a new sense of strength by having had to work her way through this crisis. Queer moments, according to Ahmed, are vital moments where new objects may come into reach and where it may be possible to extend into space in a new shape: "We might even find joy and excitement in the horror."[117] We might, as Ahmed puts it, "come into contact with other bodies to support the action of following paths that have not been cleared."[118] Participation in queer, feminist and lesbian porn film culture involves "coming into contact with other bodies" both on the screen and at physical sites. On the new paths that bodies follow together in this interpretive community, the collective political fantasy of safe space for sexual empowerment is supported and explored. *Much More Pussy* worked as a fantasy for me because it addressed, acknowledged and worked through queer, feminist and lesbian feelings of unsafety and disorientation, as well as of joy and excitement, that I also experience in my life and that were reactivated by the action next to me in the Moviemento theater. What touched me most in this film was the power of the openness and trust between these women, in the face of threat and risk. The next chapter discusses how queer, feminist and lesbian pornography as a collective political fantasy invokes an ethics of shared embodiment.

---

[116] Ibid., 4.
[117] Ibid.
[118] Ahmed, 2006, 170.

# 6. The ethics of shared embodiment

*Phone Fuck* explores the idea of longing and absence – and the tension between touching and not touching – as a trigger for desire. The film is a post breakup phone sex scene between two women. It is an erotic encounter played out in fantasy while the women masturbate in their separate apartments. The phone call is cross-edited with fragments of intimate contact between them – images that can be seen as memories or fantasies alike.

I wanted to work with the theme of a sexual experience played out on different levels – not necessarily physically between the two women in my film, but as a meeting created verbally between them, in a shared fantasy. A meeting produced in imagination, but also an autoerotic meeting, as well as a meeting between the film and the viewer. Where the viewer is invited to interact with the fantasy scenario and perhaps inspired to reach for and feel herself.

Even though the women cannot physically reach eachother over the phone they still manage to touch eachother. Likewise, I think an erotic encounter with a pornographic – or any other kind of film – is characterized precisely by the tension between touching and not touching, between touching and still not reaching. Watching film is a sensual experience. It is about how the film touches the viewer. *Phone Fuck* wants to enhance this encounter.[1]

Throughout this research project my production of the short *Phone Fuck* and participation in *Dirty Diaries* has served as the basis for investigating this interpretive community. Following the process of *Dirty Diaries*, at meetings with the other filmmakers in the project, through the practices and concerns related to my own filmmaking, as well as through the collection's wide circulation in different contexts, has made up a central part of the fieldwork. Producing *Phone Fuck* has also been one way of investigating questions about the relationships at play in this film culture creatively and in practice. Quite evidently, my presentation of *Phone Fuck* from the *Dirty Diaries* DVD booklet is influenced by Vivian Sobchack's discussions about how the lived body carnally identifies with and makes sense of the film and by her description of how she in the film experience "reflexively [turns] toward [her] own carnal, sensual, and sensible being to touch [herself] touching, smell [herself] smelling, taste [herself] tasting, and, in sum, sense [her] own sensuality."[2] In *Phone Fuck* the technologically mediated sexual encounter between the two women reflects the technologically mediated sexual en-

---

[1] Ingrid Ryberg, "Phone Fuck," *Dirty Diaries* DVD booklet, 2009.
[2] Sobchack, 2004, 77.

counter between film and spectator. It thematizes how the lived body in the film experience makes sense of the flesh on the screen, both figurally and literally, similarly to how the masturbating women turn back to their own respective bodies to sense physically what they together imagine figurally, and how this may be an enhanced sensual experience.[3] The short, as the presentation also reflects, was also influenced by Teresa de Lauretis' discussion about film as fantasy. The film thematizes the central role of fantasy in sexuality, as the setting for desire, rather than its object.[4] In their conversation over the phone the women describe in detail what they imagine doing together. The actions and movements that they describe partly correspond, but also contradict the fantasy images, as well as their respective movements in their separate bedrooms. The film explores the incoherence of fantasy, but also the sharing of it, between the two women in the film, as well as in public. As *my* fantasy *Phone Fuck* has functioned as a working through of some of the questions raised through my own participation in this film culture that this dissertation as a whole grapples with.

Through Sobchack's and de Lauretis' theories of embodied spectatorship and notions of carnal identification and fantasy, chapter 5 discussed spectatorial processes in queer, feminist and lesbian pornography as potentially shaping experiences of sexual empowerment. This chapter further addresses queer, feminist and lesbian pornography as, in de Lauretis' words, a "public form of fantasy,"[5] and in Elizabeth Freeman's a "collective political fantasy."[6] Drawing on Sobchack it discusses the ethical sensibilities and responsibilities that this publicly and collectively shared fantasy calls forth.[7] Sobchack argues that lived embodiment is shaped and conditioned by different forms of technology that form part of our everyday lives and alter "both our sense of the world and our sense of ourselves."[8] This chapter focuses on embodiment in this interpretive community as conditioned and shaped by media technology, by the practice of recording and screening queer, feminist and lesbian pornography. In *Phone Fuck* and other shorts in *Dirty Diaries* technology forms part of sexuality. As Feona Attwood points out, sex in our present culture is intertwined with new communication and media technologies allowing ordinary people to make and circulate their own sexual images.[9] In her words, "sex and technology are stitched together" and enable

---

[3] Ibid.
[4] De Lauretis, 1994, 84; 1995, 67.
[5] De Lauretis, 1995, 68. De Lauretis suggests that gay and lesbian subcultural practices work as public forms of fantasy. See also Terralee Bensinger, 1992, 72. Bensinger also proposes an understanding of lesbian pornographic activity as a matter of fantasy and of "making community."
[6] Freeman, 65.
[7] Sobchack, 2004, 3, 8-9.
[8] Sobchack, 2004, 8.
[9] Attwood, 2009, xiv.

new forms of sexual encounters in the sense that, for example, "phone sex, email affairs and cybersex are now part of the late modern repertoire of sexual *practices* and are becoming part of people's everyday lives [emphasis in original]."[10]

As a comment on this condition, the *Dirty Diaries* short *Body Contact* stages an amateur porn shooting where two women pick up a man over a dating site on the Internet, after he, at their request, displays and has his penis approved. *Flasher Girl On Tour*, where the director Joanna Rytel is filmed as she exposes herself in public, also poses questions about new media technology in the sexualized public sphere. At our third *Dirty Diaries* meeting in December 2008, where a rough cut of the film is showed and discussed, Rytel tells us that the reactions from people who became witnesses to her flashing were rather modest: "People maybe thought that we were only fooling around with a mobile phone – or perhaps Paris is such a big city that people do not really care," she says.[11] In Mia Engberg's short *Come Together* the mobile phone camera is passed around between a group of women who film their own faces as they masturbate and have orgasms. The mobile phone technology is intimately shared between these women, but the film was also publicly shared on Stockholm International Film Festival's website and later also circulated as part of *Dirty Diaries* in a wide range of contexts.

Thus, as Attwood points out, the stitched-togetherness of sex and technology includes both the making of images of one's own sexuality but also the sharing of these images in public. *Dirty Diaries* also actualizes Linda Williams' discussion about how "the very act of screening [sex] has become an intimate part of our sexuality."[12] Williams' point is that through publicly screening sex, in movie theaters in the 1970s, on video in the 1980s and since the 1990s over Internet and on smaller portable screens of all kinds, our bodies have become habituated to representations of sex, but also to the very act of screening to the degree that screening itself now forms part of our sexuality. My statement in the presentation of *Phone Fuck* that "watching film is a sensual experience," echoes Sobchack' discussion about the cinesthetic subject, but also Williams' contention that "[t]]he very act of screening [sex] is desirable, sensual, and erotic in its own right."[13]

This chapter discusses the ethical implications of the particular embodiment shaped through the stitched-togetherness of sex and technology in queer, feminist and lesbian pornography. Building on Laura U. Marks' discussions about video haptics and erotics and about indexicality, I argue that

---

[10] Attwood, 2009, xiv.
[11] Joanna Rytel, *Dirty Diaries* meeting, 2008-12-16.
[12] Williams, 2008, 326.
[13] Williams, 2008, 326.

this interpretive community invests in a shared embodiment.[14] I emphasize the locatedness of this shared embodiment in the specific shared contexts of production, distribution and consumption that make up this film culture. Most crucially, I claim that the shared knowledge, concerns and embodiment that constitute this interpretive community also evokes an "ethics of shared embodiment," to borrow from Marks.[15] As a "site of struggle," in Lynne Pearce's words, queer, feminist and lesbian pornography calls forth an ethics capable of accommodating disagreements and heterogeneity.[16] Drawing on Ann Cvetkovich, Sara Ahmed and José Esteban Muñoz, the chapter argues that queer, feminist and lesbian pornography is not so much about leaving difficulties behind or reaching a fixed goal (safe space), as it is about reaching out for and casting pictures of this goal.[17] As such, the "tension between touching and not touching, between touching and still not reaching," that *Phone Fuck* aims at thematizing also characterizes the ethics evoked in queer, feminist and lesbian pornography.[18]

## Inviting shared embodiment

> The body is dripping. All desires and dreams about an undefined body are making it soft and flowing and hard as stone. Your legs are my arms and someone else's dildo. All words for body parts are misspelled, all words rhyme.
>
> In *Fruitcake* the body is melting into a soup, mixing into fruit salad. The anus is the centre of the dissolution process, this is where we will all end up, sooner or later, sucked in towards the center. Saliva, lube and desire are spilling over, making the journey easy and inevitable.
>
> The anus is a hole, more hungry than the mouth and thirstier than the throat. But the anus, unlike the stomach, is never satisfied. It is there and it is waiting for us. The whole world is the other way around.
>
> We know that the anus is making you wet, moist in the mouth you put your desire around the opening. You're getting slippery, sliding around.
>
> The history of the sex, that is everybody's sex, that is the ultimate pleasure is pressing around your fingers. You are holding it in your hands. All bodies are one and the ultimate pleasure of them is spelled A-N-U-S.
>
> How do you spell dissolution? We spell it A-N-U-S.
> How do you spell revolution? We spell it A-N-U-S.
> How do you spell utopia? We spell it A-N-U-S.[19]

---

[14] Laura U. Marks, "Video Haptics and Erotics," in *Touch: Sensuous Theory and Multisensory Media* (Minneapolis & London: University of Minnesota Press, 2002), 1-20.
[15] Marks, 2002, 8.
[16] Pearce, 1997, 212.
[17] José Esteban Muñoz, *Cruising Utopia: The Then and There of Queer Futurity* (New York: New York University Press, 2009); Cvetkovich, 2003; Ahmed, 2004, 2006.
[18] Ingrid Ryberg, "Phone Fuck," 2009. See also Ahmed, 2006, 106.
[19] Ester Martin Bergsmark & Sara Kaaman, "Fruitcake," *Dirty Diaries* DVD booklet, 2009.

In Ester Martin Bergsmark's and Sara Kaaman's *Dirty Diaries* short *Fruitcake* bodies, fruits, sex toys and random and mundane details from different domestic settings, such as plants and electrical cords, blend together in a discontinuous and disorienting collage where boundaries between bodies and technology and female and male genitals are blurred. The film and its voice-over, as well as Bergsmark's and Kaaman's presentation of it in the *Dirty Diaries* DVD booklet, propose the anus as "everybody's sex," as a sex organ undoing hierarchically defined differences and producing another, more collectively shared embodiment, where "all bodies are one." In its unfocused close-ups the short also explores the aesthetic potential of the mobile phone camera technology as such, as also enabling conditions for such shared embodiment.

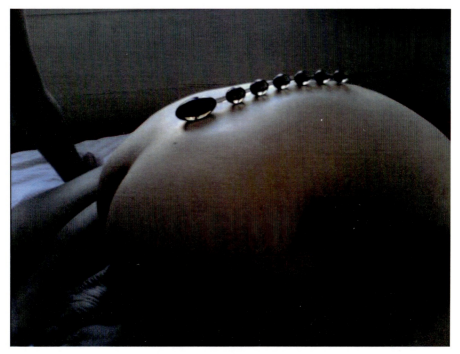

*Fruitcake (Ester Martin Bergsmark & Sara Kaaman, 2009). Courtesy of the filmmakers.*

This exploration of the mobile phone camera as providing conditions for dissolved boundaries between bodies and for shared embodiment also takes place in a number of other films in the *Dirty Diaries* collection. *Night Time* (Nelli Roselli) features a heterosexual "goth" couple having sex in a dark bedroom. The film thematizes the stitched-togetherness of sex and technology in its inclusion of a vibrator, but also through the increasingly unstable, random and shaky camera movements. The woman is filming the action herself, resulting not only in a visual representation of her and her sex partner's bodies, but also in an embodiment of the movements of their sexual encounter and her pleasure. *Night Time,* as well as Tora Mårtens' *Red Like Cherry,* invokes Carolee Schneemann's experimental portrayal of her and her partner's sex life in *Fuses* (1965). *Red Like Cherry* with its dissolves of images of skin, water, sand and light proposes an embodiment not primarily guided by visibility, as Mårtens' presentation of the film in the DVD booklet also brings up. Mårtens writes that: "*Red Like Cherry* elaborates on detail, not for the sake of detail, but as a tension-builder and carrier of desire and want. Sometimes what you don't see is better for getting-off than what you see."[20]

The film and Mårtens' presentation of it echoes Laura U. Marks' discussion about the erotic quality of "haptic images" that "[r]ather than making the object fully available to view [...] [put] the object into question, calling on the viewer to engage in its imaginative construction."[21] Applying Aloïs Riegl's notions of haptic and optical, Marks discusses the tactile qualities and the giving up of visual mastery enabled by the diminished capacity of video images. When the viewer's look is denied depth vision and is pushed back to the surface of the image, an embodied perception is enabled where "the viewer [responds] to the video as to another body and to the screen as another skin."[22] In "[pulling] the viewer [...] too close to see properly,"[23] haptic images involve an erotics of "giving up" of "visual control" and "separateness from the image."[24] In Marks' terms, these *Dirty Diaries* shorts, where the camera often come too close for the eye to see properly what is represented, all invite a "haptic look" and "encourage a bodily relationship between the viewer and the image."[25] Marks further argues that the oscillation between haptic and optical images creates an erotic relationship. Such an oscillation is explored in *Fruitcake* where blurred images are cross-edited with visually more readable images of bodies, as well as in Jennifer Rainsford's *For the Liberation of Men*. The short features an old woman's fantasies of three young men in different colored wigs and lace tights. In the DVD booklet Rainsford writes:

> I told the oldest woman I know to put on the silverdress. I filmed and interviewed her about her sexual fantasies. Together we sank into her demented landscape where the border between old memories, real events and fantasies are blurred. I came back with the three wigmen.
> One of them was a kind of elevator-prostitute, he never left the elevator, people came for rides in the elevator and sometimes used him to get rid of

---

[20] Tora Mårtens, "Red Like Cherry," Dirty Diaries DVD booklet, 2009.
[21] Marks, 2002, 16.
[22] Ibid., 4.
[23] Ibid., 16.
[24] Ibid., 13.
[25] Ibid., 3.

some frustration. His dick was constantly hard. He had red hair. She visited him in the elevator once or twice, but made contact only by talking to him.
- He is still hard, she repeats in her clear voice.

The second man wears blue tights, a short fur and has yellow hair. He is the most violent masturbator, but also the least destructive. It is very beautiful to see him, like watching someone very skilled get to work.

The last of the three is a blonde, nervous and quite fragile soul who never wants to touch ground. She enjoys visiting him the most, because of his spastic movement and fiery breath.[26]

*For the Liberation of Men (Jennifer Rainsford, 2009). Courtesy of the filmmaker.*

*For the Liberation of Men* visually explores texture, surface and tactility as the camera slowly and closely moves over the fabric of the woman's silver colored dress and wrinkled skin, as well as over the men's legs and crotches in lace tights. The film oscillates between haptic and optical images as the close caressing camera movement over the surface of the silverdress and the skin is cross-edited with images of the three masturbating men in medium shots.[27] Rainsford's presentation of the film also brings up the sharing of fantasy and embodiment between the filmmaker and the woman in the film

---

[26] Jennifer Rainsford, "For the Liberation of Men," *Dirty Diaries* DVD booklet, 2009.
[27] Marks, 2002, 6.

and as such raises questions about intimacy and trust. Marks argues that the interactive and intersubjective relationship enabled by haptic images ethically grounds "being susceptible to contact with"[28] as well as "respect for otherness."[29]

*Dirty Diaries*, as well as other examples of queer, feminist and lesbian pornography, such as Emilie Jouvet's *One Night Stand*, resonates with Marks' discussions about video haptics and erotics not least because of the low capacity of cheap and accessible technology.[30] In a discussion about a low-resolution digital pornographic photograph, Susanna Paasonen relates Marks' notion of haptic images to "a specific kind of fluidity and liveness"[31] and the elusive and accidental quality of digital images.[32] She refers to Luciana Parisi and Tiziana Terranova's discussion about digital culture as presenting "an intensification of the material qualities of the image."[33] Williams also discusses interactivity enabled by new media technology and what kind of embodied relationship to the user this entails.[34] According to Williams, small size screens alter the viewer's embodied relation to the film in the sense that "[i]nstead of being engulfed by the immaterial moving images of the film screen, my body can surround the material object that carries the image."[35] She argues that small screens invite an interactive relation with the viewing body: "Where the big screen configures me as a spectator or viewer, the small screen configures me as a user-participant invited to do more than just watch a moving image across the gulf between me and the screen."[36] She notes that "much of the pornography out there today has a built-in expectation that users will be 'in touch' with themselves and often masturbating before their computer or television monitors or new touch screens."[37]

However, the case of *Dirty Diaries*, the examples of the web comments about *Come Together* and the chat log from the discussion about *Dirty Diaries* at Malmö högskola in September 2009, demonstrate that to be a user-

---

[28] Ibid., 19.
[29] Ibid., 20.
[30] When I interviewed Emilie Jouvet in Berlin in 2008, she told me that she made *One Night Stand* with "a children's camera." See Marks, 10. Marks comments on how for instance Sadie Benning has used the toy camera format Pixelvision.
[31] Paasonen, 2010, 68.
[32] Paasonen, 2010, 62. See also Marks, 15. Addressing the question whether pornography can be haptic, Marks contends that instead of hypervisibility, "haptic cinema depends on limited visibility and the viewer's lack of mastery over the image."
[33] Luciana Parisi and Tiziana Terranova, "A Matter of Affect: Digital Images and the Cybernetic Re-Writing of Vision," *Parallax*, 7: 4 (2001), 124. Quoted by Paasonen, 2010, 68.
[34] Williams, 2008, 299-326; Williams, 1999, 300-315. See also Chuck Kleinhans, "The Change from Film to Video Pornography: Implications for Analysis," in *Pornography*, ed. Lehman, 2006, 154-167.
[35] Williams, 2008, 305.
[36] Ibid., 312.
[37] Ibid., 314.

participant in the interactive online world of the Internet does not necessarily imply an ethical and respectful relationship between images and bodies on screen and the bodies off screen. In her discussion about embodied engagements with photographic, cinematic and electronic image technologies, rather than celebrating new forms of interactivity enabled by technology, Sobchack contrarily argues that the electronic entails a loss of material and moral grounding:

> Digital electronic technology atomizes and abstractly schematizes the analogic quality of the photographic and cinematic into discrete pixels and bits of information that are then transmitted serially, each bit discontinuous, discontiguous, and absolute – each bit 'being-in-itself' even as it is part of a system. Television, videocassettes and digital discs, VCR and DVD recorders/players, electronic games, personal computers with Internet access, and pocket electronics of all kinds form an encompassing perceptual and representational system whose various forms 'interface' to constitute an alternative and absolute electronic world of immaterialized – if materially consequential – experience. And this electronic world incorporates the spectator/user uniquely in a spatially decentered, weakly temporalized and quasi-disembodied (or diffusely embodied) state.[38]

Sobchack argues that the electronic provides a "metaworld" where users are liberated from "the pull of [...] moral and physical gravity – and [...] the weight of its real-world consequences."[39] The sexist, racist and homophobic chat from Malmö högskola (see chapter 4), especially in relation to the much more respectful conduct in the auditorium, raises questions precisely about such liberation from moral gravity. In her discussion about the phenomenological consequences of new media technologies Marks, however, is more optimistic. She discusses the specific embodiment of analog and digital video and how "our own perceiving bodies respond to each medium."[40] Marks contends that "the body of analog video is constituted from flows of electrons that maintain an indexical link with the physical world."[41] Therefore, "[a]s analog video perceives and embodies the world, so we in turn share video's embodied perception."[42] In digital images, on the other hand, this indexical link is lost when reality is translated into information units (pixels, 1s and 0s), which is precisely Sobchack's concern. Nevertheless, Marks argues, "[d]igital phenomena also have properties that mimic our bodies' exceptional abilities," such as synesthesia, "our own bodily way of translating information among modalities, [...] a kind of embodied think-

---

[38] Sobchack, 153.
[39] Sobchack, 154.
[40] Marks, "Video's Body, Analog and Digital," in *Touch*, 2002, 147.
[41] Marks, 2002, 148.
[42] Ibid.

ing."[43] She argues that, despite the loss of the indexical link, "[d]igital and other electronic images are constituted by processes no less material than photography, film, and analog video are."[44] Building her argument on quantum physics and electronic engineering she claims that "digital images are existentially connected to the processes that they image."[45] Paasonen points out that in Parisi and Terranova's discussion, digital images possess an affective intensity owing to their "autonomy from the regimes of representation and identification" and "notions of the real."[46] Marks contrarily highlights that "[p]aradoxically, the age of so-called virtual media has hastened the desire for indexicality."[47] She points out that digital video "allows artists to restore authenticity and embodiment to their performances."[48] The desire for indexicality also characterizes queer, feminist and lesbian pornography, and this indexicality contributes to its investment in and shaping of shared embodiment.

## Shared spaces

One of the films that Marije Janssen talks about when I interview her during the Pornfilmfestival Berlin in 2008 is Morty Diamond's *Trans Entities: The Nasty Love of Papi and Wil* (2006).[49] She finds that the couple in the film had a "raw energy" and "powerfulness" that made her discover new desires. *Trans Entities* is also an example of the "desire for indexicality" that characterizes queer, feminist and lesbian pornography. The film features a female-to-male couple and interweaves interviews with sexual role-play. The presentation of the film reads:

> *Trans Entities: The Nasty Love of Papi and Wil* is a unique, sexy, thought provoking and above all touching portrait of a real transgender couple, Papi and Wil, who open themselves up to the camera like you have never seen before. They are a perverted, loving, polyamourous couple who identify as Trans Entities, a word they have coined to describe their gender identity.
> This film is 4 parts BDSM, polyamory, sexuality and gender documentary and 3 parts hot sex scenes. They discuss their gender expression, the perils and joy of poly love, and you see them negotiating a role-play scene. The film gives the viewer an engagingly raw look into Papi and Wil's uninhibited, joyous and exploratory life.[50]

---

[43] Marks, 2002, 149.
[44] Marks, "How Electrons Remember," in *Touch*, 2002, 163.
[45] Marks, 2002, 161.
[46] Paasonen, 2010, 69. Paasonen references Parisi and Terranova, 2001, 125.
[47] Marks, 2002, 152.
[48] Ibid., 159.
[49] Interview with Marije Janssen, Berlin, 2008-10-27.
[50] "Trans Entities," Morty Diamond website, http://www.mortydiamond.com/video/trans-entities/ (accessed 2011-11-20).

As discussed in chapter 3, queer, feminist and lesbian pornography is a hybrid film practice combining narrative, experimental, educational and not least documentary features. In queer, feminist and lesbian pornography the "documentary impulse" or "guarantee that we will behold 'the thing itself', caught in the indexical grain of cinematographic sound and image," as Christian Hansen, Catherine Needham and Bill Nichols put it, also involves a documentation of the reality of queer, feminist and lesbian sexual cultures and bodies.[51] The "thing itself" in queer, feminist and lesbian pornography include not only proof of sexual pleasure, but is related also to notions of visibility, authenticity and education. It forms part of a consciousness-raising project and the creation of alternative knowledge and publicity. Therefore, in the sense that "the photograph's existence as an object and a possession with fixed yet increasing value materializes and authenticates experience, others, and oneself as empirically real," as Sobchack puts it, photographic presence is central in queer, feminist and lesbian pornography, even if its photographic technology is digital.[52] The films exist as objects in production, distribution and consumption contexts, but also in activist archives and collections, such as the collection belonging to Club LASH. In Ann Cvetkovich's terms, queer, feminist and lesbian pornography functions as "an archive of feelings."[53] In this sense, *Trans Entities* both authenticates Papi and Wil as empirically real, and represent an archive of feelings. The film centers on their reflections and feelings in relation to a world marked by racism and homophobia. In the film the embodied indexical traces of these experiences are brought in to sexual role-playing.

In Marije Janssen's reflections about *Trans Entities* and about the same couple's appearance in Shine Louise Houston's *In Search of the Wild Kingdom*, which screens at the Pornfilmfestival Berlin the same year that I interview her, she underscores how these films have made her more sexually open. She talks about how she during the screening of *In Search of the Wild Kingdom*, similarly to her experience of the screening of *One Night Stand* at the festival in 2006, felt the energy changed in the theater and how she left aroused. In regard to *One Night Stand* she talks about how:

> For me it was just mind-blowing to see these women who were so powerful and so... sexual, but also so thoughtful about their sexuality and making it into something political... I was already in the feminist porn thing so I knew that... pornography could be much more political than I ever expected it to be,

---

[51] Hansen, Needham and Nichols, "Pornography, Ethnography, and the Discourse of Power," in *Representing Reality,* ed. Bill Nichols, 1991, 211; See also Dyer, "Idol Thoughts: Orgasm and Self-Reflexivity in Gay Pornography," in *More Dirty Looks,* 2004, 102-109.
[52] Sobchack, 2004, 143.
[53] Cvetkovich, 2003. See also Halberstam, 2005, 159; and Laura U. Marks, *The Skin of the Film: Intercultural Cinema, Embodiment, and the Senses* (Durham: Duke University Press, 2000).

but they did it in such a powerful way and it really changed my view on female sexuality as well and how you can pursue it.[54]

In her discussion about the interactive relationship enabled by haptic images and how this ethically grounds "respect for otherness," Marks references Bill Nichols' and Jane Gaines' discussions about "documentaries whose haptic, visceral intimacy engenders an ethical relationship between viewer and viewed, by inviting the viewer to mimetically embody the experience of the people viewed."[55] Marije Janssen's accounts of her experiences of *One Night Stand*, *Trans Entities* and *In Search of the Wild Kingdom*, where she was surprised about her strong physical reaction to the bodies in the films, can be read as such mimetic embodiment of *politicized* sexual experiences. When I interview Emilie Jouvet, the director of *One Night Stand*, also during the Pornfilmfestival Berlin 2008, I ask her what she thinks about the relation between politics and sexual pleasure. Jouvet stresses that she sees them as interrelated. She talks about the choice to open *One Night Stand* with interviews with the performers and how she wanted the viewers to see more of their personalities than they show in the sex scenes.

> I think it changes the perception when you see someone having sex, I mean having a certain sort of practice… when you listen to her… what she thinks about that or what she feels – it changes your mind about what you see. It becomes more complex and takes on other dimensions… It is easier to find yourself in it.[56]

This discussion also echoes Eithne Johnson's analysis of the "erotic, participative corporeality" in community-based sexpert videos that she contrasts to "the discursive-inscriptive corporeality of scientia sexualis" in professional sex education films.[57] Johnson's statement also directs attention to how shared embodiment in queer, feminist and lesbian pornography is invited through the physically shared spaces that make up this interpretive community, where the films circulate and are seen. Marije Janssen's account is characterized by what Miriam Hansen calls a "multiple and dynamic transaction" between the "phantasmagoric space on the screen" and the "theater's physical space and the social environment it [assimilates]."[58] In Jennifer's

---

[54] Interview with Marije Janssen, Berlin, 2008-10-27.
[55] Marks, 8. Marks references Bill Nichols, "The Ethnographer's Tale," in *Visualising Theory: Selected Essays from V.A.R., 1990-1994*, ed. Lucien Taylor (New York: Routledge, 1994), 60-83, and Jane M. Gaines, "Political Mimesis," in *Collecting Visible Evidence*, ed. Jane M. Gaines and Michael Renov (Minneapolis: University of Minnesota Press, 1999), 84-102.
[56] Interview with Emilie Jouvet, Berlin, 2008-10-25. See Ingrid Ryberg, "Tips från pornografen," *FLM* 5 (2009), 16-17.
[57] Johnson, 1999, 235.
[58] Hansen, 1991, 18.

account of her experiences of lesbian pornography at Club LASH, the exhibition context is similarly crucial. Jennifer talks about Club LASH as "an oasis with safe and warm atmosphere and acceptance."[59] The women in the films she saw there became role models for her.

Hence, and as argued in chapter 4, meanings of pornographic texts are shaped by their contexts of production, distribution and consumption, by the reality of the sites, practices and situations that they traverse. Similarly to how Marije Janssen found an "added value" in watching porn with others in the theater at the Pornfilmfestival Berlin, Marks also discusses her own experience at a screening of independent gay male pornography at New York Lesbian and Gay Film Festival. She accounts for how these films invited "a playful look that oscillates between distance and involvement" as well as "multiple sorts of erotic looks confined neither to particular subjects nor to particular objects, looks that, as well as dominating, may be submissive or take some other relation to their object."[60] Marks underscores how this invitation was produced also within the context of the audience in the theater. She argues that "[i]n an audience that is a coalition of different interests, the contract exists not just between the viewing individual and the screen space but among a group."[61] "The mutual participation of a group of people – an audience – in these fantasy situations enhances the experience of forming identifications *across* identities [emphasis in original]."[62] In this context she proposes an "S/M model of looking" that "accounts for the specificity of looks, for their contextuality and, most important, the ability to inhabit erotic and political relations that change with the situation."[63] Importantly, according to Marks, "[t]he negotiation that characterizes the S/M looking relation is particularly characteristic of the spectator's relation to independent films, because of the small-scale production context.[64] She argues that independent films invite a look "closely tied to a relation among the individuals involved in the production," often a documentary encounter between filmmaker and actor.[65] Furthermore, the documentary character of pornography especially "calls on a relation of identification that is different from the fantasy relations at work in fiction cinema."[66] "Identification in porn is not simply an immersion in fantasy but also a relation to the dynamics at work between filmmaker [...] and actor/subject."[67] In Marks' discussion, as well as in the

---

[59] Interview with Jennifer, Stockholm, 2008-11-04.
[60] Marks, "Love the One You're With: Straight Women, Gay Porn, and the Scene of Erotic Looking," in *Touch*, 2002, 74.
[61] Marks, 2002, 88.
[62] Ibid., 89.
[63] Ibid., 90.
[64] Marks, 2002, 87.
[65] Ibid.
[66] Ibid.
[67] Ibid.

different examples of how a shared embodiment is invited in queer, feminist and lesbian pornography, notions of the haptic and the indexical interrelate with the social contexts of this film culture. The rest of this chapter argues that the sharing of space, knowledge and fantasy that characterizes this interpretive community call forth an ethics of shared embodiment.

## Embracing trauma, imagining utopia

Marit Östberg's film *Share* (2010) opens with a black frame and a voiceover. Flickering fragments with black frames in between cuts of a naked woman masturbating on a floor gradually turn into a more seamless sequence where images of the woman are cross-edited with images of two other women getting undressed and caressing each other. The voiceover reads:

> When I think about my lover and her lover
> It is a thrill, a disease
> I don't think
> I think repeatedly
> Your presence in me
> Me and my lover's lover know how
> Her face we watch
> Her eyes we share
> Image of her eyes
> It's different, the same, the shame
> It is hard my love to think about your love, my love
> I want to touch their thoughts, bodies
> I want to see them, be them

After the woman orgasms she puts her clothes on and walks over to her lover's apartment where she finds the two women, her lover and her "lover's lover," having sex. She tells them to continue so she can watch, but after a while interrupts them and a violent threesome evolves. Afterwards she gets dressed and leaves her lover and "her other lover" together in the apartment. Walking home through the now dark city her voiceover reads:

> Me and my lover's lover know
> We watch
> We share bodies, loneliness
> A play of love
> To play love, my love
> Next time I'll bring my other lover

The film ends with a short clip with the three women together having sex again, but this time also with a fourth woman, the main character's "other lover."

*Publicity still, Share (Marit Östberg, 2010). Courtesy of the filmmaker.*

As a film about poly-amorous relationships and jealousy the film brings up both the pain and the pleasure of sharing a lover with somebody else. In the film the "thrill" and "disease" of jealousy is played out and turned into a sex scene between the women who share "bodies," "eyes," "loneliness" and are "present" in each other. I propose the film also thematizes, especially through the voiceover's articulation of the words "watch," "image," "eyes" and "touch," the sharing of embodiment in this interpretive community as such, through the circulation of images, thoughts and feelings. In Marit Östberg's accounts of the production of *Share*, as discussed in chapter 4, she talks about the importance of being close to and sharing the sexual energy of her performers. The performers in *Share* also form part of the consciousness-raising group that Marit Östberg started in Berlin after her experience of personal crisis during the screening of her film *Authority* at the London Lesbian and Gay Film Festival in March 2010. Her accounts of participation in this film culture over the course of three years demonstrate how shared embodiment in this interpretive community is also a matter of how distinctions between performers, directors and audience are blurred. Marit Östberg's reflections support Marks' discussion about independent pornography as testifying to "the dynamics at work between filmmaker and actor/subject."[68]

As *Share* demonstrates, the sharing of bodies, experiences and fantasy is not without pain, conflict and difficulties. As argued in previous chapters, queer, feminist and lesbian pornography, as a collective political fantasy about a safe space for sexual empowerment, embodies a number of conflicts and tensions. *Share* thematizes some of these and evokes Ann Cvetkovich's account of lesbian sexual public cultures as a matter of "[celebrating] the hard-won experience of sexual pleasure without denying its roots in pain and difficulty."[69] Cvetkovich argues that the emotional knowledge produced in public cultures around sex, such as in butch-femme sexual discourse by Joan Nestle, Cherríe Moraga and Leslie Feinberg, where intimate lives are situated "in relation to classism, racism, and other forms of oppression,"[70] serves an important function of "providing the space for emotional expression that is not available elsewhere."[71] She accounts for how this public emotional knowledge and expression regards in particular negotiations related to the notion of vulnerability as a question of touching and being touched, sexually and emotionally. As commented upon in chapter 5, Cvetkovich points out that vulnerability is a privilege and "a desirable and often difficult achievement."[72] Relating queer studies to trauma studies she discusses the everyday life of queer trauma, where "the normalization of sex and gender identities can be seen as a form of insidious trauma."[73] Cvetkovich discusses how trauma is acknowledged, worked through and explored in sexual practices where touch and untouchability are negotiated. She argues that "[w]ithout being essentializing, [butch-femme discussions of sexuality] use the body as

---

[68] Marks, 2002, 87.
[69] Cvetkovich, 4.
[70] Ibid.
[71] Cvetkovich, 82. Cvetkovich discusses in particular Joan Nestle's *A Restricted Country* (Ithaca, N.Y.: Firebrand Books, 1987), Cherríe Moraga's *Loving in the War Years: Lo Que Nunca Pasó Por Sus Labios* (Boston: South End Press, 1983) and Leslie Feinberg's *Stone Butch Blues* (Ithaca, N.Y.: Firebrand Books, 1993).
[72] Cvetkovich, 58.
[73] Ibid., 46.

a ground for negotiating social relations, finding, for instance, within the sexual intimacy of the couple practices that address experiences of homophobia, shame and abjection in the public world."[74] She forwards a "healing" potential in the publicly shared acknowledgment of the traumatic dimension of sexuality.[75] I propose that *Share*, in line with Cvetkovich's discussion, explores the healing potential of bringing the pain of jealousy into sexual practice and play.

Similarly, in her discussion about BDSM and especially about race role-play, for instance in Isaac Julien's *The Attendant* (1992), Freeman argues that "S/M relentlessly physicalizes the encounter with history and thereby contributes to a reparative criticism that takes up the materials of a traumatic past and remixes them in the interests of new possibilities for being and knowing."[76] This analysis is actualized also in the case of *Trans Entities*, where BDSM is explored precisely as a reparative criticism of the trauma of racism. In the film the couple, Papi and Wil, engages in a sexual role-play with a third, and unlike them, white, partner. In an interview the three of them explain: "We engage in race play that is very taboo... But there's honesty that lives here and there's struggle that lives here. We, you know, we wanna work through that." Furthermore, the couple's self-identification as "Trans Entities" can also be understood as a struggle for and an exploration of "new possibilities for being and knowing," as Freeman puts it. The inclusion of negotiations of the role-playing in *Trans Entities*' and *Share*'s non-verbal, yet emphasized physical communication about the women's different roles in the sex scene also echo Cvetkovich's contention that "[b]eing made to feel, and especially the physical or sensuous experience of being penetrated, is a rich locus of social meaning, and the physical and sexual are linked not just to the emotional but to conceptions of gender, sexuality, race, and nationality."[77]

Both Cvetkovich and Freeman engage in discussions about the notion of queer "antisociality" as associated with the works of Leo Bersani and Lee Edelman.[78] Bersani argues that across the fields of the Sex Wars, in the writings of MacKinnon and Dworkin as well as Gayle Rubin and Pat Califia, a "*redemptive reinvention of sex*" is entertained [emphasis in original].[79] In this discourse sex is imagined as "less disturbing, less socially abrasive, less violent, more respectful of 'personhood' than it has been in male-dominated

---

[74] Ibid., 56.
[75] Ibid., 88-89.
[76] Freeman, 144.
[77] Cvetkovich, 70-71.
[78] Leo Bersani, "Is the Rectum a Grave?" *October*, 43 (Winter 1987), 197-222; Lee Edelman, *No Future: Queer Theory and the Death Drive* (Durham: Duke University Press, 2004); Judith Halberstam, "The Anti-Social Turn in Queer Studies," *Graduate Journal of Social Science*, 5:2 (2008): 140-156.
[79] Bersani, 215.

phallocentric culture."[80] Drawing on George Bataille and Freud, Bersani opposes the redemptive enterprise with notions of "self-shattering," "masochism" and "disintegration and humiliation of the self."[81] He argues that, instead of accepting "our culture's lies about sexuality," the dysfunctionality of sexuality should be celebrated. Cvetkovich's discussion about lesbian public sex cultures distances itself from notions of the "self-shattering" violence of sexuality. She argues that "[f]emme lesbians also value 'loss of control,' and they don't prettify powerlessness."[82] She points out how Bersani's discussion concerns how a "specifically masculine self is humiliated, and hence threatened with disintegration, by anal penetration,"[83] and argues that "femme accounts of receptivity avoid a redemptive reading of sex, insisting on the fear, pain, and difficulty that can block the way to and be conjured up by making oneself physically and emotionally vulnerable or receptive."[84] Invoking these discussions Bergsmark's and Kaaman's *Dirty Diaries* short *Fruitcake* can be read as celebrating dissolution, not as self-shattering, and the rectum, not as "grave," but as a path to utopia.

This "embracing" of trauma, as Cvetkovich puts it, as a potentially healing and reparative practice, actualized in *Share* and *Trans Entities,* also invokes José Esteban Muñoz' work on queerness as horizon, utopia, futurity and hope.[85] In a conversation about queer hope and hopelessness between Muñoz and Lisa Duggan they discuss hope as a "risky reaching out for something else that will fail."[86] Even if "experimental intimacies often falter," as *Share* in some sense also acknowledges, "those failures and efforts to fail have a certain value despite their ends."[87] In line with their argument, queer, feminist and lesbian pornography can be considered in terms of "a politics oriented towards means and not ends."[88] They contend that hope "is not about announcing the way things *ought* to be, but, instead, imagining what things *could* be [emphasis in original]."[89] In this sense the collective political fantasy of safe space for sexual empowerment is more about imagining safe space, than about announcing correct solutions for realizing this space. The strategies explored in queer, feminist and lesbian pornography are many and sometimes conflicting. Throughout this dissertation I have

---

[80] Ibid., 215.
[81] Ibid., 217.
[82] Cvetkovich, 62.
[83] Ibid.
[84] Cvetkovich, 63.
[85] Cvetkovich, 88-89; Muñoz, 2009. Cvetkovich and Muñoz as well as Freeman all refer to Eve Kosofsky Sedgwick's discussions about queer performativity and paranoid and reparative criticism. See Sedgwick, 2003.
[86] Lisa Duggan and José Esteban Muñoz, "Hope and Hopelessness: A Dialogue," *Women & Performance: A Journal of Feminist Theory*, 19:2 (2009): 279.
[87] Duggan and Muñoz, 2009, 281.
[88] Ibid.
[89] Duggan and Muñoz, 2009, 278. See also Bensinger, 79-82.

brought up examples and situations that complicate and even question the figure of queer, feminist and lesbian pornography as a safe space for sexual empowerment, such as how my friend was sexually harassed in a theater in Berlin or the heterogeneous and contested political and aesthetic legacies of this film culture. In the case of *Dirty Diaries*, some filmmakers chose to participate anonymously and during the production there were disagreements, for instance around whether Marit Östberg's film *Uniform* should end with bloopers or not. One of the performers in the short chose to withdraw her participation and the film did not come part of the final collection. In different screening situations of *Dirty Diaries*, filmmakers, including myself, also experienced feelings of unsafety.

Queer, feminist and lesbian pornography hence is characterized by an activism of striving toward a goal, despite risks, unsafety and failures. The politics of imagining, rather than realizing safe space evokes an ethics that is not either necessarily practiced or realized, but is called forth by the investment in shared struggles and fantasies in this interpretive community. I contend that queer, feminist and lesbian pornography calls forth an ethics of shared embodiment. This ethics is located in the process of collectively imagining and reaching out, in taking the risk of failure, *and* in accommodating the failures, conflicts and traumas that this fantasy entails. Such ethics involves acknowledging past traumas and their traces, but also taking the risk of hoping and continuing to reach out for another world; in Cvetkovich's words to making oneself vulnerable, and in Marks' to be susceptible to otherness. The called forth ethics of shared embodiment in queer, feminist and lesbian pornography consists in reaching out for safe space, but still accommodating the difficulties that this shared endeavor entails.[90] It involves both acknowledging trauma and still taking the risk of hoping for something else.

Importantly, this process of reaching out and taking risks also shapes bodies. As Muñoz puts it, "[q]ueerness is also a performative because it is not simply a being but a doing for and toward the future."[91] In his discussion about queer cultural production around the time of the Stonewall rebellion in 1969, he argues for the world-making potential and performativity of queer cultural production as it insists on the possibility for another world.[92] Importantly, "utopia is not about simply achieving happiness or freedom; utopia is in fact a casting of a picture of potentiality and possibility."[93]

> Utopia is always about the not-quite-here or the notion that something is missing. Queer cultural production is both an acknowledgement of the lack that is

---

[90] See also de Lauretis, "Upping the Anti [sic] in Feminist Theory [1990]," in *Figures of Resistance*, ed. White, 2007a, 197.
[91] Muñoz, 2009, 1.
[92] Ibid.
[93] Muñoz, 2009, 125.

endemic to any heteronormative rendering of the world and a building, a 'world-making,' in the face of that lack. A nothing is a utopian act insofar as it acknowledges a lack that is normalized as reality and attempts to work with and through nothingness and ephemerality: it is both a critique and an additive or reparative gesture. Queer utopian practice is about 'building' and 'doing' in response to that status of nothing assigned to us by the heteronormative world.[94]

Echoing Muñoz, Marit Östberg talks about how queer feminist film productions can work as "temporary coalitions" where one can try building alternative relations outside of the hierarchies related to capitalism, patriarchy and racism. She reflects on how the very act of filmmaking produces "solidarity" in an activist community, but also how the films represent an idea about a community, sometimes in "a utopian way."

> The stories in queer films, what this can create, the representation of a community that may not exist, that may exist as an idea but that does not work in practice – I mean everyone feels alone and everyone feels excluded, which may depend on one's own low self-esteem, and thinks that they're not really a part of the gang... But also there is no community where everyone has always time for each other. This sisterhood idea that I think queer feminist filmmaking can be, it may not exist in reality always but it exists in the productions.[95]

This is the last research interview I do with Marit Östberg. It is June 2011 and three years have passed since we both attended the first meeting with *Dirty Diaries* at Café Copacabana. She is in Stockholm organizing a workshop on "The Lesbian Body and Queer Sexuality – Artistic and Pornographic Practices" together with the artist Malin Arnell. The workshop forms part of a program called "Community Action Center and Beyond – Two days of sociosexual affinity" where *Share* is screened along with the film *Community Action Center* (A.K. Burns and AL Steiner, 2010), films by Barbara Hammer and Malin Arnell. *Community Action Center* is an experimental video "inspired by 1970s porn-romance-liberation films,"[96] which evokes Muñoz's discussions about "queerness as a temporal arrangement in which the past is a field of possibility in which subjects can act in the present in the service of a new futurity."[97] The presentation of the film reads:

> This project is a small archive of an intergenerational community built on collaboration, friendship, sex and art. The work attempts to explore a consideration of feminist fashion, sexual aesthetics and an expansive view of what is defined as 'sex'. Burns and Steiner worked with artists and performers who

---

[94] Ibid., 118.
[95] Interview with Marit Östberg, Stockholm, 2011-06-09.
[96] "Community Action Center and Beyond," Konsthall C website, http://www.konsthallc.se/index.php?q=Community+Action+ (accessed 2011-11-21).
[97] Muñoz, 2009, 16.

created infinitely complex gender and performance roles that are both real and fantastical.[98]

After the screening Marit Östberg does a Q&A session with the filmmakers of *Community Action Center*. Burns and Steiner underscore how the project is anchored in the practices of exploring and challenging notions of gender and sexuality within their own subcultural community.[99] In my interview with Marit Östberg she also talks about how her Berlin-based consciousness-raising group for queer porn performers functions as a kind of building of "sisterhood." "What I do now builds on a close relationship to the people I work with… and the will to create things together," she says.[100]

These discussions resonate with both Muñoz's insistence on "the essential need for an understanding of queerness as collectivity,"[101] and Ahmed's contention that "[t]he queer body is not alone; queer does not reside in a body or an object, and is dependent on the mutuality of support."[102] "When we tread on paths that are less trodden, which we are not sure are paths at all (is it a path, or is the grass just a little bent?), *we might need even more support*," Ahmed argues [emphasis in original].[103] The reaching out for and imagining of a new world in queer, feminist and lesbian pornography, drawing on Ahmed, also creates "new lines," "new patterns and new ways of making sense."[104] In this sense the collective political fantasy of safe space for sexual empowerment has the potential to shape bodies in their different present realities. In collectively imagining new paths, queer, feminist and lesbian pornography also allows and provides conditions for new orientations and pleasures. I contend that rather than announcing fixed solutions or reaching specific goals, this film culture is about the public and collective sharing of

---

[98] "Community Action Center and Beyond," Konsthall C website, http://www.konsthallc.se/index.php?q=Community+Action+ (accessed 2011-11-21).
[99] A.K. Burns and AL Steiner in artist conversation with Marit Östberg, Konsthall C, Stockholm, 2011-06-09.
[100] Interview with Marit Östberg, Stockholm, 2011-06-09.
[101] Muñoz, 2009, 11.
[102] Ahmed, 2006, 170.
[103] Ibid.
[104] Ahmed, 2006, 171. See also Ahmed, 2006, 107.

trauma, hope and pleasure. It is also in this sense that screening – and recording – queer, feminist and lesbian sex forms an intimate part of sexuality. In Williams' terms, screening queer, feminist and lesbian porn is "to play at sex," just as the voiceover in *Share* talks about "a play of love, to play love."[105] In queer, feminist and lesbian pornography this play is a play at a representation of sex, which is also about playing at sex. It is a playful, but sometimes also painful and risky, exploration of the fantasy of a safe space for this play.

---

[105] Williams, 2008, 18.

# 7. The wave and the undertow: summary and conclusions

As this research project comes to an end, *Dirty Diaries* continues to circulate and gain attention internationally at different festivals and events. During the fall of 2011 the film screens at the feminist culture festival BeFem in Belgrade and wins The Feminist Porn Film Awards Europe, a prize honoring work "demonstrating female pleasure and expanding the range of sexual expression for women."[1] The Feminist Porn Film Awards Europe takes place in Berlin a week before the sixth Pornfilmfestival Berlin, which in 2011 has a record attendance of 5,500 visitors.[2] This year the festival screens a new short from one of the participating filmmakers in *Dirty Diaries*, Joanna Rytel. Her film *Gang Bang Barbie* (2010) wins the festival's Short Film Competition.[3] Moreover, during the fall of 2011 the international performance art festival Feminists in Space in Copenhagen screens Marit Östberg's film *Share* along with her new film *Sisterhood* (2011).[4] *Sisterhood* is a documentary based on interviews with participants in her other films and discusses pornography "as an important feminist and activist strategy."[5] Marit Östberg is also one of the performers in Cheryl Dunye's lesbian feature *Mommy Is Coming* that premieres at the Berlinale in February 2012. The film is set in Berlin and mixes romantic comedy with explicit sex scenes.

In this research project, I have studied one portion of a vibrant and expanding transnational queer, feminist and lesbian porn film culture. The category queer, feminist and lesbian pornography has been constructed in order to account for an ongoing wave of interest in pornography as a vehicle for queer, feminist and lesbian activism. This category has been examined as

---

[1] "About Befem," BeFem website, http://www.befem.org/ accessed 2011-11-08, "Feministischer Pornofilmpreis Europa,"
http://www.poryes.de/index.php?option=com_content&view=article&id=34&Itemid=138ontent&view=article&id=34&Itemid=138 (accessed 2011-11-07).
[2] According to Facebook post on 2011-10-31,
https://www.facebook.com/pages/Pornfilmfestival-Berlin/259816320725799 (accessed 2011-11-07).
[3] "And the winners are…" 6. Pornfilmfestival Berlin website,
http://www.pornfilmfestivalberlin.de/pffb_2011/en/?p=4682 (accessed 2011-11-08).
[4] Feminists in Space website, http://warehouse9.dk/fis/?page_id=247 (accessed 2011-11-08).
[5] "Marit Östberg (SE)," Feminists in Space website, http://warehouse9.dk/fis/?page_id=44 (accessed 2011-11-08).

a film culture made up by the transnational circulation of films, discourses, people and practices. I have accounted for this film culture through case studies of the Swedish feminist porn film collection *Dirty Diaries* where twelve filmmakers made shorts with mobile phone cameras, the annual Pornfilmfestival Berlin and Club LASH, a Stockholm-based S/M, fetish and kinky club for women and transsexual people where pornography is regularly screened. These cases have been discussed as three examples of how the film culture intertwines with queer, feminist and lesbian struggles for sexual empowerment in a wide range of contexts of production, distribution and consumption. Focusing on these three cases the study has not charted or provided a complete picture of the recent proliferation of productions and events engaged in queer, feminist and lesbian pornography. The film culture's online existence has also fallen outside of the scope of this research project.

The aim of this study has been to account for this film culture and to understand its political and ethical meanings and historical and cultural legacies. I have addressed three research questions about 1) the discourses, aesthetics, sites, practices and situations that make up this film culture; 2) what queer, feminist and lesbian pornography means for participants in this film culture; and 3) the politics and ethics of queer, feminist and lesbian pornography. In order to respond to these questions I have examined this film culture through the concept of *interpretive community*. Building on Lynne Pearce's definition of this concept, queer, feminist and lesbian pornography has been studied as a "site of struggle" and disagreement, but as nevertheless defined by certain shared knowledge and concerns.[6] The concept of interpretive community has shed light on how this film culture, despite its multi-sited and contingent character, articulates, in particular, one common political concern. Throughout this study, I have argued that the defining feature of this interpretive community is a recurrent figure of queer, feminist and lesbian pornography as a potentially safe space for sexual empowerment. I have demonstrated how this figure is mobilized in the context of the small members-only Club LASH, as well as at screenings of *Dirty Diaries* in such diverse contexts as the London International Lesbian and Gay Film Festival, the Swedish Cinematheque in Stockholm and Malmö University. I have also highlighted the centrality of this figure throughout the political and aesthetic legacies that this film culture belongs to. Hence, a main argument in this dissertation has been that queer, feminist and lesbian pornography, is characterized by a politics of constructing safe space. I have maintained that safe space, in Elizabeth Freeman's terms, is the "collective political fantasy" that this film culture engages in.[7]

---

[6] Pearce, 1997, 212, 2004, 223; Bobo, 59.
[7] Freeman, 65.

The concept of interpretive community, in my definition, has also enabled an examination of how meanings of queer, feminist and lesbian pornography are shaped not only by the discourses and aesthetics, but also by the sites, practices and situations that make up this film culture. Drawing on Miriam Hansen and Jane Juffer, I have argued that meanings and experiences of queer, feminist and lesbian pornography should be analyzed in relation to specific sites, practices and situations of reception. For example, I have highlighted how the exhibition site of Club LASH, a club dedicated to providing conditions for safe and consensual sexual encounters and BDSM role-play, contributes to research subjects' experiences of queer, feminist and lesbian pornography as a safe space for sexual exploration. I have also pointed out how practices of participation in this film culture often blur boundaries between the audience, directors, performers and organizers and that this affects how films are experienced. In bringing out specific situations of reception and experiences of exposure and unsafety, such as during the screening of *Much More Pussy* at the Pornfilmfestival Berlin in 2010, where my friend was sexually harassed, I have also directed attention to the contingent and contradictory character of the figure of safe space.

In this study, ethnographic fieldwork has been a crucial method for locating the meanings of queer, feminist and lesbian pornography in specific contexts of production, distribution and consumption. The fieldwork was designed around the cases of *Dirty Diaries*, Pornfilmfestival Berlin and Club LASH and consists of questionnaires, interviews and participant observation. Interviews with members of Club LASH, attendance at the Pornfilmfestival Berlin, in 2008, 2009 and 2010, and regular meetings with the filmmakers during the production phase of *Dirty Diaries* and a number of screenings of the completed film, amount to a large body of material that has provided crucial insights into the questions that this project set out to investigate. The ethnographic material from these different contexts of production, distribution and consumption has served as a correction of the lack of empirically based research on practices of porn production and reception and has provided an important basis for contributing to the field of porn studies.[8] Importantly, therefore, this dissertation would not have been possible without the valuable contributions of the many research subjects who chose to participate in the project in various ways.

Furthermore, in this study the concept of interpretive community and the method of ethnographic fieldwork have accentuated my own participation in this film culture and how my account of it has been articulated from this position. Participant observation has allowed me to draw from my own experiences of participating in this film culture and to underscore the situatedness of this research project.[9] The dissertation has analyzed accounts

---

[8] Attwood, 2002, 103; Paasonen, 2007, 18.
[9] Haraway, 1988.

of others' as well as my own film experiences, for instance from specific reception situations of *Dirty Diaries*. In this regard, my participation as one of the filmmakers in *Dirty Diaries* and the production of my short *Phone Fuck* have also formed a vital part of the research process. This part of the fieldwork has provided an empirical basis for outlining the political and aesthetic concerns of queer, feminist and lesbian pornography. Scrutinizing the production of *Dirty Diaries* in relation to a history of queer, feminist and lesbian representations of sex has brought out safety and consent as central concerns in this film culture. Aside from serving as an examination of production processes, the production of *Phone Fuck* has served as an exploration of issues raised through my own participation in this film culture. The short, which features a lesbian phone sex scenario, reflects on my own experiences of queer, feminist and lesbian pornography and in particular of the film *Hard Love*. *Phone Fuck* and the scene from *Hard Love* that became the inspiration for it contributed significantly to this project's focus on embodied spectatorship.

In discussing how experiences and meanings of queer, feminist and lesbian pornography are shaped by their location within this interpretive community, this work has directed attention to their corporeal dimension. Thus, I have defined interpretive community as involving embodied spectatorial processes, different practices of participation in this film culture and their situatedness in specific contexts and situations. Building on Linda Williams, Vivian Sobchack and Teresa de Lauretis, the dissertation has examined how queer, feminist and lesbian pornography as a collective political fantasy of safe space engages and shapes the embodied subjectivities of participants in this interpretive community.[10] Their work on embodied spectatorship has been discussed in order to open up and analyze research subjects' accounts of experiences of empowerment and arousal, but also of disgust and anger.

With reference to Williams' discussion about habituation to public screenings of sexual images, I have argued that queer, feminist and lesbian porn film culture provides an arena where bodies are habituated and opened up not only to "new forms of socialized arousal," but also to being porn spectators.[11] I have also stressed the necessity of considering such habituation in relation to specific bodies' location in intersecting power structures. Drawing from, but also interrogating Sobchack's notion of carnal identification through detailed interview accounts of how films are felt in the body, I have stated that the embodied experience of pornography is shaped not only by a general ability to make sense of moving images corporeally, but also by personal histories and practices. This argument has been further elaborated through de Lauretis' work on the notion of fantasy and her emphasis on taking into account who produces the fantasy and the difference between public

---

[10] Williams, 2008, 18, 309-326; Sobchack, 2004, 53-84; De Lauretis, 1994, 81-148. 1999.
[11] Williams, 2008, 18.

and private fantasies. Looking into accounts from interviews, *Dirty Diaries* meetings and films where identification, desire and "politically incorrect" fantasies are discussed, I have traced how experiences of queer, feminist and lesbian pornography are located in the "slide [...] between the subjective and the social," in de Lauretis' words.[12]

Through this theoretical framework, the study has mapped out queer, feminist and lesbian pornography's potential to form part of processes of sexual empowerment and enhanced agency. Research subjects' accounts of improved sexual self-esteem have been read also in relation to Sara Ahmed's discussions about how bodies take shape through how they extend differently in space and come into contact with other bodies.[13] Drawing from Ahmed, I have discussed queer, feminist and lesbian pornography as providing a surface where bodies constricted by dominant gender and sexual norms can expand their reach and take new shapes. The corporeal and social dimension of such processes has been underscored. However, with refernece to de Lauretis, I have also stressed that embodied subjectivities are not reshaped by willpower and that fantasies do not simply correlate with political ideals. Still, I have argued that as a public fantasy, queer, feminist and lesbian pornography can become part of the psychic reworkings of internal and external realities that constitute subjectivity.[14]

Queer, feminist and lesbian pornography has at the outset of this study been described as forming a wave of interest in pornography as activism. Drawing from Ahmed, I have discussed how this film culture opens up new paths and draws new lines for bodies to follow.[15] Thought as a wave, queer, feminist and lesbian pornography is a forceful line to follow. On its surface it gathers and shapes bodies, but it also shapes and leaves marks on the social surfaces that it traverses.[16] Importantly, as a wave, queer, feminist and lesbian pornography is not a straight line. As a wave it also embodies several intertwining undercurrents. As Elizabeth Freeman points out, a wave is constituted also by an undertow. In her terms, "the movement time of collective political fantasy" is characterized both by a forward movement and by a pull back, by a temporal drag.[17] This study has aimed at understanding and historicizing this pull or undertow of queer, feminist and lesbian pornography.

In this dissertation I have contended that queer, feminist and lesbian pornography belongs to the legacies of second wave feminism's politicization of sexuality and the emergence of feminist and lesbian porn production companies during the so-called 'Sex Wars' of the 1980s. Through reading

---

[12] De Lauretis, 1995, 64.
[13] Ahmed, 2006, 1-21.
[14] De Lauretis, 1999a, 307.
[15] Ahmed, 2006, 171.
[16] Ahmed, 2004, 165; 2006, 19-20.
[17] Freeman, 65.

the production of *Dirty Diaries* in relation to these legacies the study has highlighted the political and aesthetic heterogeneity of this film culture. Throughout this study I have argued that queer, feminist and lesbian pornography, as a "site of struggle," activates a constitutive tension between affirmation and critique that de Lauretis defines as characteristic of the women's movement and of women's cinema.[18] Drawing from de Lauretis, I have demonstrated how this "pull in opposite directions" is played out politically and aesthetically in this film culture, in debates about pornography as well as in discussions about film practice.[19] With *Dirty Diaries* as a main example, I have defined queer, feminist and lesbian pornography as a hybrid film practice incorporating documentary, narrative, experimental and educational styles. This study has aimed at historicizing the internal pull and tensions in queer, feminist and lesbian pornography, not as a progressive or decade-specific timeline, but in Clare Hemmings' words, as a "series of ongoing contests and relationships."[20] Drawing from Chris Straayer, Jane Gerhard and Lynn Comella this work has disrupted a linear chronology of queer, feminist and lesbian discussions and productions of sexual representations. For instance, I have forwarded how sexual consciousness-raising is central across this film culture and its legacies.

The inherent tension between affirmation and critique has also been discussed in terms of a tension between the notions of intimate and a counter public.[21] Building on Lauren Berlant and with examples from the interview material, I have contended that queer, feminist and lesbian pornography, as an intimate public, provides a promise of recognition and belonging for participants in this interpretive community. Drawing on Michael Warner and others, I have also contended that queer, feminist and lesbian pornography, as a counter public, challenges dominant notions of gender and sexuality and claims public visibility and accessibility. Through fieldwork examples from different reception contexts and situations, the dissertation has demonstrated that the two functions of intimate and counter public intertwine, but also at times clash in queer, feminist and lesbian porn film culture. For instance, I have discussed how the wide public circulation of *Dirty Diaries* at times has put the figure of a safe space for sexual empowerment at stake. The notions of intimate and counter public have further contributed to the disruption of a linear narrative of queer, feminist and lesbian activism and its recent past. As an "affective scene for identification" queer, feminist and lesbian pornography challenges a progressive chronology from identity politics to queer activism.[22] In this project the methodological decision to conduct fieldwork

---

[18] Pearce, 1997, 212; and de Lauretis, 2007a, 25.
[19] De Lauretis, 2007, 25.
[20] Hemmings, 2005, 31.
[21] Berlant, 2008; Berlant, 2002; Warner, 2002a; Warner, 2002b; Warner and Berlant, 1998.
[22] Berlant, 2008, viii.

was based precisely on the need to reframe such binary oppositions explaining pornography as either oppression or liberation, from the point of view of either radical feminism or sex radicalism. The fieldwork has most crucially enabled this work's understanding of queer, feminist and lesbian pornography as instead illustrating the co-presence and overlapping of these discussions. They all form part of the undercurrents of queer, feminist and lesbian pornography's politics of constructing safe space for sexual empowerment.

Finally, the study has discussed the shared knowledge and concerns in this interpretive community as a question of shared embodiment shaped by media technological aspects. Building on Laura U. Marks and with the mobile phone shorts in *Dirty Diaries* as main examples, I have highlighted how shared embodiment is invited aesthetically through notions of both the haptic and the indexical, but also socially through this film culture's various shared sites for and practices of participation and interaction. This investment in shared embodiment, I have argued, also evokes an ethics of shared embodiment. The dissertation has contended that queer, feminist and lesbian pornography's both shared and internal struggles around the figure of safe space call forth an ethics of shared embodiment that can accommodate the film culture's internal pull between affirmation and critique. It evokes an ethics that can harbor both the forward movement of the wave and its undertow.

Throughout the study I have discussed how the shared spaces, concerns and fantasies in this interpretive community involve conflicts and paradoxes that call the figure of safe space into question. I have brought up examples of how participants in this film culture have been subjected to harassment and assault, but also of how disagreements over political and aesthetic strategies were articulated within *Dirty Diaries*, and how decisions to direct and perform in films have been regretted and withdrawn, anonymous and tied to feelings of shame. I have proposed that the collective political fantasy of queer, feminist and lesbian pornography as a safe space, with reference to José Esteban Muñoz and Lisa Duggan, can be understood as a "risky reaching out" and "a politics towards means" rather than towards ends.[23] Drawing on Muñoz's work on queerness as world-making and utopia, I have argued that the political and ethical implications of queer, feminist and lesbian pornography consist in the very act of its "casting pictures of potentiality and possibility."[24] Hence, it is in the very process of imagining safe space, not in achieving it, that queer, feminist and lesbian pornography matters. With reference to Ann Cvetkovich, I have discussed the process of imagining and fantasizing about a safe space for sexual empowerment, not as a matter of leaving difficulties behind, but of acknowledging them as a part of sexuality. Drawing from her work on lesbian sexual public cultures, queer, feminist and lesbian pornography has been understood as "celebrating the hard-won

---

[23] Duggan and Muñoz, 2009, 281.
[24] Muñoz, 2009, 125.

experiences of sexual pleasure."[25] As an activist movement, the current wave of queer, feminist and lesbian pornography explores and politicizes sexuality both as pleasure and danger.

---

[25] Cvetkovich, 4.

# Appendix

## List of *Dirty Diaries* screenings[1]

Bio Rio, September 2009
Stockholm, Sweden

Skiftesföreläsning Malmö högskola, September 2009
Malmö, Sweden

Malmö Queer & Art Film Festival, September 2009
Malmö, Sweden

Ladyfest Zagreb, Vox Feminae, September 2009
Zagreb, Croatia

PornFest Isra-hell, October 2009
Tel-Aviv, Israel

HBTH conference, October 2009
Stockholm, Sweden

Uppsala International Short Film Festival, October 2009
Uppsala, Sweden

Pornfilmfestival Berlin, October 2009
Berlin, Germany

Theatrical release, November 2009
Helsinki, Finland

Cinemateket Stockholm, November 2009

---

[1] Theatrical releases, festivals and other events where all or some of the shorts in the collection have been screened up until 2010-10-31.

Stockholm, Sweden

CPH:dox, November 2009
Copenhagen, Denmark

MIX NYC, November 2009
New York, USA

Festival de Films Gays Lesbiens Trans de Paris, November 2009
Paris, France

Filmidyll, Högkvarteret, November 2009
Stockholm, Sweden

Perv Filmfestival, December 2009
Sydney, Australia

Annual Youth Environmental Congress, December 2009
Hamburg, Germany

Arbetets Museum Norrköping, December 2009
Norrköping, Sweden

London Lesbian & Gay Filmfestival, March 2010
London, UK

Clermont-Ferrand Short Filmfestival, January/February 2010
Clermont-Ferrand, France

Internationales Frauenfilmfestival Dortmund/Köln, April 2010
Dortmund/Köln, Germany

Visions du Reel, Festival International de Cinema, April 2010
Nyon, France

Hamburg International Short Film Festival, June 2010
Hamburg, Germany

Theatrical release France, June 2010
France

Roskilde Music Festival, July 2010
Roskilde, Denmark

Odense International Film Festival, August 2010
Odense, Denmark

Montreal Festival of New Cinema, October 2010
Montreal, Canada

Indie Erotic Filmfest, September 2010
San Francisco, USA

Raindance Festival London, September/October 2010
London, UK

City of Women Festival, October 2010
Ljubljana, Slovenia

Genderbenderfestival, October 2010
Bologna, Italy

Pink Screens Film Festival, October 2010
Brussels, Belgium

Skeive Filmer, October 2010
Oslo, Norway

Queer Film klubb, Högkvarteret October 2010
Stockholm, Sweden

# Questionnaire[2]

*Do you watch lesbian pornography?*

I would be very grateful if you could complete this questionnaire and return it to me in the enclosed envelop.

I am a Ph.D. student conducting research on lesbian pornography at the Department of Cinema Studies, Stockholm University. I am interested in the relation between lesbian pornography and its viewers. Today Porn Studies is a well established and expanding academic field. However, there is still very little research done on lesbian pornography and none on its spectators and consumption. The purpose of this questionnaire is to collect information about consumer habits regarding lesbian pornography. This questionnaire also asks if you would be interested in participating in follow-up interviews for this research project (question 25).

This questionnaire is a pilot to test how the questions work before I conduct a larger survey and make interviews. Information from this questionnaire may be presented in my forthcoming dissertation on lesbian pornography, as well as in related articles and lectures. However, it is important to note that the information from this questionnaire will remain *confidential* and will be presented only *anonymized*.

Check or circle the option(s) that seem(s) most appropriate to you. Feel encouraged to clarify your answers in the commentary space. If you have any questions about this questionnaire or the research project in general, please do not hesitate to contact me.

Thank you very much for your contribution!

Ingrid Ryberg
Stockholm, May 2008

---

[2] Questionnaire run at Club LASH in Stockholm, 2008-05-29. With some slight changes in the information letter, the questionnaire was also run at the Pornfilmfestival Berlin, 2008-10-23. My contact information was provided on each page.

**1. What year are you born?**

**2. How do you define your gender?**

a) Woman
b) Man
c) Intergender
d) Transgender

e) Transsexual MTF
f) Transsexual FTM
g) Other

Comment:

**3. How do you define your sexual identity?**

a) Lesbian
b) Gay male
c) Bisexual
d) Heterosexual

e) Pansexual
f) Queer
g) Asexual
h) Other

Comment:

**4. Where do you live?**

a) In Stockholm
b) In another Swedish city

c) In the countryside
d) Other

Comment:

**5. I have completed the following education:**

a) Compulsory school
b) High school
c) College less than 3 years

d) College more than 3 years
e) Graduate school
f) Other

Comment:

**5. Employment**

a) Full time job
b) Part time job
c) Unemployed

d) Student
e) Other

Comment:

**6. How often do you watch lesbian pornography?**

a) Every day
b) Every week
c) Every month
d) 3-6 times a year
e) 1-2 times a year
f) Less than once a year

Comment:

**7. What kinds of media do you use in order to watch lesbian pornography?**

a) DVD
b) VHS
c) Internet
d) Magazines
e) Other

What?
Comment:

**8. Where do you watch lesbian pornography? Circle Usually, Sometimes, Rarely or Never for the different places.**

a) At Home                     Usually   Sometimes   Rarely   Never
b) At someone else's house     Usually   Sometimes   Rarely   Never
c) In clubs/bars               Usually   Sometimes   Rarely   Never
d) At festivals                Usually   Sometimes   Rarely   Never
e) Other                       Usually   Sometimes   Rarely   Never

Comment:

**9. Do you watch lesbian pornography… Circle Usually, Sometimes, Rarely or Never for the different alternatives.**

a) Alone                Usually   Sometimes   Rarely   Never
b) With another person  Usually   Sometimes   Rarely   Never
c) With other persons   Usually   Sometimes   Rarely   Never

Comment:

**10. Do you have any lesbian pornography at home?**

a) Yes                              b) No

Comment:

**11. How and where do you get hold of lesbian pornography?**

a) I buy        From?
b) I copy       From
c) I download   From?
d) I rent       From?
e) I borrow     From?
f) Other        From?

Comment:

**12. How do you find out about where to get hold of lesbian pornography?**

a) Internet    Example:
b) Magazines   Example:
c) Friends
d) Other       Example:

Comment:

**13. How would you describe the lesbian pornography that you watch?**

a) Made by, with and for lesbians
b) Made by mainstream companies
c) S/M and fetish
d) Trans inclusive
e) Bisexual
f) Other:

Comment:

**14. Please mention some film titles, magazines, webpages, production companies or directors that you watch or use in order to watch lesbian pornography:**

**15. Do you watch lesbian pornography in order to be sexually aroused?**

a) Yes                                      b) No

Comment:

**16. Do you watch lesbian pornography for any other reasons?**

a) Yes                                    b) No

Comment:

**17. If yes – what reasons?**

**18. Do you masturbate while or after watching lesbian pornography?**

a) Always                                 c) Less than half of the times
b) More than half of the times            d) Never

Comment:

**19. Do you have sex while or after watching lesbian pornography?**

a) Always                                 c) Less than half of the times
b) More than half of the times            d) Never

Comment:

**20. How important is it for you to be able to watch lesbian pornography on a regular basis? Please circle.**

5                 4                 3                 2                 1
Very important                                        Not important at all

Comment:

**21. Do you watch any other kind of pornography?**

a) Yes                                    b) No

Comment:

**22. If yes – what kind?**

**23. If yes – how often do you watch this kind of pornography?**

a) More often than I watch lesbian pornography
b) Less often than I watch lesbian pornography
c) Equally often as I watch lesbian pornography

Comment:

**24. Are you interested in participating in interviews for this research project? Note that the interview material will remain confidential and will be presented only anonymized.**

a) Yes                              b) No

**25. If yes – please write down you contact information:**

Name:
Telephone:
Email address:

**26. Other comments on lesbian pornography or on this questionnaire:**

# Sources

## Bibliography

Aghili, Nasim. "Feministisk? porr." *FUL*, 2-4 (2009): 14-31.
Ahmed, Sara. *The Cultural Politics of Emotion*. New York: Routledge, 2004.
Ahmed, Sara. "Affective Economies." *Social Text* 79, 22: 2 (2004): 117-139.
Ahmed, Sara. *Queer Phenomenology: Orientations, Objects, Others*. Durham & London: Duke University Press, 2006.
Alasuutari, Pertti, ed. "Introduction: Three Phases of Reception Studies." In *Rethinking the Media Audience: The New Agenda*. London: SAGE Publications, 1999, 1-21.
Allison, Dorothy. "Public Silence, Private Terror." In *Pleasure and Danger*, edited by Carol S. Vance. London: Pandora Press, 1992, 103-114.
Ambjörnsson, Fanny. *I en klass för sig: Genus, klass och sexualitet bland gymnasietjejer*. Stockholm: Ordfront 2004.
Ambjörnsson, Fanny. *Vad är Queer?* Stockholm: Natur & Kultur, 2006.
Ambjörnsson, Fanny. "En rosa revolution i vardagen: Om femininitet, queera strategier och motstånd." In *Motstånd*, edited by Mona Lilja and Stellan Vinthagen. Malmö: Liber, 2009, 173-195.
Andersson, Mattias. *Porr: En bästsäljande historia*. Stockholm: Pan, 2006[5].
Ang, Ien. *Watching Dallas: Soap Opera and the Melodramatic Imagination*. London: Methuen, 1985.
Armbruster, Ursula, ed. *Kvinnor i alla länder förena er*. Stockholm, 1974.
Arnberg, Klara. *Motsättningarnas marknad: den pornografiska pressens kommersiella genombrott och regleringen av pornografi i Sverige 1950-1980*. Lund: Sekel bokförlag, 2010.
Atkinson, Ti-Grace. "The Institution of Sexual Intercourse." In *Notes from the Second Year*, edited by Shulamith Firestone. New York, 1970.
Attwood, Feona. "Reading Porn: The Paradigm Shift in Pornography Research." *Sexualities*, 5 (2002): 91-105.
Attwood, Feona. "What Do People Do with Porn? Qualitative Research into the Consumption, Use, and Experience of Pornography and Other Sexually Explicit Media." *Sexuality & Culture*, 9:2 (Spring 2005): 65-86.
Attwood, Feona, ed. *Mainstreaming Sex: The Sexualization of Western Culture*. London & New York: I.B. Taurus, 2009.
Attwood, Feona, ed. "Toward the Study of Online Porn Cultures and Practices." In *Porn.com*, New York: Peter Lang Publishing, 2010, 236-244.
Attwood, Feona ed. *Porn.com: Making Sense of Online Pornography*. New York: Peter Lang Publishing, 2010.
Bain, Alison L. and Catherine J. Nash. "Undressing the Researcher: Feminism, Embodiment and Sexuality at a Queer Bathhouse Event." *Area*, 38: 1 (2006): 99-106.

Bankier, Channa, Daniel Bergqvist, Per Båvner, Xenu Cronström, Pye Jacobsson, Lisa Johansson, Lars Jonsson, Nina Lekander, Stig-Björn Ljunggren, Petra Meyer, Oscar Swartz, Jan Söderqvist, Ylva Maria Thompson, Henrik Tornberg, Petra Österberg. *Shocking Lies: sanningar om lögner och fördomar i porrdebatten*. Stockholm: Periskop, 2000.

Bauer, Robin. "Transgressive and Transformative Gendered Sexual Practices and White Privileges: The Case of the Dyke/Trans BDSM Communities." *Women's Studies Quarterly*, 36: 3-4 (2008): 233-253.

Becker, Edith, Michelle Citron, Julia Lesage and B. Ruby Rich. "Introduction to Special Section: Lesbians and Film." *Jump Cut: A Review of Contemporary Media*, 24-25 (March 1981), http://www.ejumpcut.org/archive/onlinessays/JC24-25folder/LesbiansAndFilm.html. Accessed 2011-04-04.

Bell, David. "Pleasure and Danger: The Paradoxical Spaces of Sexual Citizenship." *Political Geography*, 14:2 (1995): 139-153.

Bensinger, Terralee. "Lesbian Pornography: The Re/Making of (a) Community." *Discourse*, 15:1 (1992): 69-93.

Bergsmark, Ester Martin and Sara Kaaman. "Fruitcake," In *Dirty Diaries* DVD booklet, 2009.

Berlant, Lauren and Michael Warner. "Sex in Public." *Critical Inquiry*, 24:2, Intimacy (Winter 1998): 547-566.

Berlant, Lauren. *The Female Complaint: The Unfinished Business of Sentimentality in American Culture*. Durham & London: Duke University Press, 2008.

Berlant, Lauren. *The Queen of America Goes to Washington City: Essays on Sex and Citizenship*. Durham & London: Duke University Press, 1997.

Berlant, Lauren and Elizabeth Freeman. "Queer Nationality." In *The Queen of America Goes to Washington City*, by Lauren Berlant. Durham & London: Duke University Press, 1997. 145-173.

Bersani, Leo. "Is the Rectum a Grave?" *October*, 43, AIDS: Cultural Analysis/Cultural Activism (Winter 1987): 197-222.

Bobo, Jacqueline. *Black Women as Cultural Readers*. New York: Columbia University Press, 1995.

Bonnevier, Katarina. *Behind Straight Curtains: Towards a Queer Feminist Theory of Architecture*. Stockholm: Axl Books, 2007.

Bromseth, Janne and Jenny Sundén. "Queering Internet Studies: Intersections of Gender and Sexuality." In *The Handbook of Internet Studies*, edited by Robert Burnett, Mia Consalvo and Charles Ess. Blackwell Publishing, 2010, 270-299.

Bronstein, Carolyn. *Battling Pornography: The American Feminist Anti-Pornography Movement, 1976-1986*. Cambridge: Cambridge University Press, 2011.

Brooker, Will and Deborah Jermyn, eds. "Reading as Resistance: The Active Audience, Introduction." In *The Audience Studies Reader*. London & New York: Routledge, 2003, 91-93.

Brownmiller, Susan. *Against Our Will: Men, Women and Rape*. New York: Simon & Schuster, 1975.

Butler, Alison. *Women's Cinema: The Contested Screen*. London & New York: Wallflower, 2002.

Butler, Heather. "What Do You Call A Lesbian With Long Fingers? The Development of Lesbian and Dyke Pornography." In *Porn Studies*, edited by Linda Williams. Durham & London: Duke University Press, 2004a, 167-197.

Butler, Judith. "The Force of Fantasy: Feminism, Mapplethorpe, and Discursive Excess [1990]." In *Feminism and Pornography*, edited by Drucilla Cornell. Oxford: Oxford University Press, 2000, 487-508.

Butler, Judith. "The Lesbian Phallus and the Morphological Imaginary [1993]." In *The Judith Butler Reader*, by Judith Butler and Sara Salih. Oxford: Blackwell, 2004, 138-180.

Båvner, Per. "En reproducerad debatt: Svenska ståndpunkter om pornografi." *Res Publica*, 43:1 (1999): 85-103.

Callahan, Vicki, ed. "Reclaiming the Archive: Archeological Explorations toward a Feminism 3.0." In *Reclaiming the Archive: Feminism and Film History*. Detroit, Michigan: Wayne State University Press, 2010, 1-7.

Capino, José B. "Homologies of Space: Text and Spectatorship in All-Male Adult Theaters." *Cinema Journal*, 45: 1 (Fall 2005): 50-65.

Carlbom, Aje and Sara Johnsdotter, eds. *Goda sanningar? Debattklimatet och den kritiska forskningens villkor*. Lund: Nordic Academic Press, 2010.

Carnes, Michelle. "Bend Over Boyfriend: Anal Sex Instructional Videos for Women." In *Pornification: Sex and Sexuality in Media Culture*, edited by Susanna Paasonen, Kaarina Nikunen and Laura Saarenmaa. Oxford, New York: Berg, 2007, 151-160.

Case, Sue Ellen. "Toward a Butch-Femme Aesthetic [1988-89]." In *The Lesbian and Gay Studies Reader*, edited by Henry Abelove, Michèle Aina Barale and David M. Halperin. New York & London: Routledge, 1993, 294-306.

Champagne, John. "'Stop Reading Films!': Film Studies, Close Analysis and Gay Pornography." *Cinema Journal*, 36: 4, (Summer 1997), 76-97.

Citron, Michelle. "Women's Film Production: Going Mainstream." In *Female Spectators: Looking At Film and Television*, edited by Deidre Pribram. London, New York: Verso, 1988, 45-63.

Clover, Carol, ed. "Introduction." In *More Dirty Looks, Women, Pornography, Power*. London: BFI Publishing, 2002.

Cody, Gabrielle. "Introduction: Sacred Bazoombas." In *Hardcore from the Heart: The Pleasures, Profits and Politics of Sex in Performance*, by Annie Sprinkle and Gabrielle Cody. New York: Continuum, 2001, 1-19.

Columpar, Corinn and Sophie Mayer, eds. "Introduction." In *There She Goes: Feminist Filmmaking and Beyond*. Detroit: Wayne State University Press, 2009, 1-15.

Comella, Lynn. "Looking Backward: Barnard and its Legacies." *The Communication Review*, 11:3 (2008): 202-211.

Comella, Lynn and Carol Queen. "The Necessary Revolution: Sex-Positive Feminism in the Post-Barnard Era." *The Communication Review*, 11:3 (2008): 274-291.

Conway, Mary T. "Inhabiting the Phallus: Reading Safe Is Desire." *Camera Obscura*, 13:2 38 (1996), 133-162.

Conway, Mary T. "Spectatorship in Lesbian Porn: The Woman's Woman's Film." *Wide Angle*, 19:3 (July 1997): 91-113.

Cornea, Christine. "Introduction: Interviews in Film and Television Studies." *Cinema Journal*, 47:2 (Winter 2008): 117-123.

Cornell, Drucilla, ed. *Feminism and Pornography*. Oxford: Oxford University Press, 2000.

Cowie, Elizabeth. "Pornography and Fantasy: Psychoanalytic Perspectives." In *Sex Exposed*, edited by Lynne Segal and Mary McIntosh. New Brunswick & New Jersey: Rutgers University Press, 1993, 132-152.

Cvetkovich, Ann. *An Archive of Feelings: Trauma, Sexuality and Lesbian Public Cultures*. Durham & London: Duke University Press, 2003.

Dahl, Ulrika. "Femme on Femme: Reflections on Collaborative Methods and Queer Femme-inist Ethnography." *SQS*, 1 (2011): 1-22.

Davis, Kathy. "Feminist Body/Politics as World Traveller: Translating Our Bodies, Ourselves." *European Journal of Women's Studies*, 9 (2002): 223-247.

Davis, Nick. "The View from the Shortbus, or All Those Fucking Movies." *GLQ*, 14:4 (2008): 623-637.

De Lauretis, Teresa. *Alice Doesn't: Feminism, Semiotics, Cinema*. Bloomington & Indianapolis: Indiana University Press, 1984.

De Lauretis, Teresa. "Rethinking Women's Cinema [1985]." In *Figures of Resistance: Essays in Feminist Theory*, edited by Patricia White. Urbana & Chicago: University of Illinois Press, 2007a, 25-47.

De Lauretis, Teresa. *Technologies of Gender: Essays on Theory, Film, and Fiction*. Bloomington & Indianapolis: Indiana University Press, 1987.

De Lauretis, Teresa. "Guerilla in the Midst: Women's Cinema in the 80s [1989]." In *Queer Screen: A Screen Reader*, edited by Jackie Stacey and Sarah Street. London & New York, 2007b, 21-40.

De Lauretis, Teresa. "Upping the Anti [sic] in Feminist Theory [1990]." in In *Figures of Resistance: Essays in Feminist Theory*, edited by Patricia White. Urbana & Chicago: University of Illinois Press, 2007a, 183-198.

De Lauretis, Teresa. "Film and the Visible." In *How Do I Look? Queer Film and Video*, edited by Bad Object-Choices. Seattle: Bay Press, 1991, 223-264.

De Lauretis, Teresa. *The Practice of Love: Lesbian Sexuality and Perverse Desire*. Bloomington & Indianapolis: Indiana University Press, 1994a.

De Lauretis, Teresa. "Habit Changes [1994b]." In *Figures of Resistance: Essays in Feminist Theory*, edited by Patricia White. Urbana & Chicago: University of Illinois Press, 2007a, 199-216.

De Lauretis, Teresa. "On the Subject of Fantasy." In *Feminisms in the Cinema*, edited by Laura Pietropaolo and Ada Testaferri. Bloomington & Indianapolis: Indiana University Press, 1995, 63-85.

De Lauretis, Teresa. "Popular Culture, Public and Private Fantasies: Femininity and Fetishism in David Cronenberg's M. Butterfly." *Signs: Journal of Women in Culture and Society*, 24: 2 (1999a): 303-324.

De Lauretis, Teresa. "Gender Symptoms, or, Peeing Like a Man." *Social Semiotics*, 9:2 (1999b), 257-270.

De Lauretis, Teresa. "The Intractability of Desire [1999c]." In *Figures of Resistance: Essays in Feminist Theory*, edited by Patricia White. Urbana & Chicago: University of Illinois Press, 2007a, 219-222.

De Lauretis, Teresa. *Freud's Drive: Psychoanalysis, Literature and Film*. New York: Palgrave MacMillan, 2008.

Doane, Mary Ann. "Film and the Masquerade: Theorizing the Female Spectator." *Screen*, 23 3-4 (1982), 74-88.

Doane, Mary Ann, Patricia Mellencamp and Linda Williams, eds. "Feminist Film Criticism: An Introduction." In *Re-vision: Essays in Feminist Film Criticism*. The American Film Institute Monograph Series 3, 1984, 1-17.

Dodson, Betty. *Liberating Masturbation: A Meditation on Self Love*. Bodysex Designs, 1974.

Duggan, Lisa and Nan D. Hunter. *Sex Wars: Sexual Dissent and Political Culture*. New York & London: Routledge, 2006[96].

Duggan, Lisa and José Esteban Muñoz. "Hope and Hopelessness: A Dialogue." *Women & Performance: A Journal of Feminist Theory*, 19:2 (2009): 275-283.

Duncan, Nancy, ed. "Renegotiating Gender and Sexuality in Public and Private Spaces." In *Bodyspace: Destabilizing Geographies of Gender and Sexuality*. New York: Routledge, 1996. 127-145.

Dworkin, Andrea. *Pornography: Men Possessing Women*. London: Women's Press, 1981.

Dyer, Richard with Julianne Pidduck. "Lesbian/Woman: Lesbian Cultural Feminist Film." In *Now You See It: Studies in Lesbian and Gay Film*. London & New York: Routledge, Second Edition, 2003[90], 169-200.

Dyer, Richard. "Idol Thoughts: Orgasm and Self-Reflexivity in Gay Pornography [1994]." In *More Dirty Looks: Gender, Pornography and Power*, edited by Pamela Church Gibson. London: BFI, 2004, 102-109.

Edelman, Lee. *No Future: Queer Theory and the Death Drive*. Durham: Duke University Press, 2004.

Edelman, Lee. "Unbecoming: Pornography and the Queer Event." In *PostPornPolitics*, edited by Tim Stüttgen. Berlin: B-Books, 2009, 194-211.

Engberg, Mia. "What is feminist porn?" In *Dirty Diaries* DVD booklet, 2009.

Ekman, Kajsa Ekis. *Varat och varan: Prostitution, surrogatmödraskap och den delade människan*. Stockholm: Leopard, 2010.

Ellis, Kate, Nan D. Hunter, Beth Jaker, Barbara O'Dair and Abby Tallmer, ed. *Caught Looking: Feminism, Pornography, and Censorship*. New York, 1986.

Feinberg, Leslie. *Stone Butch Blues*. Ithaca, N.Y.: Firebrand Books, 1993.

Findlay, Heather. "Freud's 'Fetishism' and the Lesbian Dildo Debates." In *Out In Culture: Gay, Lesbian, and Queer Essays on Popular Culture*, edited by Corey K. Creekmur and Alexander Doty. London: Cassell, 1995, 328-342.

Firestone, Shulamith. *The Dialectic of Sex: The Case for Feminist Revolution*. New York: Morrow, 1970.

Fish, Stanley Eugene. *Is There a Text in This Class? The Authority of Interpretive Communities*. Cambridge, Massachusetts & London, England: Harvard University Press, 1980.

Fiske, John. *Television Culture*. London: Methuen & Co. Ltd, 1987.

Forskningsetiska principer inom humanistisk-samhällsvetenskaplig forskning (Vetenskapsrådet, 1990)

Fraser, Mariam and Nirmal Puwar, "Introduction: Intimacy in Research." *History of the Human Sciences*, 21:4 (2008): 1-16.

Fraser, Nancy. "Rethinking the Public Sphere: A Contribution to the Critique of Actually Existing Democracy." *Social Text*, 25-26 (1990): 56-80.

Fraser, Suzanne. "Poetic World-Making: Queer as Folk, Counterpublic Speech and the 'Reader'." *Sexualities*, 9 (2006): 152-170.

Freeman, Elizabeth. *Time Binds: Queer Temporalities, Queer Histories*. Durham & London: Duke University Press, 2010.

Friedan, Betty. *The Feminine Mystique*. New York: Norton, 1963.

Förråande pornografiska filmer – en översyn av 4 § lagen (1990:886) om granskning och kontroll av filmer och videogram, PM av hovrättslagmannen Mats Melin, DS 2001:5

Gaines, Jane M. "Women and Representation: Can We Enjoy Alternative Pleasure?" In *Issues in Feminist Film Criticism*, edited by Patricia Erens. Bloomington: Indiana University Press, 1990, 75-92.

Gaines, Jane M. "Political Mimesis." In *Collecting Visible Evidence*, edited by Jane M. Gaines and Michael Renov. Minneapolis: University of Minnesota Press, 1999, 84-102.

Gerhard, Jane. *Desiring Revolution: Second-wave Feminism and the Rewriting of American Sexual Thought, 1920 to 1982*. New York: Columbia University Press, 2001.

Gibson, Pamela Church, ed. *More Dirty Looks: Gender, Pornography and Power*. London: BFI Publishing, 2004.

Gorna, Robin. "Delightful Visions: From anti-porn to eroticizing safer sex." In *Sex Exposed*, edited by Lynne Segal and Mary McIntosh. New Brunswick & New Jersey: Rutgers University Press, 1993, 169-183.

Grosz, Elizabeth. *Chaos, Territory, Art: Deleuze and the Framing of the Earth*. New York: Columbia University Press, 2008.

Grosz, Elizabeth. "Lesbian Fetishism?" *differences*, 3 (Summer 1991), 39-54.

Gunning, Tom. "The Cinema of Attractions: Early Film, Its Spectator and the Avant-Garde." *Wide Angle*, 8:3-4 (1986), 1-14.

Gustafsson, Tommy and Mariah Larsson. "Porren inför lagen. Två fallstudier angående den officiella attityden till offentligt visad pornografisk film 1921 och 1971." *Historisk tidskrift*, 123:3 (2009): 445-465.

Halberstam, Judith. In a *Queer Time and Place: Transgender Bodies, Subcultural Lives*. New York: New York University Press, 2005.

Halberstam, Judith. "The Anti-Social Turn in Queer Studies." *Graduate Journal of Social Science*, 5:2 (2008): 140-156.

Hall, Stuart. "Encoding/Decoding." In *Culture, Media, Language: Working Papers in Cultural Studies, 1972-79*, edited by Stuart Hall, Dorothy Hobson, Andrew Lowe and Paul Willis. London & New York: Routledge, 2005 [1980], 117- 127.

Hallgren, Hanna. *När lesbiska blev kvinnor – När kvinnor blev lesbiska. Lesbiskfeministiska kvinnors diskursproduktion rörande kön, sexualitet, kropp och identitet under 1970- och 1980-talen i Sverige*. Göteborg: Kabusa böcker, 2008.

Hammer, Barbara. *Hammer! Making Movies Out of Sex and Life*. New York City: The Feminist Press, 2010.

Hammers, Corie. "An Examination of Lesbian/Queer Bathhouse Culture and the Social Organization of (Im)Personal Sex." *Journal of Contemporary Ethnography*, 38:3 (2009): 308-335.

Hankin, Kelly. *The Girls in the Back Room: Looking at the Lesbian Bar*. Minneapolis & London: University of Minnesota Press, 2002.

Hankin, Kelly. "And Introducing...The Female Director: Documentaries about Women Filmmakers as Feminist Activism." *NWSA Journal*, 19:1 (Spring 2007): 59-88.

Hansen, Christian, Catherine Needham and Bill Nichols. "Pornography, Ethnography, and the Discourse of Power." In *Representing Reality*, edited by Bill Nichols. Bloomington & Indianapolis: Indiana University Press, 1991, 201-228.

Hansen, Miriam. *Babel and Babylon: Spectatorship in American Silent Film*. Cambridge, Massachusetts & London, England: Harvard University Press, 1991.

Hansen, Miriam. "Early Cinema, Late Cinema: Transformations of the Public Sphere [1993]." In *Viewing Positions*, edited by Linda Williams. New Brunswick, New Jersey: Rutgers University Press, 1997, 134-152.

Hansen, Miriam. "Benjamin and Cinema: Not a One Way Street." *Critical Inquiry*, 25:2 (1999): 306-343.

Haraway, Donna. "Situated Knowledges: The Science Question in Feminism and the Privilege of Partial Perspective." *Feminist Studies*, 14:3 (Autumn, 1988): 575-599.

Harbord, Janet. *Film Cultures*. London, Thousand Oaks, California & New Delhi: Sage Publications, 2002.

Haskell, Molly. *From Reverence to Rape: The Treatment of Women in the Movies.* New York: Holt, Rinehart and Winston, 1974.

Hedling, Erik. "Breaking the Swedish Sex Barrier: Painful Lustfulness in Ingmar Bergman's The Silence." *Film International*, 6:6 (2008): 17-27.

Hemmings, Clare. "Telling Feminist Stories." *Feminist Theory*, 6 (2005): 115-139.

Henderson, Lisa. "Lesbian Pornography: Cultural Transgression and Sexual Demystification." In *New Lesbian Criticism: Literary and Cultural Readings*, edited by Sally Munt. New York: Columbia University Press, 1992, 173-191.

Henderson Lisa. "Simple Pleasures: Lesbian Community and Go Fish." *Signs: Journal of Women in Culture and Society*, 25:1 (1999): 37-64.

Henderson, Lisa. "Queer Relay." *GLQ*, 14:4 (2008a): 569-597.

Henderson, Lisa. "Slow Love." *The Communication Review*, 11 (2008b): 219-224.

Herzog, Amy. "In the Flesh: Space and Embodiment in the Pornographic Peep Show Arcade." *The Velvet Light Trap*, 62 (Fall 2009): 29-43.

Hirdman, Anja. *Den ensamma fallosen*. Stockholm: Atlas, 2008.

Hite, Shere. *The Hite Rapport: A Nationwide Study of Female Sexuality*. New York: Dell, 1976.

Hollinger, Karen. "Theorizing Mainstream Female Spectatorship: The Case of the Popular Lesbian Film." *Cinema Journal*, 37:2 (Winter 1998): 3-17.

hooks, bell. "The Oppositional Gaze: Black Female Spectators." In *Reel to Real: Race, Sex and Class at the Movies*. New York & London: Routledge, 1996, 197-213.

hooks, bell. *Ain't I a Woman: Black Women and Feminism*. Boston: South End Press, 1981.

Hubbard, Phil. "Sex Zones: Intimacy, Citizenship and Public Space." *Sexualities*, 4:1 (2001): 51-71.

Hull, Gloria T., Patricia Bell Scott and Barbara Smith. *All the Women Are White, All the Blacks Are Men, but Some of Us Are Brave: Black Women's Studies*. New York: The Feminist Press, 1982.

Hunter, Nan D. "Contextualizing the Sexuality Debates: A Chronology 1966-2005." In *Sex Wars: Sexual Dissent and Political Culture*, edited by Lisa Duggan and Nan D. Hunter. New York & London: Routledge, 2006, 15-28.

Isaksson, Emma. *Kvinnokamp: synen på underordning och motstånd i den nya kvinnorörelsen*. Stockholm: Bokförlaget Atlas, 2007.

Jacobs, Katrien. "'The Lady of the Little Death': Illuminated Encounters and Erotic Duties in the Life and Art of Maria Beatty." *Wide Angle*, 19:3 (1997): 13-40.

Jacobs, Katrien, Marije Janssen and Matteo Pasquinelli, eds. *C'lickme: A Netporn Studies Reader*. Amsterdam: Institute of Network Cultures, 2007.

Jancovich, Marc, Lucy Faire and Sarah Stubbings, eds. "From Spectatorship to Film Consumption." In *The Place of the Audience: Cultural Geographies of Film Consumption*. London: BFI Publishing, 2003, 3-15.

Johnson, Eithne. "Loving Yourself: The Specular Scene in Sexual Self-Help Advice for Women." In *Collecting Visible Evidence*, edited by Jane M. Gaines and Michael Renov. Minneapolis & London: University of Minnesota Press, 1999, 216-240.

Johnson, Eithne. "Excess and Ecstacy: Constructing Female Pleasure in Porn Movies." *The Velvet Light Trap*, 32 (Fall 1993): 30-49.

Johnston, Claire. "Women's Cinema as Counter-Cinema [1973]." In *Feminist Film Theory: A Reader*, edited by Sue Thornham. Edinburgh: Edinburgh University Press, 1999, 31-40.

Johnston, Claire. "The Subject of Feminist Film Theory/Practice." *Screen*, 21: 2 (Summer 1980): 27-34.

Jong, Erica. Fear of Flying (1973).
Juffer, Jane. *At Home with Pornography: Women, Sex, and Everyday Life*. New York & London: New York University Press, 1998.
Juhasz, Alexandra. "They Said We Were Trying to Show Reality – All I Want to Show Is My Video: The Politics of the Realist Feminist Documentary." In *Collecting Visible Evidence*, edited by Jane M. Gaines and Michael Renov. Minneapolis & London: University of Minnesota Press, 1999, 190-215.
Juhasz, Alexandra, ed. *Women of Vision: Histories in Feminist Film and Video*. Minneapolis: University of Minnesota Press, 2001.
Juhasz, Alexandra. "No Woman Is an Object: Realizing the Feminist Collaborative Video." *Camera Obscura* 54, 18: 3 (2003): 71-98.
Juhasz, Alexandra. "The Future Was Then: Reinvesting in Feminist Media Practice and Politics." *Camera Obscura* 61, 21: 1 (2006): 53.
Kaplan, E. Ann. "Women's Happytime Commune: New Departures in Women's Films." *Jump Cut: A Review of Contemporary Media*, 9 (1975), http://www.ejumpcut.org/archive/onlinessays/JC09folder/WomensHappytmCom.html. Accessed 2011-11-16.
Kendrick, Walter. *The Secret Museum: Pornography in Modern Culture*. Berkeley & Los Angeles, California: University of California Press, 1987.
Kipnis, Laura. *Bound and Gagged: Pornography and the Politics of Fantasy in America*. Durham & London: Duke University Press, 1999.
Kirkham, Pat and Beverley Skeggs. "Pornographies, Pleasures, and Pedagogies in U.K. and U.S." *Jump Cut*, 40 (March 1996): 106-113.
Kleinhans, Chuck. "The Change from Film to Video Pornography: Implications for Analysis." In *Pornography, Film and Culture*, edited by Peter Lehman. New Brunswick, New Jersey & London: Rutgers University Press, 2006, 154-167.
Koed, Anne. "The Myth of the Vaginal Orgasm." In *Notes From the First Years*, edited by Shulamith Firestone. New York, 1968.
Koivunen, Anu. "Confessions of a Free Woman: Telling Feminist Stories in Postfeminist Media Culture." *Journal of Aesthetics & Culture*, 1 (2009), http://www.aestheticsandculture.net/index.php/jac/article/view/4644. Accessed 2011-11-17.
Koivunen, Anu. "An Affective Turn? Reimagining the Subject of Feminist Theory." In *Working with Affect in Feminist Readings*, edited by Marianne Liljeström and Susanna Paasonen. New York: Routledge, 2010, 8-28.
Kuhn, Annette. *Women's Pictures: Feminism and Cinema*. London & New York: Verso, Second Edition, 1994[82].
Kuhn, Annette. *Family Secrets: Acts of Memory and Imagination*. London & New York: Verso, 1995.
Kuhn, Annette. *An Everyday Magic: Cinema and Cultural Memory*. London & New York: I.B. Tauris, 2002.
Kulick, Don. "Introduction: The Sexual Life of Anthropologists: Erotic Subjectivity and Ethnographic Work." In *Taboo: Sex, Identity and Erotic Subjectivity in Anthropological Fieldwork*, edited by Don Kulick and Margaret Wilson. London & New York: Routledge, 1995, 1-28.
Kulick, Don, ed. "Introduction." In *Queersverige*. Stockholm: Natur & Kultur, 2005a, 11-19.
Kulick, Don. "Four Hundred Thousand Swedish Perverts." *GLQ: A Journal of Lesbian and Gay Studies*, 11:2 (2005b): 205-235.
Larsson, Mariah "Drömmen om den goda pornografin: Om sextio- och sjuttiotalsfilmen och gränsen mellan konst och pornografi." *Tidskift för genusvetenskap*, 1:2 (2007): 93-107.

Larsson, Mariah. "Contested Pleasures." In *Swedish Film: An Introduction and Reader*, edited by Mariah Larsson and Anders Marklund. Lund: Nordic Academic Press, 2010, 205-214.

Lederer, Laura, ed. *Take Back the Night: Women on Pornography*. New York: William Morrow, 1980.

Lehman, Peter, ed. "Introduction: 'A Dirty Little Secret' – Why Teach and Study Pornography?" In *Pornography, Film and Culture*. New Brunswick, New Jersey & London: Rutgers University Press, 2006, 1-21.

Lehman, Peter. "Revelations About Pornography." In *Pornography, Film and Culture*. New Brunswick, New Jersey & London: Rutgers University Press, 2006, 87-98.

Lehman, Peter, ed. *Pornography, Film and Culture*. New Brunswick, New Jersey & London: Rutgers University Press, 2006.

Lennerhed, Lena. *Frihet att njuta: sexualdebatten i Sverige på 1960-talet*. Stockholm: Norstedts, 1994.

Livingstone, Sonia. "The Challenge of Changing Audiences: Or, What Is the Audience Researcher to Do in the Age of the Internet." *European Journal of Communication*, 19:1 (2004): 75-86.

Loach, Loretta. "Bad Girls: Women Who Use Pornography." In *Sex Exposed*, edited by Lynne Segal and Mary McIntosh. New Brunswick & New Jersey: Rutgers University Press, 1993, 266-274.

Loist, Skadi. "Precarious Cultural Work: About the Organization of (Queer) Film Festivals." *Screen*, 52:2 (2011): 268-273.

Love, Heather. "Rethinking Sex: Introduction." *GLQ: A Journal of Lesbian and Gay Studies*, 17:1 (2011): 1-14.

Love, Heather. "The GLQ Archive: Diary of a Conference on Sexuality, 1982." *GLQ*, 17:1 (2011): 49-50.

Lundgren, Anna Sofia. *Tre år i G. Perspektiv på kropp och kön i skolan*. Eslöv: Symposion, 2000.

MacCormack, Patricia. *Cinesexuality*. Aldershot, Hampshire: Ashgate, 2008.

MacDonald, Scott. "Confessions of a Feminist Porn Watcher." *Film Quarterly*, 36: 3 (Spring 1983), 10-17.

McDonald, Scott, Anne Severson and Yvonne Rainer. "Two Interviews: Demystifying the Female Body: Anne Severson 'Near the Big Chakra.' Yvonne Rainer: 'Privilege'." *Film Quarterly*, 45:1 (Autumn 1991): 18-32.

MacKinnon, Katharine A. "Only Words [1993]." In *Feminism and Pornography*, edited by Drucilla Cornell. Oxford: Oxford University Press, 2000, 94-120.

Magnusson, Elin. "Skin." In *Dirty Diaries* DVD booklet, 2009.

Malm. Rasmus. "Slaget om porren." *Ottar*, 2 (2008): 50-55.

Marks, Laura U. *The Skin of the Film: Intercultural Cinema, Embodiment, and the Senses*. Durham: Duke University Press, 2000.

Marks, Laura U. *Touch, Sensuous Theory and Multisensory Media*. Minneapolis & London: University of Minnesota Press, 2002.

Massumi, Brian. *Parables for the Virtual: Movement, Affect, Sensation*. Durham & London: Duke University Press, 2002.

Mayer, Vicki. "Guys Gone Wild." *Cinema Journal*, 47: 2 (2008): 97-116.

Mayer, Vicki, Miranda J. Banks and John Thornton Caldwell, eds. *Production Studies, Cultural Studies of Media Industries*. New York: Routledge 2009.

Mayne, Judith. *Cinema and Spectatorship*. London & New York: Routledge, 1993.

Mayne, Judith. "Paradoxes of Spectatorship." In *Viewing Positions: Ways of Seeing Film* edited by Linda Williams. New Brunswick, New Jersey: Rutgers University Press, 1997.

McCabe, Janet. *Feminist Film Studies: Writing the Woman into Cinema*. London & New York: Wallflower, 2004.

McDowell, Linda. "City Life and Difference." In *Unsettling Cities*, edited by John Allen, Doreen Massey and Michael Pryke. London: Routledge, 1999, 143-160.

McNair, Brian. *Striptease Culture: Sex, Media and the Democratization of Desire*. London & New York: Routledge, 2002.

McRobbie, Angela. *Feminism and Youth Culture*. London: Macmillan Press Ltd, 1991.

McRobbie, Angela. *The Aftermath of Feminism: Gender, Culture and Social Change*. London: SAGE, 2009.

McRobbie, Angela. "Pornographic Permutations." *The Communication Review*, 11 (2008), 225-236.

Metz, Christian. *The Imaginary Signifier: Psychoanalysis and the Cinema*, translated by Celia Britton et al. Bloomington: Indiana University Press, 1986[77].

Millet, Kate. *Sexual Politics*. Garden City N.Y., 1970.

Moorman, Jennifer. "Gay for Pay, Gay For(e)play: The Politics of Taxonomy and Authenticity in LGBTQ Online Porn." In *Porn.com: Making Sense of Online Pornography*, edited by Feona Attwood. New York: Peter Lang Publishing, 2010, 155-170.

Moraga, Cherríe and Gloria Anzaldúa, eds. *This Bridge Called My Back: Writings by Radical Women of Color*. Persephone Press, 1981.

Moraga, Cherríe. *Loving in the War Years: Lo Que Nunca Pasó Por Sus Labios*. Boston: South End Press, 1983.

Mulvey, Laura. "Visual Pleasure and Narrative Cinema." *Screen*, 16:3 (1975): 6-18.

Munford, Rebecca. "BUST-ing the Third Wave: Barbies, Blowjobs and Girlie Feminism." In *Mainstreaming Sex: The Sexualization of Western Culture*, edited by Feona Attwood. London & New York: I.B.Tauris, 2009, 183-198.

Muñoz, José Esteban. *Disidentifications: Queers of Color and the Performance of Politics*. Minneapolis, London: University of Minnesota Press 1999.

Muñoz, José Esteban. *Cruising Utopia: The Then and There of Queer Futurity*. New York: New York University Press, 2009.

Mühleisen, Wenke. "Mainstream Sexualization and the Potential for Nordic New Feminism." *NORA – Nordic Journal of Women's Studies*, 15:2-3 (2007): 172-189.

Mårtens, Tora. "Red Like Cherry." In *Dirty Diaries* DVD booklet, 2009.

Nash, Catherine Jean and Alison Bain. "'Reclaiming Raunch'? Spatializing Queer Identities at Toronto Women's Bathhouse Events." *Social & Cultural Geography*, 8:1 (2007): 47-62.

Nestle, Joan. *A Restricted Country*. Ithaca, N.Y.: Firebrand Books, 1987.

Nichols, Bill. "The Ethnographer's Tale." In *Visualising Theory: Selected Essays from V.A.R., 1990-1994*, edited by Lucien Taylor. New York: Routledge, 1994, 60-83.

Nikunen, Kaarina. "Cosmo Girls Talk: Blurring Boundaries of Porn and Sex." In *Pornification: Sex and Sexuality in Media Culture*, edited by Susanna Paasonen, Kaarina Nikunen and Laura Saarenmaa. Oxford, New York: Berg, 2007, 73-85.

O'Connell Davidson, Julia. "If No Means No, Does Yes Mean Yes? Consenting to Research Intimacies." *History of the Human Sciences*, 21: 4 (2008): 49-67.

*Our Bodies, Ourselves: A Book By and For Women by The Boston Women's Health Book Collective*. New York: Simon and Schuster 1973[71].

Paasonen, Susanna, Kaarina Nikunen and Laura Saarenmaa, ed. "Pornification and the Education of Desire." In *Pornification: Sex and Sexuality in Media Culture*. Oxford, New York: Berg, 2007, 1-20.

Nikunen, Kaatarina, Susanna Paasonen and Laura Saarenmaa, eds. *Pornification, Sex and Sexuality in Media Culture*. Oxford & New York: Berg, 2007.

Paasonen, Susanna. "Disturbing, Fleshy Texts: Close Looking at Pornography." In *Working with Affect in Feminst Readings: Disturbing Differences*, edited by Marianne Liljeström and Susanna Paasonen. London and New York: Routledge, 2010, 58-71.

Paasonen, Susanna. "Strange Bedfellows, Pornography, Affect and Feminist Reading." *Feminist Theory*, 8 (2007): 43-57.

Paasonen, Susanna. "Labors of Love: Netporn, Web 2.0 and the Meanings of Amateurism." *New Media and Society*, 12 (2010): 1297-1312.

Parisi, Luciana and Tiziana Terranova. "A Matter of Affect: Digital Images and the Cybernetic Re-Writing of Vision." *Parallax*, 7: 4 (2001), 122-127.

Pearce, Lynne. *Feminism and the Politics of Reading*. London, New York, Sydney & Aukland: Arnold, 1997.

Pearce, Lynne. *The Rhetorics of Feminism: Readings in Contemporary Cultural Theory and the Popular Press*. London & New York: Routledge, 2004.

Phelan, Peggy. *Unmarked: The Politics of Performance*. London and New York: Routledge, 1993.

Pidduck, Julianne. "New Queer Cinema and Experimental Video." In *New Queer Cinema: A Critical Reader*, edited by Michele Aron. Edinburgh: Edinburgh University Press, 2004, 80-97.

Preciado, Beatriz. *Manifiesto Contra-sexual*. Opera Prima, 2002.

Probyn, Elspeth. *Sexing the Self, Gendered Positions in Cultural Studies*. London & New York: Routledge, 1993.

Queen, Carol. "Sex Radical Politics, Sex-Positive Feminist Thought, and Whore Stigma." In *Whores and Other Feminists*, edited by Jill Nagle. New York & London: Routledge, 1997, 125-137.

Rabinovitz, Lauren. *Points of Resistance: Women, Power & Politics in the New York Avant-garde Cinema, 1943-71*. Urbana & Chicago: University of Illinois Press, 1991.

Radway, Janice. *Reading the Romance: Women, Patriarchy and Popular Literature*. Chapel Hill, NC, & London: Univeristy of North Carolina Press, 1984a.

Radway, Janice. "Interpretive Communities and Variable Literacies: The Functions of Romance Reading." *Daedalus*, 113:3 (Summer 1984b): 49-73.

Rainsford, Jennifer. "For the Liberation of Men." In *Dirty Diaries* DVD booklet, 2009.

Reich, June L. "Genderfuck: The Law of the Dildo [1992]." In *Camp: Queer Aesthetics and the Performing Subject: A Reader*, edited by Fabio Cleto. Edinburgh: Edinburgh University Press, 1999, 254-265.

Rich, B. Ruby. *Chick Flicks: Theories and Memories of the Feminist Film Movement*. Durham, North Carolina: Duke University Press, 1998.

Rhyne, Ragan. "Hard-core Shopping: Educating Consumption in SIR Video Production's Lesbian Porn." *The Velvet Light Trap*, 59 (Spring 2007): 42-50.

Rodgerson, Gillian. "Lesbian Erotic Explorations." In *Sex Exposed: Sexuality and the Pornography Debate*, edited by Lynne Segal and Mary McIntosh. New Brunswick, New Jersey: Rutgers University Press, 1993, 275-279.

Rooke, Alison. "Queer in the Field: On Emotions, Temporality, and Performativity in Ethnography." *Journal of Lesbian Studies*, 13 (2009): 149-160.

Rosen, Marjorie. *Popcorn Venus: Women, Movies & the American Dream.* New York: Coward, 1973.
Rosenberg, Tiina. *Queerfeministisk agenda.* Stockholm: Bokförlaget Atlas, 2002.
Rosenberg, Tiina. "Varför så rädda för sex?" *Arena,* 3 (2003): 15-17.
Rosenberg, Tiina. *L-ordet: Vart tog alla lesbiska vägen?* Stockholm: Normal förlag, 2006.
Ross, Becki L. "'It's Merely Designed for Sexual Arousal': Interrogating the Indefensibility of Lesbian Smut[1997]." In *Feminism and Pornography,* edited by Drucilla Cornell. Oxford: Oxford University Press, 2000, 264-317.
Royalle, Candida. "Porn in the USA." In *Feminism and Pornography,* edited by Drucilla Cornell. Oxford: Oxford University Press, 2000, 540-550.
Rubin Gayle. "Thinking Sex: Notes for a Radical Theory of the Politics of Sexuality." In *Pleasure and Danger: Exploring Female Sexuality,* edited by Carol S. Vance. London: Pandora Press, 1992[84], 267-319.
Russell, Diana E. "Pornography and Rape: A Causal Model [1988]." In *Feminism and Pornography,* edited by Drucilla Cornell. Oxford: Oxford University Press, 2000, 48-93.
Ryberg, Ingrid. "Tant eller queer?" In *Femkamp: Bang om nordisk feminism,* edited by Gunilla Edemo and Ulrika Westerlund. Stockholm: Bang Förlag, 2004, 397-409.
Ryberg, Ingrid. "Röra upp." *Kom ut,* 7 (2007): 20-21.
Ryberg, Ingrid. "Tips från pornografen." *FLM: En kulturtidskrift om film,* 5 (2009), 16-17.
Ryberg, Ingrid. "Flattaktik." *FLM: En kulturtidskrift om film,* 9/10 (2010), 16-17.
Ryberg, Marjorie. "Maximizing Visibility." *Film International,* 6:6 (2008), 72-79.
Ryberg, Ingrid. "Phone Fuck." In *Dirty Diaries* DVD booklet, 2009.
Rytel, Joanna. "Flasher Girl On Tour." In *Dirty Diaries* dvd-booklet, 2009.
Sarrimo, Christine. *När det personliga blev politiskt.* Stockholm/Stehag: Brutus Östlings Bokförlag Symposion, 2000.
Scharf, Laura. *National Organization for Women (NOW).* New York City, 1974, New York Chapter, Conference Proceedings, Women's Sexuality Conference: To Explore, Define and Celebrate Our Own Sexuality.
Sedgwick, Eve Kosofsky. "Paranoid Reading and Reparative Reading, Or, You're so Paranoid, You Probably Think This Essay Is About You." In *Touching Feeling: Affect, Pedagogy, Performativity.* Durham: Duke University Press, 2003, 123-151.
Segal, Lynne and Mary McIntosh, ed. *Sex Exposed.* New Brunswick & New Jersey: Rutgers University Press, 1993.
Sjöholm, Carina. *Gå på bio: Rum för drömmar i folkhemmets Sverige.* Stockholm/Stehag: Brutus Östlings Bokförlag Symposion, 2003.
Skeggs, Beverley. "Matter Out of Place: Visibility and Sexualities in Leisure Spaces." *Leisure Studies,* 18 (1999): 213-232.
Skeggs, Bev, Nancy Thumim and Helen Wood. "'Oh Goodness, I Am Watching Reality TV': How Methods Make Class in Audience Research." *European Journal of Cultural Studies,* 11:1 (2008): 5-24.
Smyth, Cherry. "The Pleasure Threshold: Looking at Lesbian Pornography on Film." *Feminist Review,* 34 (1990): 152-159.
Sobchack, Vivian. *Carnal Thoughts, Embodiment and Moving Image Culture.* Berkeley & Los Angeles: University of California Press, 2004.
Sobchack, Vivian. *The Address of the Eye: A Phenomenology of Film Experience.* Princeton, New Jersey: Princeton University Press, 1992.

Sowards Stacey K. and Valerie R. Renegar. "The Rhetorical Functions of Consciousness-raising in Third Wave Feminism." *Communication Studies*, 55:4 (Winter 2004), 535-552.

Spigel, Lynn. "Theorizing the Bachelorette: 'Waves' of Feminist Media Studies." *Signs: Journal of Women in Culture and Society*, 30:1 (2004), 1209-1221.

Stacey, Jackie. "Desperately Seeking Difference." *Screen*, 28:1 (Winter 1987), 48-61.

Stacey, Jackie. *Star Gazing: Hollywood Cinema and Female Spectatorship*. London & New York: Routledge, 1994.

Staiger, Janet. *Interpreting Films: Studies in the Historical Reception of American Cinema*. Princeton, New Jersey: Princeton University Press, 1992.

Staiger, Janet. "Fans and Fan Behavior," in *Media Reception Studies*. New York & London: New York University Press, 2005, 95-114.

Stein, Arlene. "The Year of the Lustful Lesbian." In *Shameless: Sexual Dissidence in American Culture*. New York & London: New York University Press, 2006, 39-58.

Straayer, Chris. *Deviant Eyes, Deviant Bodies: Sexual Re-orientation in Film and Video*. New York: Columbia University Press, 1996.

Stüttgen, Tim, ed. *PostPornPolitics*. Berlin: B-Books, 2009.

Svensson, Ingeborg. *Liket i garderoben: En studie av sexualitet, livsstil och begravning*. Stockholm: Normal, 2003.

Turner, Graeme, ed. "Editor's Introduction." In *The Film Cultures Reader*. London & New York: Routledge, 2002, 1-10.

Ullén, Magnus. *Bara för dig: Pornografi, konsumtion, berättande*. Stockholm/Sala: Vertigo förlag, 2009.

Vance, Carol S., ed. "More Danger, More Pleasure: A Decade After the Barnard Sexuality Conference." In *Pleasure and Danger: Exploring Female Sexuality*. London: Pandora Press, 1992[84], xvi-xxi.

Vance, Carol S., ed. *Pleasure and Danger: Exploring Female Sexuality*. London: Pandora Press, 1992[84].

Wallace, Lee. *Lesbianism, Cinema, Space: The Sexual Life of Apartments*. New York & London: Routledge, 2009.

Wallenberg, Louise. "Transgressive Drag Kings Defying Dildoed Dykes: A Look at Contemporary Swedish Queer Film." In *Queer Cinema in Europe*, edited by Robin Griffiths. Bristol: Intellect, 2008, 207-227.

Warner, Michael. "Publics and counterpublics." *Public Culture*, 14:1 (Winter 2002a): 49-90.

Warner, Michael. "Introduction." In *Publics and Counterpublics*. New York: Zone Books, 2002b, 7-20.

White, Patricia. "Lesbian Cinephilia." In *UnInvited: Classical Hollywood Cinema and Lesbian Representability*. Bloomington & Indianapolis: Indiana University Press, 1999a, 29-60.

White, Patricia, B. Ruby Rich, Eric O. Clarke and Richard Fung. "Queer Publicity, A Dossier on Lesbian and Gay Film Festivals." *GLQ*, 5:1 (1999b): 73-93.

White, Patricia, ed. "Introduction: Thinking Feminist." In *Figures of Resistance: Essays in Feminist Theory*. Urbana & Chicago: University of Illinois Press, 2007, 1-22.

White, Patricia. "Feminist Commitment and Feminized Service: Nonprofits and Journals." *Cinema Journal*, 49: 3 (Spring 2010): 99-103.

Williams, Linda. "Film Bodies: Gender, Genre and Excess." Film Quarterly, 44:4 (1991): 2-13.

Williams, Linda, ed. "Introduction." In *Viewing Positions: Ways of Seeing Film*. New Brunswick, New Jersey: Rutgers University Press, 1997, 1-20.

Williams, Linda. "Pornographies On/scene, or Diff'rent Strokes for Diff'rent Folks." In *Sex Exposed*, edited by Lynne Segal and Mary McIntosh. New Brunswick & New Jersey: Rutgers University Press, 1993, 233-265.

Williams, Linda. *Hard Core: Power, Pleasure and the "Frenzy of The Visible"*. Berkeley, Los Angeles & London: University of California Press, Expanded Paperback Edition, 1999[89].

Williams, Linda, ed. *Porn Studies*. Durham & London: Duke University Press, 2004a.

Williams, Linda, ed. "Porn Studies: Proliferating Pornographies On/Scene: An Introduction," in *Porn Studies*. Durham & London: Duke University Press, 2004a. 1-23.

Williams, Linda. "Second Thoughts on Hard-Core: American Obscenity Law and the Scapegoating of Deviance[1993]." In *More Dirty Looks: Gender, Pornography and Power*, edited by Pamela Church Gibson. London: BFI Publishing, 2004b, 165-175.

Williams, Linda. *Screening Sex*. Durham & London: Duke University Press, 2008.

Wilton, Tamsin, ed. "Introduction: On invisibility and mortality." In *Immortal, Invisible: Lesbians and the Moving Image*. London & New York: Routledge, 1995, 1-19.

Witt-Brattström, Ebba. *Å alla kära systrar!* Stockholm: Norstedts, 2010.

Wolf Madame, "On Your Back Woman." In *Dirty Diaries* DVD booklet, 2009.

Wood, Helen. *Talking With Television: Women, Talk Shows and Modern Self-Reflexivity*. Urbana & Chicago: University of Illinois Press, 2009.

Young, Iris Marion. "Unruly Categories: A Critique of Nancy Fraser's Dual Systems Theory." *New Left Review*, 1/222 (March-April 1997), http://www.newleftreview.org/?page=artivle&view=1899. Accessed 2010-08-25.

Young, Iris Marion. *On Female Body Experience: "Throwing Like a Girl" and Other Essays*. Oxford: Oxford University Press, 2005.

Östberg, Marit. "Nu kör vi!" *Ottar*, 3 (2009): 20-23.

Östberg, Marit. "Hjälteporr," *Kom ut*, 3 (2009), 45.

Östberg, Marit. "Authority." In *Dirty Diaries* DVD booklet, 2009.

Östergren, Petra. "Kvinnorummets gränser." *Bang*, 2 (1998): 54-55.

Östergren, Petra. *Porr, horor och feminister*. Stockholm: Natur och Kultur, 2006.

## Newspapers articles

A.P. "Porno Au Féminin." *Libération*, 2010-06-30.

Bergsmark, Ester Martin. "Rätt att skattebetalarna finansierar våra porrfilmer." *Newsmill*, 2009-08-27, http://www.newsmill.se/artikel/2009/08/27/r-tt-att-skattebetalarna-finansierar-v-ra-porrfilmer. Accessed 2011-11-12.

Böhlin, Lars. "Inte ens feministisk porr känns lovande." *Västerbottens dagblad*, 2009-09-04, http://www.folkbladet.nu/154385/2009/09/04/inte-ens-feministisk-porr-kanns-lovande. Accessed 2011-06-06.

Carnmo, Camilla. "Dirty Diaries." *Smålandsposten*, 2009-09-04. http://smp.se/noje_o_kultur/film/dirty-diaries(1504761).gm. Accessed 2009-09-08.

Curman, Sofia and Maria Ringborg. "Porr för feminister?" *DN.se Kultur&Nöje*, 2009-08-28, http://www.dn.se/kultur-noje/film-tv/porr-for-feminister-1.940378. Accessed 2010-06-17.

Fagerström, Linda. "Subversivt på sängkanten." *Helsingborgs Dagblad*, 2009-09-03, http://hd.se/kultur/2009/09/03/subversivt-paa-saengkanten/. Acessed 2011-05-17.

Fredriksson, Beatrice. "Taxpayers should not have to fund feminist porn." *The Local*, 2009-09-03, http://www.thelocal.se/21870/20090903/. Accessed 2011-09-14.

Frey, Anna. "Intervju med Mia Engberg: 'Feministisk porr vill skaka om.'" *Dagens Nyheter*, 2009-07-25, http://www.dn.se/kultur-noje/film-tv/intervju-med-mia-engberg-feministisk-porr-vill-skaka-om. Accessed 2011-11-10.

Heberlein, Ann. "Ge oss bra porr – för båda könen." *Aftonbladet*, 2004-05-13, http://www.aftonbladet.se/debatt/article210841.ab. Accessed 2009-03-16.

Kvarnkullen, Tomas. "Våldsporren i tv ska bort." *Aftonbladet*, 2000-02-14, http://wwwc.aftonbladet.se/nyheter/0002/14/porr.html. Accessed 2009-03-16.

Malm, Rasmus. "Ett annat sätt att berätta om lusta." *Göteborgsposten*, 2009-09-03, http://www.gp.se/kulturnoje/1.16170-rasmus-malm-ett-annat-satt-att-beratta-om-lusta. Accessed 2009-09-11.

Marklund, Annika. "Dirty Diaries är som hederlig hemmaporr." *Aftonbladet*, 2009-09-11.
http://www.aftonbladet.se/nyheter/kolumnister/annikamarklund/article5774851.ab?service=print. Accessed 2010-06-21.

Mårtenson, Mary. "'Jag är så trött på gubbporren'." *Aftonbladet*, 2001-11-28, http://www.aftonbladet.se/vss/kvinna/story/0,2789,109691,00.html. Accessed 2006-06-09.

Rouyer, Philippe. "Dirty Diaries." *Premiere*, June 2010.

Sandberg, Elin. "Mer provokation än erotik i feministisk porrfilm." *Tidningen Kulturen*, 2009-09-05,
http://www.tidningenkulturen.se/artiklar/film/filmkritik/4990-film-dvddirty-diaries-12-short-stories-of-feminist-porn-prod-mia-engberg. Accessed 2011-11-11.

S.D. "Dirty Diaries." *Cahiers du Cinema*, June 2010.

T.S. "Dirty Diaries." *Le Monde*, 2010-06-30.

TT Spektra, "Filminstitutet förklarar porrfilmen." In *Dagens Nyheter* 090922, *Göteborgs Posten* 090922, *Svenska Dagbladet* 090922, *Smålandsposten* 090922, *Upsala Nya Tidning* 090922 and *Helsingborgs Dagblad* 090922.

Östberg, Marit. "Vi behöver fler kåta kvinnor i offentligheten." *Newsmill*, 2009-08-27, http://www.newsmill.se/artikel/2009/08/27/vi-behover-fler-kata-kvinnor-i-offentligheten?page=1. Accessed 2010-06-21.

Östberg, Marit. "Rätt att ge skattepengar till feministisk porr." *Aftonbladet*, 2009-09-05, http://www.aftonbladet.se/debatt/debattamnen/samhalle/article5741067.ab. Accessed 2009-09-08.

# Blogs

Mad Kate, "27 July 2009." The blog The Queer X Show, 2009-08-03. http://queerxshow.wordpress.com/2009/08/03/27-july-2009/. Accessed 2010-03-13.

Munthe, Emma Gray. "Dirty Diaries – bra eller anus?" The blog Weird Science, 2009-09-14, http://www.weirdscience.se/?p=6269. Accessed 2011-11-11.

## Websites

"About Befem," BeFem website, http://www.befem.org/. Accessed 2011-11-08,

"And the winners are…" 6. Pornfilmfestival Berlin website, http://www.pornfilmfestivalberlin.de/pffb_2011/en/?p=4682. Accessed 2011-11-08).

Brüning, Jürgen et al. "What is the difference between pornography and art? ART IS MORE EXPANSIVE!" Pornfilmfestival Berlin 2006 website, http://www.pornfilmfestivalberlin.de/archiv/background.html. Accessed 2011-02-12.

"Community Action Center and Beyond." Konsthall C website, http://www.konsthallc.se/index.php?q=Community+Action+. Accessed 2011-11-21.

"Dirty Diaries: Twelve Shorts of Feminist Porn." Dirty Diaries website, http://www.dirtydiaries.se/. Accessed 2011-10-13.

"Dirty Diaries." Svensk Filmdatabas, http://www.sfi.se/sv/svensk-film/Filmdatabasen/?type=MOVIE&itemid=66210&ref=%2ftemplates%2fSwedishFilmSearchResult.aspx%3fid%3d1225%26epslanguage%3dsv%26searchword%3ddirty+diaries%26type%3dMovieTitle%26match%3dBegin%26page%3d1. Accessed 2009-05-09.

"Feministischer Pornofilmpreis Europa." Feminist Porn Awards Europe website, http://www.poryes.de/index.php?option=com_content&view=article&id=34&Itemid=138ontent&view=article&id=34&Itemid=138. Accessed 2011-11-07.

"Hamburg International Short Film Festival." Hamburg International Short Film Festival website, http://festival.shortfilm.com/index.php?id=festivalnews&L=1. Accessed 2011-10-21.

Ingo & The Fukk Crew X, "Klub Fukk – The End." Klubb Fukk website, http://woteverworld.com/2010/11/klub-fukk-the-end/. Accessed 2011-11-17.

Joy, Petra. "Sensuality, Creativity and Respect/Humor/Inspiration." Petra Joy website, http://www.petrajoy.com/vision.asp. Accessed 2011-11-18.

Kinney, Nan. "About." Fatale Media website, http://www.fatalemedia.com/about.html. Accessed 2008-04-04.

"Marit Östberg." Feminists in Space website, http://warehouse9.dk/fis/?page_id=44. Accessed 2011-11-08.

"Moviemento." Moviemento website, http://www.moviemento.de/. Accessed 2011-10-10.

"Om Njutafilms." Njutafilms website, http://www.njutafilms.nu/. Accessed 2011-11-19.

"Paris Porn Film Fest." Paris Porn Film Fest website, http://parispornfilmfest.com. Accessed 2010-08-03.

"Queer Porn TV." Queer Porn TV website, http://queerporn.tv. Accessed 2011-11-10.

"Selma & Sofie," Sexyfilm website, www.sexyfilm.se. Accessed 2006-06-09.

Sundahl, Deborah. "Fatale Media Newsletter August 2005." Fatale Media website, http://www.fatalemedia.com/newsletter/082005.html. Accessed 2011-11-18.

"The Crash Pad Series." The Crash Pad Series website,
   http://www.crashpadseries.com. Accessed 2011-11-10.
"The Feminist Porn Awards." The Feminist Porn Awards website,
   http://goodforher.com/feminist_porn_awards. Accessed 2011-11-15.
"Trans Entities," Morty Diamond website,
   http://www.mortydiamond.com/video/trans-entities/. Accessed 2011-11-20.
"6.PornfilmfestivalBerlin." Pornfilmfestival Berlin website,
   http://www.pornfilmfestivalberlin.de/pffb_2011/en/. Accessed 2011-11-15.

## Facebook pages

Fatale Media. https://www.facebook.com/#!/FataleMedia. Accessed 2011-11-15.
Pornfilmfestival Berlin. Published 2011-10-31.
   https://www.facebook.com/pages/Pornfilmfestival-Berlin/259816320725799.
   Accessed 2011-11-07.
The Queer X Show. Published 2010-03-02.
   https://www.facebook.com/note.php?note_id=334096238387&id=119867167658&ref=mf. Accessed 2011-11-15.
Too Much Pussy. Published 2010-03-02.
   http://www.facebook.com/?ref=logo#!/note.php?note_id=334096238387&id=119867167658&ref=mf. Accessed 2010-03-09.

## Films

*After School Special* (Fatale Media, 2001)
*Airport* (Silke Dunkhorst & Manuela Kay, 1994)
*A Hole in My Heart* (*Ett hål i mitt hjärta*, Lukas Moodysson, 2004)
*Baise-Moi* (Virginie Despentes, 2000)
*Bathroom Sluts* (Fatale Media, 1991)
*Belladonna's Fucking Girls Part 3* (Belladonna, 2006)
*Bend Over Boyfriend 2* (SIR Video, 1999)
*Bitch & Butch* (Mia Engberg, 2002)
*Black Widow* (Bob Rafelson, 1987)
*Body Contact* (Pella Kågerman, 2009)
*Clips* (Fatale Media, 1988)
*Come Together* (Mia Engberg, 2009)
*Comedy In Six Unnatural Acts* (Jan Oxenberg, 1975)
*Community Action Center* (A.K. Burns and AL Steiner, 2010)
*Crash Pad, The* (Shine Louise Houston, 2005)
*Deep Throat* (Gerard Damiano, 1972)
*Destricted* (Marina Abramovic, Matthew Barney, Marco Brambilla, Larry Clark, Gaspar Noé, Richard Prince, Sam Taylor-Wood, 2006)
*Dildoman* (Åsa Sandzén, 2009)
*Dirty Diaries* (Mia Engberg, 2009)
*Dragkingdom of Sweden* (Åsa Ekman & Ingrid Ryberg, 2002)
*Dyketactics* (Barbara Hammer, 1974)
*Erotic In Nature* (Tigress Productions, 1985)
*Female Ejaculation: The Workshop* (Deborah Sundahl, 2008)
*Female Fist* (Kajsa Dahlberg, 2006)

*Flasher Girl on Tour* (Joanna Rytel, 2009)
*Flossie* (Mac Ahlberg, 1975)
*For the Liberation of Men* (Jennifer Rainsford, 2009)
*Fruitcake* (Ester Martin Bergsmark & Sara Kaaman, 2009)
*Fuses* (Carolee Schneemann, 1965)
*Hard Love & How to Fuck in High Heels* (Shar Rednour and Jackie Strano, 2002)
*Gang Bang Barbie* (Joanna Rytel, 2010)
*Home Movie* (Jan Oxenberg, 1972)
*How to Female Ejaculate* (Deborah Sundahl, 1992)
*I Am Curious Yellow* (*Jag är nyfiken gul*, Vilgot Sjöman, 1967)
*In Search of the Wild Kingdom* (Shine Louise Houston, 2007)
*Mann & Frau & Animal* (Valie Export, 1973)
*Menses* (Barbara Hammer, 1974)
*Mommy Is Coming* (Cheryl Dunye, 2012)
*Much More Pussy* (Emilie Jouvet, 2010)
*Multiple Orgasm* (Barbara Hammer, 1976)
*Near the Big Chakra* (Ann Severson, 1972)
*Night Games* (*Nattlek*, Mai Zetterling, 1966)
*Night Time* (Nelli Roselli, 2009)
*On Your Back Woman!* (Wolf Madame, 2009)
*One Night Stand* (Emilie Jouvet, 2006)
*Owls, The* (Cheryl Dunye, 2010)
*Pansexual Public Porn* (Del La Grace Volcano, 1998)
*Phineas Slipped* (Keri Oakie, 2003)
*Phone Fuck* (Ingrid Ryberg, 2009)
*Piano, The* (Jane Campion, 1993)
*Pornographlics* (Dirty Pillows Inc, 2003)
*Post man Always Rings Twice, The* (Bob Rafelson, 1981)
*Pretty Baby* (Louis Malle, 1978)
*Red Like Cherry* (Tora Mårtens, 2009)
*Romance* (Catherine Breillat, 1999)
*Safe Is Desire* (Fatale Media, 1991)
*Selma & Sofie* (Mia Engberg, 2002)
*Share* (Marit Östberg, 2010)
*Shocking Truth* (Alexa Wolf, 2000)
*Shortbus* (John Cameron Mitchell, 2006)
*Silence, The* (*Tystnaden*, Ingmar Bergman, 1963)
*Sisterhood* (Marit Östberg, 2011)
*Skin* (Elin Magnusson, 2009)
*Special Delivery* (Carolyn Caizzi, 2007)
*Suburban Dykes* (Fatale Media, 1990)
*Summer With Monica* (*Sommaren med Monika*, Ingmar Bergman, 1953)
*Swedish Marriage Manual* (*Ur kärlekens språk*, Torgny Wickman, 1969)
*Tampopo* (Juzo Itami, 1986)
*Three Daughters* (Candida Royalle, 1986)
*Trans Entities: The Nasty Love of Papi and Wil* (Morty Diamond, 2006)
*Too Much Pussy: Feminist Sluts in the Queer X Show* (Emilie Jouvet, 2010)
*Uniform* (Marit Östberg, 2008)
*Virgin Spring, The* (*Jungfrukällan*, Ingmar Bergman, 1960)
*Watermelon Woman, The* (Cheryl Dunye, 1996)
*Women I Love* (Barbara Hammer, 1976)
*Women of Vision* (Alexandra Juhasz, 1998)

*491* (Vilgot Sjöman, 1964)

## Television

*The Tonight Show*. 10 September 2009, NBC.
*Evolution of Erotica, The*. Episode 3 in television mini-series documentary *Lesbian Sex and Sexuality* (Katherine Linton, 2007).

## Art installations and performances

*Dinner Table, The* (Judy Chicago, 1979)
*Cut Piece* (Yoko Ono, 1965)
*Genital Panik* (Valie Export, 1968)
*Post Porn Modernist* (Annie Sprinkle, 1989-)
*Queer X Show, The* (Mad·Kate, Judy Minx, Wendy Delorme, Sadie Lune, DJ Metzgerei, Madison Young, Emilie Jouvet, 2009)

## Other sources

A.K. Burns and AL Steiner in artist conversation with Marit Östberg, Konsthall C, Stockholm, 2011-06-09.
Chat log from Skiftesföreläsning at Malmö högskola, 2009-09-07. Received by email from project coordinator Evelina Mildner Lindén, 2009-10-06.
Email conversation with friend in Berlin, February 2011.
Frenkel, Cissi Elwin. Letter written to Lena Adelsohn Liljeroth 17 September 2009, received 21 September 2009.
LASH newsletter, "LASH-info maj 2008." Received by email 2008-05-26.
*On Our Backs,* years 1984-1987.
"Queers Read This." Queer Nation Manifesto, 1990. Published in Tiina Rosenberg's *Queerfeministisk agenda*. Stockholm: Bokförlaget Atlas, 2002, 167-178.
Royalle, Candida. Presentation Pornfilmfestival Berlin, 2009-10-22.
Åman, Kajsa. Panel discussion at Stockholm Pride Festival, 2006-08-04.

## Interviews

2008-08-11, Marit Östberg, Skype
2008-09-01, Marit Östberg, Berlin
2008-09-19 Mia Engberg, Stockholm
2008-10-22, Marit Östberg, Berlin
2008-10-24, Laura Méritt, Berlin
2008-10-25, Anonymous research subject, Berlin
2008-10-25, Emilie Jouvet, Berlin
2008-10-26, Iris Segundo, Berlin
2008-10-26, Manuela Kay, Berlin
2008-10-27, Flora Schanda, Berlin
2008-10-27, Marije Janssen, Berlin

2008-11-04, Jennifer, Stockholm
2008-11-06, Chris, Stockholm
2008-11-11, Chris and Jennifer, Stockholm
2008-11-25, Helene Delilah and anonymous research subject, Stockholm
2008-11-25, Rosa Danner, Skype
2009-02-26, Marit Östberg, Stockholm
2009-10-23, Shine Louise Houston, Berlin
2009-10-24, Marit Östberg, Berlin
2010-01-25, Mia Engberg, Stockholm
2010-06-05, Marit Östberg, Hamburg
2010-06-11, Barbara Hammer, Stockholm
2010-09-28, Marit Östberg, Stockholm
2011-06-09, Marit Östberg, Stockholm

## Participant observation

2008-05-29 Club LASH

Pornfilmfestival Berlin
October 2008
October 2009
October 2010

*Dirty Diaries* meetings
2008-06-12
2008-09-18
2008-12-16
2009-03-10
2009-08-25
2010-01-14

*Dirty Diaries* screenings
Bio Rio, Stockholm, September 2009
Malmö University, September 2009
Malmö Queer Art & Film Festival, September 2009
HBTH conference in Stockholm, October 2009
Uppsala International Short Film Festival, October 2009
Pornfilmfestival Berlin in October 2009
The Cinematheque in Stockholm, November 2009
FilmIdyll in Stockholm, November 2009
Hamburg International Short Film Festival, June 2010

# Index

access, 32, 59, 61, 66, 70, 102, 114, 117, 118, 119, 123, 126, 133, 139, 145, 146, 147, 154, 175

affirmation and critique, 26, 42, 43, 75, 81, 85, 88, 92, 93, 96, 104, 106, 112, 115, 194, 195

Ahmed, Sara, 30, 32, 40, 43, 109, 133, 142, 145, 146, 158, 164, 165, 170, 187, 193

anti-porn feminism, 20, 21, 22, 23, 24, 26, 81, 89, 90, 91, 92, 93, 94, 95, 99, 162

Attwood, Feona, 15, 29, 35, 36, 62, 63, 64, 124, 144, 168, 169, 191

authenticity, 27, 49, 53, 61, 63, 73, 74, 84, 103, 104, 105, 111, 119, 131, 176, 177

*Authority*, 18, 56, 80, 89, 95, 110, 111, 121, 126, 135, 137, 182

Barbara Hammer, 17, 57, 60, 75, 84, 90, 186

Barnard Conference, 17, 23, 75, 76, 91, 92

BDSM, 15, 17, 23, 24, 52, 58, 70, 80, 89, 94, 111, 116, 117, 118, 148, 153, 161, 176, 183, 191

Bensinger, Terralee, 27, 36, 50, 93, 94, 106, 168, 184

Bergsmark, Ester Martin, 27, 28, 56, 77, 100, 170, 171, 184

Berlant, Lauren, 29, 34, 109, 120, 121, 123, 136, 137, 140, 144, 194

Bersani, Leo, 30, 183, 184

*Bitch & Butch*, 21, 56, 73, 79, 80, 100, 104

Bobo, Jacqueline, 18, 31, 33, 34, 35, 48, 49, 61, 65, 121, 190

*Body Contact*, 25, 56, 108, 130, 169

Butler, Judith, 15, 24, 26, 27, 50, 90, 93, 94, 99, 105, 106, 116, 157, 162, 163

Candida Royalle, 23, 24, 36, 54, 57, 84, 92, 95, 96, 97, 109, 120

carnal identification, 43, 149, 150, 153, 154, 168, 192

Club LASH, 18, 36, 42, 43, 51, 52, 54, 58, 59, 60, 70, 113, 115, 117, 118, 119, 139, 140, 158, 177, 178, 190, 191

collective political fantasy, 43, 163, 165, 168, 182

*Come Together*, 56, 100, 101, 102, 103, 105, 110, 122, 169, 174

Comella, Lynn, 17, 75, 82, 84, 91, 92, 93, 99, 194

consciousness-raising, 17, 56, 78, 80, 81, 84, 85, 88, 89, 91, 93, 99, 110, 123, 124, 134, 139, 158, 160, 165, 177, 182, 187, 194

consent, 71, 77, 79, 80, 117, 118, 158, 163, 192

Conway, Mary T., 24, 90, 93, 94, 152

counter public, 34, 65, 112, 115, 121, 122, 126, 133, 134, 135, 139, 142, 194

cultural feminism, 23, 26, 75, 90, 91, 93
Cvetkovich, Ann, 30, 40, 41, 43, 48, 94, 144, 146, 170, 177, 182, 183, 184, 185, 195, 196
De Lauretis, Teresa, 25, 26, 33, 37, 39, 40, 41, 43, 75, 81, 85, 88, 94, 103, 104, 106, 142, 144, 145, 146, 147, 154, 155, 156, 157, 158, 159, 161, 162, 164, 168, 185, 192, 193, 194
desire, 23, 29, 38, 39, 53, 67, 69, 83, 92, 96, 97, 105, 116, 121, 140, 143, 149, 152, 156, 157, 158, 159, 161, 167, 168, 170, 172, 176, 193
digital, 174, 175, 177
*Dildoman*, 25, 56, 108, 121, 130, 223
*Dirty Diaries*, 13, 14, 18, 19, 20, 22, 24, 25, 26, 27, 28, 29, 30, 36, 42, 43, 45, 46, 47, 49, 51, 54, 55, 56, 63, 64, 65, 69, 71, 73, 74, 76, 77, 78, 79, 80, 81, 83, 85, 86, 87, 88, 89, 96, 98, 100, 101, 102, 107, 108, 110, 111, 114, 121, 123, 124, 125, 126, 127, 130, 131, 132, 133, 134, 135, 136, 137, 139, 147, 152, 153, 160, 163, 167, 168, 169, 170, 171, 172, 173, 174, 184, 185, 186, 189, 190, 191, 192, 193, 194, 195
disorientation, 146, 147, 164
documentary, 21, 26, 47, 48, 54, 73, 74, 79, 100, 102, 103, 104, 105, 111, 126, 127, 160, 176, 177, 179, 189, 194
Duggan, Lisa, 16, 23, 24, 92, 184, 195
Dworkin, Andrea, 23, 91, 162, 183
Dyer, Richard, 84, 105, 177

embodied spectatorship, 37, 38, 39, 40, 43, 61, 62, 141, 142, 168, 192
Emilie Jouvet, 14, 54, 57, 60, 79, 80, 83, 95, 123, 135, 141, 148, 174, 178
empowerment, 14, 17, 19, 21, 31, 34, 37, 40, 42, 43, 59, 61, 73, 74, 75, 81, 99, 106, 114, 118, 120, 121, 123, 136, 140, 142, 147, 165, 168, 182, 184, 187, 190, 192, 193, 194, 195
erotica, 15, 17, 26, 53, 80, 89, 126, 157
ethnographic fieldwork, 18, 32, 42, 47, 49, 51, 56, 62, 64, 71, 113, 167, 191, 192, 194, 195
Fanon, Frantz, 146
fantasy, 39, 41, 42, 43, 53, 69, 74, 76, 103, 106, 110, 111, 120, 142, 144, 154, 155, 156, 157, 159, 161, 162, 163, 164, 165, 167, 168, 173, 179, 182, 184, 185, 187, 190, 192, 193, 195
Fatale Media, 16, 24, 36, 57, 90, 92, 93, 94, 95, 99, 105, 110, 111, 152
female ejaculation, 95
Femme Productions, 16, 23, 92, 97, 110, 153
Fish, Stanley, 18, 31, 61, 65, 116
*Flasher Girl On Tour*, 25, 56, 107, 108, 169
*For the Liberation of Men*, 56, 172, 173
Freeman, Elizabeth, 30, 40, 41, 76, 89, 106, 109, 120, 121, 123, 161, 168, 183, 184, 190, 193
*Fruitcake*, 56, 100, 130, 170, 171, 172, 184
*Fuses*, 90, 96, 172
Gaines, Jane, 25, 95, 106, 126, 161, 178

genital display, 26, 96, 99, 100

Gerhard, Jane, 17, 22, 23, 36, 75, 78, 81, 82, 84, 85, 86, 87, 90, 91, 92, 194

habituation, 38, 43, 143, 144, 148, 152, 158, 169, 192

Halberstam, Judith, 30, 41, 48, 70, 75, 76, 109, 111, 177, 183

Hallgren, Hanna, 17, 21, 22, 23, 81, 82, 84, 90, 91, 104

Hansen, Miriam, 32, 33, 34, 63, 66, 67, 105, 114, 120, 123, 127, 132, 134, 142, 143, 177, 178, 191

haptic, 43, 172, 173, 174, 178, 179, 195

Haraway, Donna, 49, 65, 191, 212

*Hard Love*, 57, 68, 69, 192, 224

Helena Lindblom, 13, 64

Hemmings, Clare, 40, 41, 51, 76, 88, 106, 194

heterogeneity, 26, 27, 51, 96, 105, 170, 194

identification, 34, 50, 60, 120, 147, 149, 150, 153, 156, 157, 158, 159, 162, 176, 179, 183, 193, 194

implicated reading, 38, 61, 67, 145, 146

indexicality, 43, 169, 175, 176, 177, 179, 195

interpretive community, 18, 19, 22, 27, 30, 31, 32, 33, 34, 35, 37, 39, 42, 43, 45, 47, 49, 50, 51, 59, 60, 61, 62, 63, 65, 66, 70, 74, 76, 86, 106, 112, 114, 118, 120, 131, 135, 139, 142, 143, 147, 163, 165, 167, 168, 170, 178, 180, 181, 185, 190, 191, 192, 194, 195

intimate public, 34, 115, 120, 134, 135, 139, 142, 194

Johnson, Eithne, 95, 98, 99, 178

Juffer, Jane, 17, 32, 50, 61, 62, 66, 82, 84, 99, 110, 114, 117, 119, 126, 127, 139, 144, 145, 153, 157, 160, 191

Kay, Manuela, 53, 54, 60, 99, 152, 163

Kuhn, Annette, 18, 26, 35, 76, 104, 106

Kulick, Don, 20, 22, 28, 29, 46, 67, 74

Larsson, Mariah, 15, 20, 21, 22, 23, 29, 130, 132

London Lesbian and Gay Film Festival, 137, 146, 165, 182

male gaze, 102, 103, 147

Marit Östberg, 56, 60, 79, 80, 89, 95, 110, 111, 121, 134, 135, 136, 137, 138, 139, 140, 146, 158, 163, 165, 180, 182, 185, 186, 187, 189

Marks, Laura U., 43, 96, 169, 170, 172, 173, 174, 175, 176, 177, 178, 179, 182, 185, 195

maximum visibility, 36, 97, 99, 100, 106

McNair, Brian, 15, 29, 216

Mia Engberg, 13, 21, 24, 26, 45, 46, 47, 56, 59, 60, 64, 73, 74, 75, 76, 77, 78, 79, 87, 88, 89, 90, 98, 100, 101, 102, 103, 104, 111, 122, 125, 126, 133, 147, 160, 163, 169

*Much More Pussy*, 55, 57, 67, 83, 123, 124, 141, 142, 143, 144, 148, 154, 164, 165, 191

Mulvey, Laura, 25, 33, 102, 103

Muñoz, José Esteban, 40, 41, 43, 106, 170, 184, 185, 186, 187, 195

Mühleisen, Wencke, 20, 74, 124, 133, 134

*Night Time*, 56, 130, 171

Njutafilms, 14, 46, 126, 222

Nordic new feminism, 20, 74, 124

NOW, 76, 81, 82, 91, 218
*Off Our Backs*, 89, 90, 91
*On Our Backs*, 23, 57, 89, 90, 92, 93, 116
*On Your Back Woman!*, 56, 86, 88, 94, 111
*One Night Stand*, 57, 80, 95, 105, 135, 147, 148, 149, 153, 174, 177, 178
*Our Bodies, Ourselves*, 23, 82, 83, 84, 85
Paasonen, Susanna, 15, 16, 18, 35, 36, 37, 38, 40, 62, 66, 67, 68, 124, 153, 174, 176, 191
Pearce, Lynne, 18, 31, 50, 61, 65, 67, 86, 170, 190, 194
*Phone Fuck*, 13, 18, 54, 55, 56, 64, 68, 69, 79, 110, 132, 167, 168, 169, 170, 192
porn studies, 35, 36, 50, 152, 191
Pornfilmfestival Berlin, The, 15, 18, 36, 42, 51, 53, 54, 56, 57, 58, 59, 60, 64, 67, 79, 80, 97, 99, 113, 119, 123, 127, 139, 141, 143, 145, 148, 152, 153, 163, 176, 177, 178, 179, 189, 190, 191
Probyn, Elspeth, 61, 65
Queen, Carol, 34, 57, 75, 84, 91, 92, 93, 99, 109, 121
queer feminism, 20, 46, 74
Queer Nation, 123, 142, 164
recognition, 34, 61, 115, 116, 120, 135, 136, 139, 142, 149, 158, 194
*Red Like Cherry*, 56, 96, 172, 216
Rhyne, Ragan, 24, 34, 69, 95, 99, 105, 116, 152, 153
Rich, B. Ruby, 48, 49, 78, 90, 91, 103, 104, 123
S/M, 18, 51, 91, 93, 113, 161, 179, 183, 190
*Safe is Desire*, 99, 100, 110, 152

safe space, 19, 31, 34, 41, 42, 43, 61, 66, 73, 75, 80, 92, 106, 111, 114, 118, 120, 121, 127, 133, 140, 164, 165, 170, 182, 184, 185, 187, 190, 191, 192, 194, 195
safer sex, 79, 93, 99, 110, 118
Sandström, Helena, 65
scientia sexualis, 36, 106, 178
*Selma & Sofie*, 21, 45, 47, 56, 73, 80, 100, 104, 125
sex radicalism, 16, 23, 24, 26, 62, 75, 89, 90, 93, 95, 123, 141
Sex Wars, 16, 17, 22, 23, 24, 35, 36, 41, 75, 85, 88, 89, 90, 92, 94, 109, 183, 193
sexpert tradition, 54, 96, 99, 143, 178
sexualization, 15, 19, 27, 28, 29, 30, 36, 60, 61, 108, 124, 133, 134, 138, 139
*Share*, 56, 135, 136, 180, 182, 183, 184, 186, 188, 189
shared embodiment, 19, 43, 165, 167, 170, 171, 176, 178, 179, 182, 185, 195
Shine Louise Houston, 14, 54, 57, 60, 64, 95, 110, 177
*Shocking Truth*, 21
SIR Video, 24, 36, 57, 68, 95, 99, 153
site of struggle, 31, 86, 112, 170, 190, 194
situated knowledge, 49
*Skin*, 56, 98, 111, 130, 177
Smyth, Cherry, 24, 36, 50, 94, 95, 116
Sobchack, Vivian, 32, 37, 38, 39, 40, 43, 65, 109, 142, 147, 149, 150, 154, 158, 167, 168, 169, 175, 177, 192
Sprinkle, Annie, 15, 36, 57, 59, 84, 92, 99, 117

Stacey, Jackie, 32, 35, 61, 72, 78, 103, 157
Straayer, Chris, 15, 17, 36, 75, 90, 93, 94, 95, 104, 105, 117, 157, 194
subjectivity, 39, 40, 63, 67, 97, 109, 115, 120, 145, 149, 155, 159, 162, 193
*Suburban Dykes*, 57, 93, 99, 100, 110
Swedish Film Institute, The, 13, 14, 20, 21, 27, 28, 45, 126, 130, 131, 133
technology, 39, 43, 69, 102, 104, 110, 143, 146, 155, 168, 169, 171, 174, 175, 177
*The Queer X Show*, 57, 83, 84, 85, 123, 141, 160
theater experience, 63, 67, 142, 164
third wave feminism, 20, 74, 87, 88
Tigress Productions, 36, 57, 90, 92, 93, 157
*Too Much Pussy*
 *Feminist Sluts in the Queer X Show*, 57, 83, 84, 123, 124, 141, 160, 164
*Trans Entities*

*The Nasty Love of Papi and Wil*, 57, 105, 111, 148, 149, 153, 176, 177, 178, 183, 184
trauma, 144, 146, 180, 182, 183, 184, 185, 188
unsafety, 43, 142, 146, 164, 165, 185, 191
utopia, 170, 180, 184, 185, 195
Wallace, Lee, 109, 110, 111
Warner, Michael, 29, 34, 109, 122, 123, 136, 194
Williams, Linda, 15, 16, 18, 23, 24, 33, 35, 36, 37, 38, 39, 40, 43, 48, 61, 67, 68, 78, 84, 91, 92, 93, 95, 96, 97, 99, 103, 104, 109, 111, 116, 117, 120, 123, 126, 130, 142, 143, 148, 149, 153, 158, 159, 161, 162, 169, 174, 188, 192
women's cinema, 25, 75, 79, 100, 105, 106, 194
world-making, 41, 185, 186, 195
voyeurism, 102, 152
vulnerability, 38, 68, 144, 182, 184, 185
Young, Iris Marion, 14, 34, 54, 57, 83, 122, 144, 145
Östergren, Petra, 21

Stockholm Cinema Studies
Published by Stockholm University
Editor: Astrid Söderbergh Widding

1. **Karl Hansson**, *Det figurala och den rörliga bilden – Om estetik, materialitet och medieteknologi hos Jean Epstein, Bill Viola och Artintact* (*The Figural and the Moving Image – On Aesthetics, Materiality and Media Technology in the Work of Jean Epstein, Bill Viola and "Artintact"*) (Stockholm, 2006): 214 pp.
2. **Eirik Frisvold Hanssen**, *Early Discourses on Colour and Cinema: Origins, Functions, Meanings* (Stockholm, 2006): 208 pp.
3. **Therése Andersson**, *Beauty Box – Filmstjärnor och skönhetskultur i det tidiga 1900-talets Sverige* (*Beauty Box – Film Stars and Beauty Culture in Early Twentieth-Century Sweden*) (Stockholm, 2006): 200 pp.
4. **Anna Sofia Rossholm**, *Reproducing Languages. Translating Bodies: Approaches to Speech, Translation and Identity in Early European Sound Film* (Stockholm, 2006): 214 pp.
5. **Åsa Jernudd**, *Filmkultur och nöjesliv i Örebro 1897-1908* (*Movies and Entertainment in Örebro 1897-1908*) (Stockholm, 2007): 204 pp.
6. **Henrik Gustafsson**, *Out of Site: Landscape and Cultural Reflexivity in New Hollywood Cinema 1969-1974* (Stockholm, 2007): 228 pp.
7. **Vreni Hockenjos**, *Picturing Dissolving Views: August Strindberg and the Visual Media of His Age* (Stockholm, 2007): 250 pp.
8. **Malena Janson**, *Bio för barnet bästa?: Svensk barnfilm som fostran och fritidsnöje under 60 år* (*Cinema of Best Intentions?: 60 Years of Swedish Children's Film as Education and Entertainment*) (Stockholm, 2007): 176 pp.
9. **Joel Frykholm**, *Framing the Feature Film: Multi-Reel Feature Film and American Film Culture in the 1910s* (Stockholm, 2009): 346 pp.
10. **Christopher Natzén**, *The Coming of Sound Film in Sweden 1928 - 1932: New and Old Technologies* (Stockholm, 2010): 284 pp.
11. **Ingrid Ryberg**, *Imagining Safe Space: The Politics of Queer, Feminist and Lesbian Pornography* (Stockholm, 2012): 233 pp.


Orders for single volumes should be addressed to any international bookseller or directly to the disributor:

Stockholm University Library
SE-10691, Stockholm Sweden
Phone: +46 8 16 2800
Web page: www.sub.su.se
E-mail: acta@sub.su.se

ACTA UNIVERSITATIS STOCKHOLMIENSIS

Corpus Troporum
Romanica Stockholmiensia
Stockholm Cinema Studies
Stockholm Economic Studies. Pamphlet Series
Stockholm Oriental Studies
Stockholm Slavic Studies
Stockholm Studies in Baltic Languages
Stockholm Studies in Classical Archaeology
Stockholm Studies in Comparative Religion
Stockholm Studies in Economic History
Stockholm Studies in Educational Psychology
Stockholm Studies in English
Stockholm Studies in Ethnology
Stockholm Studies in Film History
Stockholm Studies in History
Stockholm Studies in History of Art
Stockholm Studies in History of Ideas
Stockholm Studies in History of Literature
Stockholm Studies in Human Geography
Stockholm Studies in Linguistics
Stockholm Studies in Modern Philology. N.S.
Stockholm Studies in Musicology
Stockholm Studies in Philosophy
Stockholm Studies in Psychology
Stockholm Studies in Russian Literature
Stockholm Studies in Scandinavian Philology. N.S.
Stockholm Studies in Social Anthropology, N.S.
Stockholm Studies in Sociology. N.S.
Stockholm Studies in Statistics
Stockholm Theatre Studies
Stockholm University Demography Unit - Dissertation Series
Stockholmer Germanistische Forschungen
Studia Fennica Stockholmiensia
Studia Graeca Stockholmiensia. Series Graeca Studia Graeca Stockholmiensia. Series Neohellenica
Studia Juridica Stockholmiensia
Studia Latina Stockholmiensia
Studies in North-European Archaeology